Sustaining Language Use

Perspectives on Community-Based Language Development

Managing Editor
Eric Kindberg

Volume Editors
Dirk Kievit
Bonnie Brown

Production Staff
Lois Gourley, Compositor
Barbara Alber, Cover and Graphic Design

Cover Photo
© Copyright Marc Ewell. Used by permission.

Sustaining Language Use

Perspectives on Community-Based Language Development

M. Paul Lewis and Gary F. Simons

With a Foreword by G. Richard Tucker

SIL International®
Dallas, TX

© 2016 by SIL International®
Library of Congress Control Number: 2016955037
ISBN: 978-1-55671-267-8

No part of this publication may be reproduced, stored in a retrieval system, or transmitted in any form or by any means—electronic, mechanical, photocopy, recording, or otherwise—without the express permission of SIL International®. However, short passages, generally understood to be within the limits of Fair Use, may be quoted without written permission.

Copies of this and other publications of SIL International® may be obtained through distributors such as Amazon, Barnes & Noble, other worldwide distributors and, for select volumes, www.sil.org/resources/publications:

SIL International Publications
7500 W. Camp Wisdom Road
Dallas, Texas 75236-5629 USA

General inquiry: publications_intl@sil.org
Pending order inquiry: *sales_intl@sil.org*

www.sil.org/resources/publications

Contents

Figures vii
Tables ix
Foreword xi
Preface xiii
Acknowledgments xv
How to Use this Book xvii

1 The Sustainable Use Model 1
   1.1 Introduction 1
   1.2 Why the Sustainable Use Model? 2
   1.3 What is the Sustainable Use Model? 5
   1.4 How this book is organized 8
   1.5 Going deeper 12

2 Local Language Communities in a Globalizing World 15
   2.1 Introduction 15
   2.2 What is a local community? 16
   2.3 Life-crucial knowledge 19
   2.4 Multiple identities, languages, and bodies of knowledge . . . 21
   2.5 So, why should we care? 23
   2.6 Going deeper 28

3 Community-Based Language Development 35
   3.1 Introduction 35
   3.2 Community 36
   3.3 What is community-based language development? 47
   3.4 Going deeper 57

4 Local Languages in Ecological Perspective 63
   4.1 Introduction 63
   4.2 Multiple languages for multiple topics, participants, and locations 64
   4.3 Functions, topics, and bodies of knowledge 67
   4.4 Categorizing functions 68
   4.5 The quest for stable multilingualism 70

    4.6 Going deeper 70
5 **Assessing the Ecological Profile of a Speech Community** 79
    5.1 Introduction. 79
    5.2 The Expanded Graded Intergenerational Disruption
        Scale (EGIDS) 80
    5.3 The EGIDS and language revitalization 90
    5.4 Assessment of EGIDS levels 92
    5.5 Going deeper. 96
6 **Sustainable Levels of Language Use** 111
    6.1 Introduction. 111
    6.2 Sustainable levels of language use 115
    6.3 Going deeper 120
7 **Conditions of Sustainable Use** 123
    7.1 Introduction. 123
    7.2 The FAMED conditions 125
    7.3 Some general observations. 129
    7.4 Assessing the FAMED conditions 130
    7.5 Using the FAMED conditions to assess language vitality . . . 146
    7.6 Going deeper 149
8 **Language Development: Addressing the FAMED Conditions** 155
    8.1 Introduction. 155
    8.2 Building the capacity of the language 156
    8.3 Going deeper 166
9 **Language Development: Achieving Sustainable Use** 169
    9.1 Introduction. 169
    9.2 Achieving Sustainable Literacy 171
    9.3 Achieving Sustainable Orality. 181
    9.4 Achieving Sustainable Identity 193
    9.5 Going deeper 199
10 **Organizing for Community-Based Language Development** 201
    10.1 Introduction. 201
    10.2 Planning a community-based language development
         program 202
    10.3 Determining the program content 205
    10.4 Planning language development endeavors 208
    10.5 Implementing the overall language development plan
         in a single speech community 210
    10.6 Implementing programs in multiple speech communities   212
    10.7 Going deeper 212
11 **Conclusion** 215
Appendix 217
References 245
Index 263
About the Authors 269

Figures

1.1 Status of the languages of the world 4
1.2 Overview of the Sustainable Use Model 5
5.1 Multi-scalar nature of the EGIDS 103
6.1 Levels of sustainable use: The mountain metaphor 116

Tables

5.1	Expanded Graded Intergenerational Disruption Scale (Lewis, Simons, and Fennig 2016)	80
5.2	EGIDS decision tree based on four diagnostic questions	93
5.3	What is the level of official use?	93
5.4	What is the sustainability status?	94
5.5	What is the youngest generation of proficient speakers?	94
5.6	Fishman's Graded Intergenerational Disruption Scale (GIDS)	97
5.7	UNESCO's Language and Vitality Endangerment framework	109
7.1	Functions scale	131
7.2	Acquisition scale	134
7.3	Motivation scale	138
7.4	Environment scale	140
7.5	Differentiation scale	143
7.6	FAMED conditions summary table	147
10.1	Language choice in Nawdm speech communities	205

Foreword

In this clearly written monograph, Paul Lewis and Gary Simons lay the groundwork for those who will be working in the coming decades with members of local language communities to help them implement diverse activities that will most effectively lead to a sustainable level of language use. They build appropriately upon the groundbreaking work that was carried out several decades ago by sociolinguists such as Charles Ferguson, Robert Cooper, and Joshua Fishman.

The authors remind us that the challenges that face members of local language communities who aspire toward maintaining a sustainable level of language use in today's globalizing world are daunting. Access to information via television, the internet, or mobile devices is available almost everywhere around the clock—and typically in a language of wider communication such as English.

As a personal aside, when I first worked as a program advisor in language education for the Ford Foundation based in Manila, Philippines (1967–1969), the internet did not exist, and in fact we literally had no telephone in our house—and of course the world wide web did not exist and mobile phones had not yet been invented. I was fortunate to develop wonderful collegial friendships with SIL linguists and to have the opportunity to visit with them in various sites in Mindanao to observe them at work in the field with members of local language communities who wished to codify and to preserve their language(s). Although they faced many challenges, the pervasiveness of English via the internet was not one of them.

Lewis and Simons have written a monograph which will serve as a very practical, and useful guide to those working with members of local language communities. By examining and profiling a language community using the Expanded Graded Intergenerational Disruption Scale (EGIDS) together with an assessment of conditions for sustainable use gathered by examining factors related to Functions, Acquisition, Motivation, Environment, and Differentiation (FAMED), community members will be able to develop plans of action to reinforce conditions that will likely result in a sustainable level of language use. A key point that permeates the monograph is that there must be "buy in" from all of the stakeholders concerning the importance or value of the language to them for preserving or serving various functions in the future.

The rationale for, and the components of, the Sustainable Use Model (SUM) are clearly presented with what I found to be numerous informative and interesting exemplars drawn from ongoing work in diverse areas throughout the world.

I strongly recommend this monograph to those interested in, and committed to community-based language development.

G. Richard Tucker
Paul Mellon University Professor of Applied Linguistics
Carnegie Mellon University

Preface

This volume is the result of more than ten years of reflection and discussion by the authors and a large and experienced group of colleagues regarding SIL International's corporate learning, after 80 years of working in local communities, to develop less-commonly known languages. Of course not all the details of that corporate experience are documented here, nor is all of that experience necessarily useful for the purposes of this book, but the distillation of that experience, its refinement and reformulation in light of current realities, has led us to the elaboration of a model of language development, the Sustainable Use Model (SUM), which we present here.

As with any model, we base our approach on sound theoretical principles. The aim of this book is to provide a practical explanatory framework for understanding the dynamics of language and culture maintenance. This framework can be used by those working with communities, including community members themselves—who are experiencing the pressures created by increasing contact with the world around them. This book is aimed at activists, consultants, and advisers who, confronted with the contemporary context, are searching for a way to address the issues in terms that make sense to members of local speech communities. We don't discard theory, nor do we discount the concerns of academics, but we don't want knowledge of theory or academic rigor to become prerequisites for well-informed action. Instead, we want the important ideas that local speech communities need to understand to be framed in such a way that they resonate with what some members of those communities are thinking and feeling.

This book is aimed at those who are "on the ground" working with a community to address the issues that arise from language and culture contact. Ideally, many in that audience will themselves be members of those communities. Others may be concerned outsiders who bring with them both their concern and some particular area of expertise. A third audience are those in positions of influence regarding language and diversity policy. We believe that all three of these audiences can benefit greatly by looking at diversity issues through the twin lenses we present here: a focus on local community-based development and a focus on sustainable knowledge transmission as foundational to the sustainability of language use.

Collectively, we refer to these three audiences as reflective practitioners. Whatever their role, our audience is made up of those who are reflective practitioners of language development. Not only are they doing the hard work of language and culture maintenance and revitalization, but they are also committed to growing in their understanding and professionalism in that work. Readers of this volume are excluded from that audience only to the degree that they exclude themselves by either failing to be reflective or by isolating themselves from praxis. Though we build on well-established theoretical concepts, this book is not intended for armchair theorists who will very likely point out its many omissions of literature citations, its incomplete coverage of the many alternatives available to practitioners, and a host of other lapses. We are sure that there are many valuable theoretical contributions that we are unaware of, have ignored, or have chosen not to mention. Our primary effort has been to lay a conceptual groundwork, a single coherent model, for effective action. We are more concerned about what needs to be done and with providing a theoretically sound, but practical, rationale for those actions, than we are with tracing the historical development of scientific thinking or defending one theoretical approach against another.

While we present the SUM as a whole and expect it to represent a coherent perspective, we do not present it as complete or as the final answer. As stated above, the SUM represents a distillation of many years of experience resulting in a framework which brings some order and organization to the complexities of each distinctive language ecology. There is still much to learn about those complexities. Our hope in presenting this material is that, as practitioners reflect on their own experiences, they will be able to add to the model in ways that will make it even more useful and productive as a tool for community-based language development.

M. Paul Lewis
Gary F. Simons
November 2015, Dallas, TX

Acknowledgments

The development of the SUM has not happened in isolation. Numerous colleagues have sat with us for long hours as we've attempted to step back from our long-developed habits of the mind in order to take a fresh look at what happens when a community begins to engage in its own language planning in the current global context. The authors of this volume are the scribes, collators, and organizers of the substance of those conversations. We have reflected on those discussions and the model that has emerged is an attempt to apply these new perspectives to the issues that communities face. We have framed our questions (and answers) in light of current global realities. A significant review of the overall approach and a serious test of the EGIDS as a tool for developing an ecological perspective on the status of languages within a country was provided by a symposium that we organized in 2011. The papers presented there are available in a companion volume (Lewis and Simons 2015) with several cases studies which demonstrate the application of the SUM. Those same case studies also raised several very helpful questions which facilitated the further development of the model.

By involving those with years of experience in all parts of the world, we have a good deal of confidence that the model we present can be used widely and beneficially. Our discussants and collaborators collectively represent centuries of field experience. It is rare to have such resources to call upon and we are grateful for the opportunity. Participating with us, and meriting considerable credit for what follows, are: Stan Anonby, Bagamba Araali, Eric Bartels, Douglas Boone, Wes Collins, Kathy Dadd, Ken Decker, Tefera Endalew, Paul Frank, Maik Gibson, Raymond Gordon, Bryan Harmelink, Richard Harmon, Sue Hasselbring, Deborah Hatfield, Ellen Jackson, Mark Karan, Amy Kim, Georgetta MacDonald, Tom Marmor, Hannah Paris (especially for her research for the Appendix), David Pearson, Doyle Peterson, Todd Poulter, Steve Quakenbush, Frank Robbins, Brian Schrag, James Stahl, Janet Stahl, John Stark, Barbara Trudell, Catherine Young, and many others.

We are grateful to participants in the workshops, seminars, and courses in Australia, Canada, Indonesia, Nepal, Peru, the Philippines, Thailand, and the United States where initial versions of this material have been presented. Especially helpful in those pilot programs were Ken Decker, David Eberhard, David Jeffery, Mark Karan, Alex Larkin, Mary Morgan, and Chari Viloria. We have benefited greatly from the interactions with the participants and students as they applied the model to their own situations, struggled with the concepts, and asked questions and made suggestions about both content and presentation. We also acknowledge the valuable contributions, comments, and suggestion of those who have responded to our progress reports and summaries in Bangkok, Dallas, Nairobi, and elsewhere.

This work has also benefited greatly from the editorial and development assistance of Bonnie Henson and the proofreading and commenting skills of Sue Hasselbring, Dirk Kievit, Alan Rogers, and Linda Simons who have reviewed the manuscript making helpful suggestions regarding the clarity of the content, providing additional examples, and especially, doing careful copy editing of the text. The authors accept full responsibility for any remaining shortcomings.

We are grateful to the administrators and leadership of SIL International who have encouraged us in this multi-year effort and who willingly set us free to engage with the concepts and develop and test the model as it emerged.

How to Use this Book

We have divided each chapter of this book into two sections. The first part of each chapter contains what we hope are fairly clear and logical explanations of concepts for planners, decision makers, and implementers. The second part is a "Going Deeper" section which provides a rudimentary literature review, identifying references to the academic and theoretical literature. In the Going Deeper section, we try to cover the ground of relevant literature, but we have made no attempt to be comprehensive. Most often we provide the references to the literature and discuss the approaches that we have mentioned or are following in the first part of the chapter. It is expected that this volume may, on occasion, be used in conjunction with other introductory works on sociolinguistics. Where that is the case, on some topics, there may be some overlap in coverage in the Going Deeper section, but we include our general summary to ensure that the volume can stand on its own. For the reflective practitioner, the first part of each chapter will be of primary interest. In general, we avoid bibliographic citations there which might distract from the main points being emphasized. For those who wish to do even more reflection, the Going Deeper section will provide the references to the academic literature that we have drawn upon pointing the reader towards a more in-depth study of the topics we've discussed.

The chapters are organized to facilitate the understanding of the concepts. Each chapter begins with a box that encapsulates the big idea that is about to be discussed. Examples and points to ponder are included in shaded boxes throughout. The chapter topics follow the logical sequence of the SUM beginning with a presentation of the general situation that local language communities encounter, moving to an overview of the model, and then progressively working through each of the components. This organization not only follows the logic of the SUM but traces a planning process that community planners and decision makers can follow in evaluating their situation. In practice, language development practitioners will very likely find themselves dealing with various parts of the SUM and different levels of assessment, evaluation, action, and implementation all at the same time and, almost certainly, iteratively.

Where no previous overt language development has been attempted, or for those completely unfamiliar with the model, it may be helpful to start at the beginning and follow the SUM's logical progression from start to finish. In most cases, however, there will already be a history of language development efforts that needs to be taken into account. Some activities may have been tried with varying degrees of success. Some may have failed. Others may have produced unexpected or very mixed outcomes. In such cases, it may be more fruitful for language development planners to begin (after reading this book!) somewhere in the middle or nearer to the end of the process that we have described here. They may wish to address a particular set of issues first and then work back through the model to fill in, dig deeper, or explore anomalies. The SUM is as much a lens through which to view the situation of a speech community as it is a set of procedures to be followed. Using the SUM as a guide for planning, however, will inevitably require community-based language developers to account for the missing pieces and make adjustments to their plans and activities as needed.

1

The Sustainable Use Model

The Sustainable Use Model helps members of local speech communities and those working with them to think about how they will transmit life-crucial knowledge to future generations.

1.1 Introduction

The loss of linguistic diversity is one of the primary areas of current focus and concern in linguistics. It is, however, most-of-all a matter of critical concern for members of local speech communities who daily confront the pressures of a globalizing world. As the world grows smaller and "flatter" there is increasing contact of those communities with those around them and with each other. The totally isolated, monolingual, uncontacted community is increasingly rare. Where in the past we measured contact primarily in terms of physical access (via roads, rivers, and air transport) and to a lesser extent in terms of access to information (mainly through broadcast and print media), we must now also consider telephony and internet as additional means, the virtual highways, by which people initiate and maintain contact with each other.

In addition, urbanization and mobility have emerged as increasingly powerful phenomena. Motivated by perceived economic benefits and by the ease of movement afforded by advances in both transportation and communication, the growth of cosmopolitan cities with burgeoning populations of both domestic and international immigrants brings into much sharper focus the dynamics of language and culture contact.

These technological and socioeconomic developments certainly bring great benefits but they also change the linguistic ecology in which local language communities live and function. We find ourselves and those in smaller and less powerful local communities in the midst of an unprecedented sociolinguistic climate change.

None of the phenomena we are observing are, in themselves, particularly new. Contact between users of different languages has always occurred in the past, and it will continue into the future. What is different is the scale and scope of the contexts which bring about that contact. The pace of the contact-induced processes themselves, aided by a global economy and advances in technology, has increased. The current movement of people into the cities, both through domestic and international migration, ranks with other historical periods of massive global migration. Physical migration is paralleled by virtual migration as people from all languages and cultures interact with each other in cyberspace.

Though this volume is primarily about language development and focuses on the important role that language plays in the construction and maintenance of a community's identity, it starts by recognizing how the current environment of heightened contact poses risks not only for local languages but for local communities and the knowledge that they possess. With that larger context in view, the Sustainable Use Model provides a theoretical perspective that will assist reflective practitioners of language development to find a way forward in addressing the needs and desires of local communities that are, in some cases unwittingly, endangered or threatened by the current environment.

1.2 Why the Sustainable Use Model?

The Sustainable Use Model (SUM) begins, not with language, but with the notion that local communities must concern themselves with the preservation and transmission of knowledge that is, for them, crucial to their way of life (like their history, traditions, folklore, and other arts) or crucial in other ways to their well-being (be it physical, spiritual, social, or economic). The basic decision that members of these communities must make is how they will sustain their identity and how the essential bodies of knowledge associated with that identity will be transmitted to succeeding generations.

This initial focus on knowledge management, rather than language maintenance, allows the community to recognize that in addition to their own traditional bodies of life-crucial knowledge, they must also consider how they will manage new bodies of knowledge which they are encountering as they come into contact with people from other communities. The SUM has been developed to help local communities think through their current circumstances and design responses that will meet their ongoing needs in all areas of life. Language, of course, is an important, perhaps the most important, means by which life-crucial knowledge can be transmitted. The choice of communication genres to be used, and provisions for the preservation, development, acquisition, and transmission of those communication genres within a community's total communication repertoire are major areas of concern. Any knowledge management strategy must take into account the realities of the contemporary world.

1.2.1 Multilingualism and language shift

In a world where contact is the norm, local language communities are, of necessity, becoming increasingly multilingual. Multilingualism *per se* is beneficial both for an individual and for a community. However, the competition that language contact often creates between a more prestigious language and a local variety often results in users abandoning the local language in favor of the more dominant and prestigious language. The result is language shift. In many cases, language shift ultimately leads to language death, the situation where there are no remaining speakers of the local variety. Since languages are closely associated with particular bodies of knowledge, the loss of a language may also bring about the loss of a body of knowledge. That is why knowledge management efforts must take into account the entire linguistic repertoire of a community. The perception that the bodies of knowledge of more economically developed and powerful communities are of greater value and usefulness leads some to abandon their heritage languages in favor of the languages which are most closely associated with those more highly valued bodies of knowledge. Increasingly, local speech communities are needlessly giving up their local languages based on the belief that by doing so they will increase their opportunities and better their immediate circumstances or the prospects of success for their children. In the process, however, they may lose much of their heritage life-crucial knowledge, impoverishing themselves and generations to come.

Not too many years ago, language contact was understood in terms of physical access. The development of national infrastructure, roads, schools, broadcasting, telephony, were the primary means by which contact was facilitated. More recently, language contact must be additionally understood in terms of new networks of communication and interaction, primarily via digital means. These networks are larger, more diverse, and are not necessarily confined by geographical or even social space. The anonymity of electronic communications systems overcomes the social barriers that may exist where communication is more localized or confined to face-to-face interactions. People who might be unlikely to interact with each other face-to-face, now are able to interact frequently online and may participate in a broad range of bodies of knowledge that extend well beyond their physical, geographical, cultural, or social settings.

Participants in these networks have a larger set of interactional tools that they can use to construct, modify, and hybridize their identities. Their online virtual personae may enable them to participate in social networks that were previously inaccessible to them. This opens a new world of opportunity for some members of local communities but it also increases the pressure on these communities to acquire the sociolinguistic and communicative capacities that give them greater mobility in this larger ecological setting. All too often this is accompanied by the abandonment of their heritage language and culture.

This increase in intergroup contacts and the resulting multilingualism means that the most significant issue confronting local communities in the twenty-first century is the endangerment of their identity, their knowledge, and their languages. The importance assigned to local bodies of knowledge that once were highly valued may not be so readily apparent in this wider global environment. And knowledge previously unknown or inaccessible is seen to have value as a means to gain access to and fuller participation in that broader set of global relationships. This is why knowledge management, planning, and strategizing by local communities inevitably must deal with the issue of language and identity maintenance.

This broad range of concerns and the activities related to them are what we are calling language development.

1.2.2 Language endangerment

Because of these global changes, observers of these trends need to better understand the state of the languages of the world. As the contact between users of different languages increases, the pressures towards language shift (and eventual death) of local languages grow. At the same time, efforts are underway in many local languages to maintain and even expand their use. A mechanism is needed to evaluate both language loss and language development on a global scale. Much attention is being given to language endangerment as a growing crisis in need of urgent action. At the same time language development activities that might address and remedy the endangerment crisis need to be developed, implemented, evaluated, and modified to meet the knowledge management needs of local communities.

The 19th edition of the *Ethnologue* (2016) provides a current comprehensive, albeit approximate, assessment of the state of vitality of all the world's languages. That assessment uses the Expanded Graded Intergenerational Disruption Scale (EGIDS), the vitality assessment scale that is a core component of the Sustainable Use Model (see chapter 5.). The global distribution of languages on this scale is shown in figure 1.1.

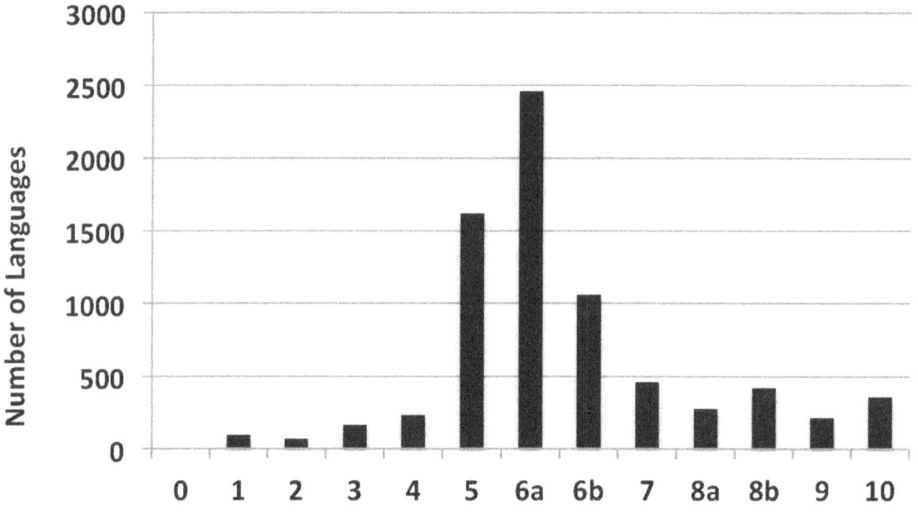

Figure 1.1 Status of the languages of the world.

An analysis of the data from the *Ethnologue* shows that of the 7,097 languages known to be in use, nearly 35% of languages fall right in the middle of the scale as being in vigorous unwritten use (EGIDS 6a). To the left of that, nearly 31% have a stronger level of development (EGIDS 0–5) while to the right just over 34% are in some stage of loss or shift (EGIDS 6b–9). The number of threatened and dying languages exceeds the number of languages that are at some stage of development. This situation is dynamic and continues to evolve. As described above, the pressures of language contact, in most cases, work against the maintenance and sustainable use of local languages. At the same time, language development work attempts to promote ongoing use of many local languages, though the effectiveness of those efforts is yet to be fully understood.

1.3 What is the Sustainable Use Model?

The overall approach of the SUM is to start with the bigger picture, gaining a general assessment of the situation, and using that as a launching point for action as early as possible. More in-depth research of the dynamics of language use in each community will inevitably be called for as language development efforts progress, but in cases where language vitality is weak or is severely threatened, waiting until an in-depth study can be completed is generally not advisable. The SUM helps reflective practitioners of language development think about the larger issues and then work down to the more detailed concerns of what to do, when, and how. The overall organization of the SUM consists of three major sets of activities, as shown in figure 1.2.

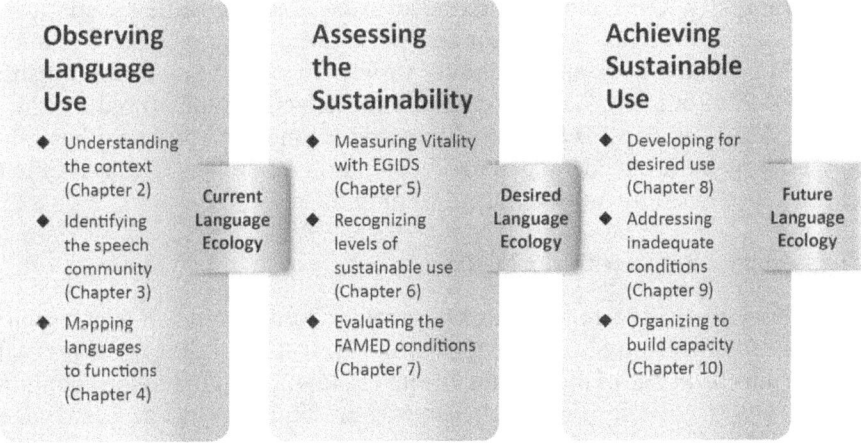

Figure 1.2 Overview of the Sustainable Use Model.

Initially, those activities are focused on observing language use in a speech community. This involves observations of the socioeconomic context and the linguistic ecology as well as the identification of the speech community that will be the focus of language development work. Then follows assessment of the sustainability of the languages in the linguistic repertoire of the speech community. Finally, based on that work, specific activities are designed that are aimed at achieving sustainable language use. The following subsections briefly introduce four of the repeating themes of the model: sustainable levels of language use, using EGIDS to assess language vitality, the role of community agency and capacity in achieving sustainable use, and using the assessment of the situation to effectively plan for results.

1.3.1 Sustainable language use

The heart of the SUM is the notion that there are only three sustainable levels of language use:

- Sustainable Literacy—in which both written and oral use of the language are maintained over the long term.
- Sustainable Orality—in which only oral use for everyday communication is maintained.
- Sustainable Identity—in which the on-going use of the language is limited to functions that maintain ethnic identity.

Other levels of use are transitory. Without some overt language development intervention they will deteriorate to the next lower level of sustainable use. The levels of use are directly related to the overall vitality of the language and so we will often use the terms level of use and level of vitality interchangeably.

There are many factors which contribute to sustainability. The level of use of a language can be measured using a graded scale that takes these factors into account. Several different scales have been proposed and used by different evaluators. In the SUM, we use the Expanded Graded Intergenerational Disruption Scale (EGIDS). Similarly, the factors which need to be assessed to determine a level of use for a language can be categorized in different ways. We have organized these within a framework of conditions which we call Functions, Acquisition, Motivation, Environment, and Differentiation, collectively identified by the acronym FAMED. The FAMED conditions provide a coherent approach that can be readily used by both outside experts and community members themselves to address the issues faced by local language communities.

1.3.2 Assessing vitality with the EGIDS

The SUM uses the EGIDS to evaluate the current vitality status of each language in the linguistic repertoire of a speech community. Not all of the languages in that repertoire may be at one of the sustainable levels. It will then fall to the community to decide how they wish to respond. The current vitality status of a language in that community serves as a baseline for making language development decisions based on the community's decisions regarding how it wishes to manage its life-crucial knowledge. The current status of a language also serves as an indicator of what will be required for the community to achieve a sustainable level of use and vitality for that language (moving either up or down the scale to one of the sustainable levels). The companion volume (Lewis and Simons 2015) provides some examples of how this kind of evaluation of the status of languages can be carried out for an entire country.

Much of what needs to be addressed, particularly at the higher, stronger levels of language development, lies outside of the purview of language development *per se*. Economic, political, religious, and social changes are needed and few communities are prepared to take on all of those at once or even one at a time. The SUM is an attempt to assist local communities in identifying how to apply their resources most effectively and efficiently. The FAMED conditions provide a way for community language development efforts to target the specific factors that are more likely to result in the needed outcomes.

The SUM stresses that vitality can be re-established most effectively in an incremental fashion by moving languages up the vitality scale (or sometimes down the scale) to a level of use that is sustainable.

1.3.3 Community agency and community capacity

Another foundational perspective of the SUM is that language development decisions are most appropriately community decisions. Outside agents, at best, can only contribute (mostly theoretical) information and provide perspective. Language development strategies must be community-based and language development goals should be developed from each community's vision, based on well-informed awareness and perspectives, of its desired future. As with medical interventions on individuals, community language development activities need to be undertaken with the informed consent of the community. The full participation of the community in the decision making constitutes their consent. And the fostering of awareness and perspective constitutes their being informed. Without both components, language development may represent an imposition by outsiders or be poorly designed or both.

While we believe that the maintenance of linguistic and cultural diversity is preferable, not every community will opt to maintain the bodies of knowledge which are life-crucial for their distinct identity. In some cases, they may wish to disengage from their heritage identity and assimilate or hybridize. These decisions, while lamentable, should be respected. Having said that, however, we should not minimize the role that the outside expert can play in providing awareness and perspective. Communities need to make informed decisions and outside expertise can provide them with important information and perspectives that they may not otherwise have access to. Many local language communities accept uncritically the prevailing views promoted by dominant communities regarding the value and potential of the heritage language. Even when local community members may not share those dominant perspectives, they may feel timid or unqualified to express their own opinions. Often neither the views of the local nor of the dominant communities are scientifically accurate or represent well-founded principles of language use and language maintenance. While it is not appropriate for an outsider to impose their views nor to usurp the decision-making role, it can be extremely beneficial for such an expert to educate and inform all those involved in an effort to increase the capacity of the community members themselves to make informed decisions and to engage in the language development program design and implementation to the greatest extent possible. This process involves much more than having an outside consultant "show up" with expert information. There is a lengthy process of relationship and trust building that must be engaged in before an outsider may have enough knowledge of the situation and achieve enough credibility to be given a platform for making a contribution to the process. Those activities, however, go beyond the scope of this volume.

1.3.4 Planning for results

Once the desired level of sustainable language use is identified by a community, a language development program can be designed to address the interconnected factors that are necessary to achieve that sustainable level.

In general, such a program of language development interventions should be designed specifically to move the community towards the desired level of sustainable use. All too often, language development activities are unfocused or attempt to include any and all areas of activity that are seen to have been effective in some other context. This frequently results in the inefficient use of resources. In the worst cases, counterproductive or unexpected consequences are the result. By providing a comprehensive and coherent theory of how to assess a situation and to identify what factors must be addressed, the SUM gives local language communities a framework for shaping and designing language development activities that will more effectively bring about the desired results.

Activities that are part of a language development program can address the specific conditions that are weak or lacking in the situation. Activities that do not effectively address those conditions can be avoided. In addition, the coherent framework found in the SUM provides a way for a more rational and well-founded planning and design process, and a framework for ongoing monitoring and evaluation of progress towards the desired outcomes.

Many development agencies have adopted a formal system for planning community-based change projects that are focused on achieving specific results. Such a system is extremely useful as a tool for planning and managing language development programs as well and merits investigation by those who wish to engage in language development work. The companion volume, *Managing Language Programs: Perspectives, Processes, and Practices* (Marmor and Bartels, forthcoming), lays out the major features of such a results-based planning and program management system with specific application to community-based language development.

1.4 How this book is organized

Each chapter in this book deals with a significant component of the model, starting with a description of the major issues confronting minoritized communities and ending with a discussion of sets of activities that can be helpful in specific contexts. The overall organization of the book into three sets of three chapters each can be seen in figure 1.2. The early chapters in particular introduce concepts and terminology that will be used throughout the book.

Chapter 2, "Local Language Communities in a Globalizing World," lays out the general problem that local communities must recognize and respond to. In a globalizing world, with increasing and often overwhelming levels of contact, it is exceedingly difficult for non-dominant communities to maintain their cultural and linguistic distinctives. We approach this problem in terms of the disruption of the transmission of life-crucial knowledge. While language plays an important role in the transmission of knowledge, most community members find the abstract concept of "language" to be too far removed from more concrete and salient daily issues of life to be much concerned about its loss. In contrast, many will readily recognize

1.4 How this book is organized

that knowledge management, both the preservation of traditional knowledge and the acquisition of new technological and scientific knowledge (among others), is important. Different segments of a community may be more concerned about different bodies of knowledge. Elders may be more focused on the loss of traditions and cultural lore. Young people may be drawn to globalized culture and actively seeking to participate in it. Often, the heritage language of the community is seen as part of the problem rather than the solution. So starting with the issue of how a community wants to manage the transmission of life-crucial knowledge—the knowledge that is important for its survival and well-being—frames the discussion in terms that are much more salient and actionable.

In chapter 3, we propose that "Community-Based Language Development" is a way to address the phenomena described in chapter 2. We describe the overall approach of community-based language development, how it builds on and differs from previous approaches, and we describe its distinctives. By starting with the notion of life-crucial bodies of knowledge and taking into account that the focus of language development needs to be the speech community (in contrast to a single language in isolation), community-based language development using the Sustainable Use Model provides a way for members of local communities to analyze the current configuration of their linguistic repertoire and identify the bodies of knowledge that they deem to be life-crucial. Once that assessment is in place, the community can make a better-informed decision regarding the language development goals they wish to achieve in each of the languages in their linguistic repertoire. At that point, a more detailed analysis of the conditions affecting sustainable language use is carried out and specific actions are designed to address the conditions that are not adequate.

Chapter 4, "Local Languages in Ecological Perspective," argues that the development of local languages cannot be addressed without consideration of the more dominant languages that are part of the context. Language development is the overt, directed, purposeful reconfiguration of the functional assignments of the languages in a speech community's linguistic repertoire. Because of heightened language contact as described in chapters 1 and 2, established domains of use are encroached on by larger, dominant languages. Because of these pressures, the linguistic ecology, the configuration of the ways in which the languages in a speech community are being used, is changing. As the dominant language becomes associated with more and more domains of use (constellations of topics, participants, and locations) and the local language is gradually losing its close associations with those domains, the overall patterns of language use change. Language development as we envision it in the SUM is the intentional altering of the linguistic ecology in order to re-establish and preserve domains of use (functions) for the local language. As with any intervention in an ecological system, change must be introduced with caution and based on as thorough an understanding of the functions and relationships among the elements that exist within that ecology as possible.

Chapter 5, "Assessing the Ecological Profile of a Speech Community," explains how the current profile of language vitality can be assessed using the Expanded Graded Intergenerational Disruption Scale, or EGIDS. This tool consists of a 13-level scale that identifies possible levels of development versus endangerment of a language. The EGIDS gives the local community a more readily understood description of the position of their language(s) on a natural scale of language development versus decline. This assessment provides the basis for establishing a desired sustainable level of language use.

Community-based language development must focus on helping local speech communities identify and achieve a sustainable level of language use for each of the languages in their linguistic repertoire. Chapter 6, "Sustainable Levels of Language Use," describes the kinds of sustainable language use that are possible for local languages. The SUM identifies three sustainable vital levels of language use: Sustainable Identity, Sustainable Orality, and Sustainable Literacy. A fourth level, Sustainable History is applied to adequately documented but no longer spoken languages. These sustainable levels correspond to EGIDS level 10 where adequate documentation also exists (Sustainable History), EGIDS 9 (Sustainable Identity), EGIDS 6a (Sustainable Orality) and EGIDS 4 (Sustainable Literacy). Other levels of language use (as measured by EGIDS) are transitory and subject to the pressures of contact. Without intervention, these unsustainable levels of language use are likely to give way over time and the language will slide down the EGIDS scale to a lower level of vitality.

Sustainable language use can only be achieved when certain conditions are met. Chapter 7, "Conditions of Sustainable Use," describes what those conditions are. The SUM identifies five conditions which are identified using the acronym FAMED: Functions, Acquisition, Motivation, Environment, and Differentiation. These five concepts are major components of the SUM and are treated as proper nouns throughout this book; when one of these words is capitalized in the middle of a sentence it is an explicit reference to one of the FAMED conditions. Each of these conditions can be assessed and specific activities designed to address inadequacies or to re-enforce conditions that are minimally adequate. The FAMED conditions provide a way to analyze the state of stable multilingualism (diglossia) in the speech community:

- The Functions condition accounts for the bodies of knowledge that are associated with the language (the content or topic component of a domain of use).
- Acquisition deals with the means by which users acquire proficiency in the language for those functions.
- Motivation addresses the perceived benefits associated with using the language for those functions.
- Environment describes the policy environment in which language use for the specified functions must operate.
- Differentiation describes the degree to which language use for the desired functions is compartmentalized into distinct niches for each language in the linguistic repertoire and how that compartmentalization is maintained and enforced.

The analysis of the FAMED conditions serves as the beginnings of the development of an action plan for language development as it provides a description of the conditions that are inadequate for the desired level of sustainable use. Planned interventions can then work towards the outcomes of a results-based plan that specifically addresses the inadequate conditions.

Chapter 8, "Language Development: Address the FAMED Conditions," discusses the kinds of language development activities that relate to sustaining a particular body of knowledge. Bodies of Knowledge correspond in large measure to functions, as introduced in chapter 7. The identification of bodies of life-crucial knowledge, both internal knowledge and external knowledge, provides a useful organizing framework for language development efforts. It is then possible to identify the specific language development activities that are needed for each body of knowledge. Some language development activities, like standardization, may apply to all functions. However, some bodies of knowledge or functions may require specific language development interventions, for example, the recovery or development of content-specific terminology, in order to achieve the desired sustainable level of use. Some segments of the speech community may be more concerned about some bodies of knowledge than others. Not all segments of the community may be willing (or able) to work together. While one part of the community may be investing in heritage lore, another may be more focused on HIV/AIDS awareness and prevention. Yet another may focus on the production of religious materials. Rather than being an obstacle to language development, this diversity of interests and participation can be leveraged to maximize the community's investment in the language development process and to expand the perceived benefits associated with the use of the local language.

In chapter 9, "Language Development: Achieving Sustainable Use," we turn to the practical problem of identifying activities that could be used to achieve the conditions of sustainable language use in a particular situation. With the association of certain bodies of life-crucial knowledge with a specific language within a speech community, and the identification of a desired level of sustainable use for that language (for at least some functions), activities specifically designed to address inadequate FAMED conditions can be designed. These tactical decisions must reflect current realities including an examination of previous similar efforts and their reception, the political, social, and economic contexts in which language development is now being implemented, expected costs, and actual and potential resources available to the overall program. There are many examples of activities that have been tried. Some have proven to be very effective, others have not. Chapter 9 describes some general principles and summarizes the primary objectives that should be in view as language development work attempts to move a language towards a sustainable level of use.

Chapter 10, "Organizing for Community-Based Language Development," introduces some of the practical issues related to planning and managing a community-based language development project. As described in chapters 8 and 9, the SUM allows for multi-faceted and diverse participation of different segments of the speech community in the overall language development effort. Organizing and coordinating that participation may not always be possible where parallel and sometimes competing efforts are being implemented simultaneously. In addition, some language development efforts may apply widely to multiple language communities that are not part of the same speech community. It is hoped that diverse segments of the community can at least reach a consensus at the strategic level (an agreed upon desired sustainable level of use, for example) and can coordinate with each other in areas of common concern such as orthography design and standardization. Apart from that, language development may be decentralized and distributed among distinct segments of a community.

Finally, chapter 11, "Conclusion," closes with a very brief summary of the SUM.

The Appendix is the beginnings of a collection of examples and case studies organized within the SUM framework by EGIDS levels and FAMED conditions. Each example has been categorized in terms of how it might be applied to moving a language from one EGIDS level to another and in terms of which of the FAMED conditions it might be most helpfully applied to. Such categorizations, of course, are not exclusive as many activities have multiple areas of application. It is our hope to see the archive of examples added to and improved upon as use of the SUM as a guiding framework grows and expands.

1.5 Going deeper

This chapter has provided an overview of the Sustainable Use Model and introduces many topics that will be discussed in much greater detail in the rest of the volume. Concepts presented above as part of the general context in which local communities find themselves are further elaborated in the following sections.

1.5.1 Diversity

Much of what this book deals with is the existence, maintenance, or loss of linguistic and cultural diversity. The loss of linguistic diversity is what currently most occupies the attention of linguists and many members of local communities. The value of linguistic diversity has been contested with some having argued that linguistic diversity correlates with lack of economic development though that idea has been widely disputed. There is now a well documented body of evidence demonstrating that linguistic diversity and economic development are not directly related to each other (e.g. Pool 1972; Fishman 1990). The first chapter of Fasold's introductory volume on sociolinguistics (1984) traces the early stages of this discussion.

The ideological position that causally linked diversity to lack of development led to polices which promoted assimilation of diverse groups into the "mainstream" cultures and languages of dominant groups in part as a means of promoting economic growth. For more on ideological orientations towards diversity, see our discussion of language planning ideologies in the Going Deeper section of chapter 3. More recently, diversity has come to be viewed as beneficial, with linguistic diversity in particular seen as a resource that enriches a nation (Ruíz 1984). In spite of this shift in ideology many local communities are motivated by the advantages of participation in the larger dominant socioeconomic system to redefine their particular identities or to abandon them all together. Generally, these dynamics can be seen at work in the approaches to multilingual and multicultural education adopted by governments (Lewis and Trudell 2008).

1.5.2 Globalization

Globalization is most specifically defined as an economic process where goods and services are spreading across national boundaries. In effect, however, globalization

1.5 Going deeper

as used in this volume is much broader than the expansion of economic markets and the wider distribution of goods and services. "Indeed, globalization is best thought of as a multi-dimensional process that cuts across various spheres of activity in the realms of economy, politics, culture, technology and so forth" (Rubdy and Alsagoff 2014:1). As a result there is a very large literature dealing with both the causes and effects of globalization in a wide range of areas of life. The volume edited by Rubdy and Alsagoff (2014) explores the interaction of globalization and language with case studies from a number of different parts of the world. That volume provides numerous links to the foundational literature on identity construction, hybridization, and other important concepts that have come into focus as a result of globalizing forces affecting local communities. For the most part, we focus on the increase in contact among ethnic groups that these advances in communication and transportation have brought about. Contact has also been increased as a result of widespread migration, largely motivated by the new economic opportunities available to previously less-resourced communities. The leveling process which globalization is bringing about has been described by Friedman (2005) as the world becoming "flatter."

The *Ethnologue* (Lewis, Simons, and Fennig 2016) is a comprehensive catalog of the languages of the world that began as a research project in the early 1950s. The *Ethnologue* database provides the best available source for analyses of the global linguistic ecology (e.g., Simons and Lewis 2013).

1.5.3 Language contact and multilingualism

Linguists have a great deal to say about the effects of language contact on both the languages-in-contact themselves and on the societal uses of those languages and the meanings associated with language choice, language mixing, code-switching, and other phenomena that occur when speakers of different linguistic varieties come into contact with each other. One obvious result of contact is that language learning begins to take place with at least some speakers of each language gaining some level of proficiency in second languages as they come into contact with those who speak them. The literature on multilingualism both in individuals and in a society as a whole is too large to even begin to review here though we will refer to some of these topics in later chapters.

Some studies focus on bilingual proficiency, second language acquisition, and the assessment of second language proficiency (e.g., Baker 1988, Cummins 1980, Grimes 1992, Jones and Spolsky 1975, Lyon 1996, and many more). Others, too numerous to mention, look at the societal aspects of multilingualism. Many of these will be mentioned in the Going Deeper sections of later chapters in this volume. Good introductory volumes that cover most aspects of the topic are Edwards 1994 and Romaine 1995.

1.5.4 Language shift and language endangerment

Language shift is another topic that has had extensive treatment in the sociolinguistic literature. Most introductory sociolinguistics textbooks (e.g., Fasold 1984, Holmes 1992, Wardhaugh 2002) describe the general phenomenon. It is most often described in terms of intergenerational shift occurring prototypically over three generations where grandparents are largely monolingual in the heritage language, their children (the childbearing generation) are bilingual in that language and a dominant language, and their children (the grandchild generation) are largely monolingual in the dominant language.

Another perspective on language shift focuses not so much on language shift over time from generation to generation, but on the diminishing use of a language in social space. This occurs when another language spreads and begins to be used for more and more functions within a community, displacing the local language for those uses. This spread of a language is the inverse of language shift. A good foundational work on the dynamics of that process can be found in Cooper 1982. In effect, the two perspectives on language shift, loss of intergenerational transmission and loss of functions, go hand in hand. As a language is used for fewer functions, there is less opportunity and need for it to be learned. As there are fewer fully proficient users of a language, there are fewer and fewer opportunities and needs to use it.

When language shift is widespread in a community or when it occurs in all of the communities in which a language is spoken, language shift can lead to complete loss of speakers resulting in language death. The death of local languages is a focus of concern for linguists and community members alike and is the motivation for a volume such as this one aimed at sustaining language use.

Language endangerment refers to the growing trend of language loss through the processes of language shift and death. Local languages have long been subject to these pressures but the severity of the crisis was declared clearly in a series of related presentations published in 1992 (Hale et. al. 1992). Most often cited among these is a set of predictions regarding the potential loss of up to 90% of the world's languages (Krauss 1992). A more recent look at the state of the world's languages in crisis can be found in Simons and Lewis 2013.

1.5.5 Sustainability and vitality

For more detail on sustainability of a language and its overall vitality see elsewhere in this book. These concepts are dealt with in considerable depth in chapters 5 (vitality) and 6 (sustainability).

2

Local Language Communities in a Globalizing World

If local communities lack the capacity and resources to sustainably transmit life-crucial knowledge to future generations, their languages and identities are at risk.

2.1 Introduction

We live in a world where communications and transportation are making it easier and easier for people in even the farthest removed locations to be in contact with others. In the past, some locations were isolated and the people who lived there were uncontacted and unable to contact others. Now, there are fewer and fewer situations that fit that description. While some locations may remain geographically isolated, fewer and fewer are completely unreached by technology. Even where there are no roads providing physical access, there are radio and television, cellular telephones, and increasingly, internet access.

The spread of cultural phenomena that we are experiencing today is unprecedented in human history. Globalization—the seemingly all-encompassing process of contact and interaction in terms of economy, politics, culture, technology and worldview—is a fact of life for all of us on the planet. The spread of dominant languages is part of this globalizing trend. One significant feature of globalization is that the traditional linkages between location and language are being broken down. Users of a particular language can be found in multiple locations, often separated from each other by great distances, and in any one location there may be users of multiple languages. In addition, people are more mobile, moving from one location to another with greater frequency, and therefore in much greater contact with people from other locations who use different languages. This new environment presents particular challenges for members of smaller, non-dominant societies and cultures, which we will refer to generically as local communities. And it is a situation that is of particular interest to applied sociolinguists and others who study patterns of language use, as well as to those who concern themselves with the preservation and even expansion of the languages spoken by those local communities. Given the growing pressures to participate in global culture, along with the ease of access to it, speakers of local languages find themselves increasingly pressured to abandon their languages and acquire others which are judged to be more broadly useful or prestigious.

The marked increase in migration, both domestic and international, is characterized by significant shifts in population from rural areas to rapidly growing urban centers. Cities are places where people from all over the world are in day-to-day contact with each other and thus serve as fertile environments for language and culture contact. This concentration of diverse populations fosters contact between possessors and users of different bodies of knowledge. Inevitably in such an environment, local bodies of knowledge are placed in competition with global knowledge and are often at a disadvantage in that struggle.

Although the same principles of language use and contact operate in all social groupings whatever their size or status, our focus in this book is primarily on local communities and the new realities that they confront. These are communities which can be distinguished by their status within the larger context around them. For them, a language related to their history and heritage may play a significant role in the maintenance of their distinctive identity. This book starts from the premise that it is important for these communities to maintain their cultural identities and the knowledge associated with those identities. We also recognize that local communities need to recognize the roles of the multiple languages that comprise their linguistic repertoire in this new world. Each of these languages plays a part in helping community members meet their ongoing needs in all areas of life. In particular this volume focuses on how local language communities can identify and transmit life-crucial knowledge across geographic and social space and from one generation to the next.

In this chapter, we define and describe several key concepts that we will make frequent reference to in the chapters that follow.

2.2 What is a local community?

We use the term community to refer to any group which is unified to a significant degree by a sense of shared identity. Shared identity is a group's conviction that they belong together and that they are different from other groups. It is this sense of identity that causes people who belong or want to belong to a particular group to behave in ways that will identify them as members of that group. This may be reflected in the place they live, the clothing they wear, the food they eat, the customs they observe, the religion they practice, and the language variety (or varieties) that they speak. Participation in those behaviors, in turn, re-enforces the sense of shared identity.

A community is also characterized by a heightened level of internal interaction. Not only do the members of a community share behavior patterns, they interact with each other and affirm and reinforce those behavior patterns through multiple and frequent contacts. They marry, work, engage in ceremonies together,

2.2 What is a local community?

and participate in communal governance along with many other spheres of shared activity. All of these are carried out in the ways prescribed by the group's identity, the shared set of norms that distinguish them as a group from all other groups. Most importantly for our discussion of community-based language development, all of these interactions are carried out using a language or some combination of languages (the community's linguistic repertoire). While there may be a good deal of variation in the behaviors associated with a particular identity, especially where segments of the group are widely dispersed geographically, it is the shared identity which fundamentally unifies a community and simultaneously distinguishes it from all others.

2.2.1 Language communities

Frequently, a particular language variety comes to be associated with a group's identity and often that language is so tightly bound to the identity that a group may be identified by the name of their language. Alternatively, their language may be identified by the name of the group or by the location where they live. The terms language group or language community may be used to identify such a community where group identity is clearly and tightly associated with a particular language (or closely related varieties that essentially function as a single language). More broadly, and perhaps more frequently, the term is applied to all those who use a particular language as their first or primary language. In some cases, as for example, Russian speakers in the Ukraine, Latvia or Azerbaijan, the language community spans national borders and may consist of a number of dispersed local communities around the world. Language may be the most significant feature that links these dispersed communities to each other though often there are other shared behaviors, beliefs, and bodies of knowledge which these communities maintain and pass on from generation to generation.

2.2.2 Minority or minoritized communities

Frequently, the term "minority" is applied to local language communities. These communities are not necessarily categorized as minorities because of their smaller numbers. In some cases, so-called minority communities actually represent the majority population in their nation-state. Some prefer to use the term "minoritized" with its connotation that minority status is one that has been imposed on the communities that the term is applied to. These communities are so described because of inequalities in resources and capacity to meet communicative and other needs. We have generally tried to avoid using these terms because of this ambiguity and because negative connotations often accompany that usage. In an increasingly globalizing world, local language communities encounter a number of significant (and growing) obstacles that hinder their ability to meet their needs. Many, if not most, do not have adequate capacity to maintain the use of the languages most closely associated with their identity—the languages that they have traditionally maintained over the longer term. This lack of capacity limits them in a variety of ways.

Limited participation

Local language communities may not participate fully in their own governance nor in the political and economic systems of their nation-state. Sometimes this is attributed to their limited proficiency in the official languages of that country. More often there are other underlying economic, political, and social factors at work. As a result, local language communities are frequently less able to determine their own fates. This often leads to exploitation and discrimination against them. Because of the lack of access and participation in national or international life, local language communities may be "off the radar" or completely invisible to members of more dominant communities. With little power to influence decision-making, they are often overlooked. Their very existence may be ignored or even denied. In some cases, there is little motivation for those in power to provide them with access to the political process since this may upset the balance of power or the distribution of economic resources.

Limited opportunities

Often local communities are in the minority because the resources dedicated to the development of a country's population are allocated primarily to the dominant segments of the population. The languages used for formal education may not be languages that members of local communities speak well, if at all. Schools and teachers may not be adequately provided or trained in the regions where local languages are found. As a result, the transmission of knowledge using the language of the local community will be outside the formal education system and may be limited to traditional lore and traditional technologies. This also exposes these communities to the risk of being exploited, of having their natural resources taken away, and to health risks that might otherwise be avoided. With limited opportunity to access a broader range of knowledge, local communities may feel pressured to give up their own identity in order to have access to the benefits of participation in the dominant community.

Limited resources

Because of the limited educational opportunities, members of local language communities may be unable to engage in occupations that require formal training or that use newer technologies. With only a limited set of occupations available to them, they may not be able to adequately support themselves and may have little opportunity to generate wealth that enables them to improve their living conditions, respond to health issues, or educate their children. Often the clearest marker of minority status is economic disadvantage or poverty, but there are other kinds of impoverishment that accompany minoritization resulting in limitations on cognitive, psychological, social, and spiritual resources as well.

Limited sustainability

Under these kinds of social, political, and economic pressures, there may be little motivation or opportunity for members of a local community to maintain their language and identity. If the majority of the rewards and benefits in the political, economic, social, and spiritual spheres are mediated through a different language and identity, there may appear to be little reason to retain the minoritized identity and the language associated with it.

Many local communities are experiencing loss of language vitality. As shown in figure 1.1, approximately one third of the world's languages are in some stage of language loss. And many of those that are currently in vigorous oral use, are subject to socioeconomic pressures that might easily cause them to "tip" towards language shift as well. The dominance of larger, more powerful communities, and of their ostensibly more useful languages, places increasing pressure on members of the local community to use those more powerful languages more frequently and to pass those languages on to their children as replacements for the local languages. Even though ongoing day-to-day oral use of the language is vigorous and may remain so for a long time, the pressures placed upon these communities by their minority status mean fewer and fewer opportunities for them to increase or even maintain the number of bodies of knowledge for which their language is used. Increasingly the tendency is for them to experience culture shift with accompanying changes in language use. Ultimately, this process can result in complete loss of the local language. If this happens in all of the communities where the language is used, language death occurs.

2.3 Life-crucial knowledge

It is helpful to make a distinction between information and knowledge. Information consists of data, facts, and technologies. Knowledge consists of information that has become useful as a community interacts with it, evaluates it, and incorporates it into its way of life. Information becomes empowering when it becomes part of a community's knowledge-base and is actively engaged with and made use of.

For example, demographic researchers or census takers may gather information about individuals or entire communities. They may be able to produce profiles of those individuals or communities which describe their significant features (age, gender, educational level, residential location, employment, etc.). They may be able to describe spending patterns, religious affiliations, and the like. All of this information may exist in a database or a research notebook, or in a dust-covered box or file cabinet in a warehouse or library basement. In that form, it is simply information and is not useful to anyone until it is interacted with, evaluated, and put to use for some purpose. At that point, it becomes knowledge and not simply a collection of data.

In an electronic and digital world, information can be readily and rapidly created, transmitted, stored, and widely broadcast. For local communities, that information isn't necessarily knowledge until they have the capacity and resources to interact with it, evaluate it, and make use of it for their purposes. The capacity for such interaction is only in small measure related to access to the relevant technologies. The greatest obstacle for many local communities is that information that has the potential to affect their well-being (and thereby become knowledge) is unavailable to them in a language in which they are proficient.

The function of language in meeting the needs of local communities is significant. The capacity of the communities to use the linguistic resources they have at their disposal to communicate with each other, to reinforce their identity, to educate their children, and to participate in a meaningful way in governance, economic activity, health maintenance, and spiritual development becomes a central aspect of their ability to maintain their existence as a community.

The kinds of knowledge that local communities need to transmit in order to achieve these functions is what we call life-crucial knowledge. This is knowledge that is crucial for the ongoing well-being of the community. Life-crucial knowledge can be described in terms of two general categories: internal and external.

2.3.1 Internal knowledge

Part of what enables a local community to distinguish itself from other communities and maintain its own identity is a sense of shared origins and history. These are embodied in a shared body of knowledge and lore. Often this may take the form of stories and legends, ritual uses of language, ceremonies, as well as nonverbal activities such as cuisine, ways of dress, dance, music, and the visual arts. If the local community cannot pass this knowledge from one generation to the next, it will be less able to maintain its distinct identity.

In addition, local communities must be able to transmit knowledge that will enable them to sustain governance, economic activity, health maintenance, and religious practice. This traditional knowledge may be part of their cultural heritage. Information about these traditional life ways may be documented, but that information becomes knowledge when it affects how people think, feel, and behave. Frequently, for example, communities have knowledge of local flora and fauna that may have medicinal uses or provide economic benefit. Kinship and genealogical information, traditional technologies and art forms (and ways of talking about them) are other examples of such internal practical knowledge that are part of a local community's cultural patrimony. They also affect how people in the community interact with each other and with their environment.

> **Agta ethnobotanical knowledge**
>
> Until recently, the Agta people in the Philippines were exceptionally skilled ethnobotanists with a vocabulary of many hundreds of terms to express that knowledge. The plant world was a central theme of their culture. Every Agta adult used several species of plants every day for food, medicines, ritual, art, and social activities. Agta knowledge of their biological world (including plant medicines) probably constituted the largest single body of knowledge, more than all of the other bodies of knowledge combined. It was estimated that the Agta had between 700 and 800 names for plants in their language. For older Agta, this was still the case as recently as 2008. But younger adults, and especially teenagers, have lost most of this knowledge today. (Headland 2010:114)

2.3.2 External knowledge

In addition to maintaining identity and passing on traditional life-crucial political, economic, health, and spiritual knowledge, local communities need to be able to transmit knowledge that will enable them to interact with the outside world more effectively, take advantage of the resources that others may have to offer, and enable them to incorporate innovations in the most appropriate and advantageous ways. If there is no way for a community to transmit this kind of knowledge it will increasingly find itself cut off and marginalized. If this external knowledge fails to enter into the community or to be passed on from one generation to the next, the ability to benefit from these resources may be lost. If a dominant language is the exclusive means by which such external life-crucial knowledge is transmitted, a gap may develop between those who are proficient in the language (and thus have access to the knowledge and its benefit) and those who have low levels of proficiency in the language by which that body of knowledge is communicated. For instance, if all of the medical and health terminology exists only in a dominant language, local community members are likely to have a great deal of difficulty accessing knowledge about diseases and their treatment.

2.4 Multiple identities, languages, and bodies of knowledge

While it is convenient for our purposes to categorize knowledge, identity, and language as we have, it is important to recognize that individuals and communities live in a world where the categories are not so clear cut. Local communities may have multiple identities with which they wish to associate. One identity might be that of their heritage and tradition. Another might be that associated with the external world—the national culture or the global society with which they are in increasing contact. It is very likely that there are distinct language varieties that are closely associated with each of those contexts and with the bodies of knowledge which constitute those distinctive identities.

2.4.1 Multiple identities

Many local communities may be sharing and managing multiple identities. While they have their traditional heritage identity (and the internal knowledge associated with it) they also may participate in larger external contexts at the regional, national, and global levels. This may be a source of conflict or stress as they attempt to reconcile a heritage identity with a more cosmopolitan orientation. There may be pressures to leave the heritage identity behind or to re-interpret it in terms that will make it more compatible with cosmopolitan values and practices. Issues of authenticity, synergy, and hybridity arise as traditional ways of life meet modern technological innovations. Some communities fragment along generational lines with young people participating more in the cosmopolitan and global identities and older people maintaining a more traditional way of life. In some cases, the fragmentation occurs along the urban-rural divide with city-dwellers blending in with the larger urban society around them but assuming their heritage identity when they return to their home communities. Many local communities are developing hybridized identities which combine some aspects of each of the multiple identities that are available to them.

2.4.2 Multiple languages

Both the formation of identity and the transmission of knowledge are mediated through language (among other means) and so local communities, as they negotiate multiple bodies of knowledge and multiple identities, often deal with multiple languages as well. Many local communities are characterized by high levels of multilingualism. It is frequently the case that the level of multilingualism in these communities exceeds that of the dominant society. Users of the dominant languages don't need to learn a second language in order to participate in the larger society whereas monolingual local language users are limited in many ways, as we have already described.

Even where inter-ethnic relationships are more equitable, there are advantages to having proficiency in the language of one's neighbors. Users of local languages therefore often acquire at least partial proficiency in the neighboring or nearby languages that can provide them with benefits.

> **Majangir**
>
> The Majangir people of Ethiopia are very widely scattered. They traditionally live in scattered small settlements. Therefore, they often live interspersed with other small language communities. But there are also larger language communities on the periphery of Majangir country. Therefore, in the northwest, many Majangir also speak Anuak. In the northeast, they also speak Oromo; in the far south, Bench, and in the south central areas, Amharic which is being spread via the school system. The Majangir language is quite homogenous, but the language repertoires of speakers in these different social networks vary. (Source: Pete Unseth, Graduate Institute of Applied Linguistics, Dallas, TX, personal communication)

2.4.3 Multiple bodies of knowledge

As described above, local communities have both internal knowledge and external knowledge that they need to be able to transmit. They may find it advantageous to transmit life-crucial knowledge in multiple languages or even a mixture of languages. They will inevitably have to choose whether to communicate these different bodies of life-crucial knowledge in their heritage language, in the language of the dominant culture, in a global language, or perhaps through some combination of all of the languages in their linguistic repertoire.

Most often, internal knowledge will have been transmitted traditionally in the heritage language of the community. Frequently, this knowledge transmission takes place orally and may also include a variety of artistic genres such as poetry, song, and dance. Typically, there will be specialized vocabulary in that language which embodies concepts that uniquely express that way of life. A shift from one language to another for the transmission of this long-held body of knowledge may require the development of new vocabulary and terminology in the new language. When this kind of translation takes place, some of the nuances and finer details of the traditional knowledge may be lost. In addition, a decision to transmit knowledge that was previously passed on orally through written media will require the development of an orthography and the acquisition of literacy skills. As these shifts in language and modality are taking place some of the artistic expressions may be lost as well.

External knowledge—new ideas and concepts that expand upon the heritage lore or that are complete innovations coming from the outside—may include outsider perspectives on such things as health, economic activity, politics, communications technologies, or religious and spiritual information. These perspectives may differ significantly from related internal information. In addition, coming from many different sources, there may be significant inconsistencies among the various bodies of external knowledge that a local community interacts with. Typically, some members of local communities are unable to evaluate and make use of this external information because it is only available to them in a language which they do not speak well if they speak it at all. In many cases, external knowledge may be primarily available in written form, thus limiting access only to those who are educated.

External knowledge can be made more accessible if it is provided in the languages and modalities most closely associated with a community's primary identity but this requires the development of vocabulary and terminology in order to express the new concepts accurately and authentically. People will need to learn these new terms and what they mean. And, as with internal knowledge, if written media are chosen as the primary means of disseminating the external knowledge, the acquisition of literacy skills needs to be planned for. Not so often considered in these sorts of language development efforts is the role of artistic genres which may be either imported along with the body of knowledge or hybridized with existing traditional genres.

The Sustainable Use Model is intended to help local communities evaluate their knowledge transmission patterns. It takes into account both internal and external bodies of knowledge that they deem to be life-crucial in light of the whole of their linguistic repertoire. This evaluation sets the boundaries and defines the scope of any needed language development. Whether maintenance of internal knowledge or the introduction of external knowledge (or both) are in focus, the work of language development involves much more than simply addressing language acquisition and language proficiency issues.

2.5 So, why should we care?

Some have questioned the need to be concerned about communities which are experiencing this loss of language and culture. Changes in language and language use patterns are normal and happen all the time. There are several reasons why minority language communities and those who wish to assist them should care about their situation.

2.5.1 The humanitarian rationale

Members of a community which is in the process of losing its language and culture experience significant amounts of disruption and stress in all areas of life. A child growing up in a community which is viewed with disdain develops a self-image that reflects that experience. As social norms are abandoned, they frequently are not replaced all at once or with adequate equivalents. This can lead to social tensions, divisions in the community, disruptive and harmful patterns of behavior, and even violence. There is evidence that communities experiencing such a transition may have elevated levels of alcoholism, drug addiction, HIV/AIDS, and suicide.

Often members of local language communities make decisions about the life-crucial knowledge they will pass on and whether to continue using their heritage language for transmitting such knowledge to their children without full awareness of the consequences of those decisions. Frequently they are also unaware of the options that are available to them. Practitioners of community-based language development can provide a valuable service to minority language communities by providing them with awareness and perspective of their current situation and of the costs and benefits of any knowledge transmission and language development decisions they may make.

2.5.2 The human rights rationale

Increasingly there is an international policy environment which recognizes the rights of individuals and communities to maintain their distinctive identities and to use their own languages. While not all governments have subscribed to all of the international agreements, there is a general consensus in the international community that linguistic and cultural heritage (referred to more broadly as intangible heritage to distinguish it from monuments and artifacts) should be preserved and maintained. Much of the world's intangible heritage resides within what we are calling local communities in the form of life-crucial knowledge that only these communities possess and can pass on. It is important that these communities be aware of their rights and that they be assisted in asserting their language and identity rights.

> **Point to ponder**
>
> The United Nations Declaration on the Rights of Indigenous Peoples, which was adopted by 144 nations in 2007, codifies this right as follows:
>
> "Indigenous peoples have the right to revitalize, use, develop and transmit to future generations their histories, languages, oral traditions, philosophies, writing systems and literatures, and to designate and retain their own names for communities, places and persons." (Article 13.1)
>
> There are similar documents and statements from other international bodies.

2.5.3 The ecological rationale

This rationale starts from the premise that diversity is good for the planet. Where there is only limited diversity, there is less redundancy and the ability of an environment to rebound from disaster is more limited. For example, the great Irish potato famine had a devastating effect because there was only one kind of potato being grown. When the blight came there were no other potato varieties that were blight resistant and so the entire economic system collapsed as the potato crops were lost. Greater diversity, redundancy of varieties, is better than a monoculture. This view is representative of an ideological orientation (See the Going Deeper section of chapter 3) which sees diversity as a resource rather than as a problem.

Beyond this general sentiment that diversity in itself is desirable, a growing number of scholars argue that there is a connection between the level of biodiversity in any given region and the level of linguistic diversity in that same area. The exact relationship between the two is unclear, however. Some propose that high levels of biodiversity lead to an enrichment of the vocabulary and structures of the local languages as people find ways to talk about the greater number of species that exist in their environmental context. The argument is that the capacity of the language expands to accommodate the greater diversity of life-crucial knowledge that must be dealt with every day and that must be passed on to the next generation. Conversely, the argument goes that as the ways of talking about these species are lost, the knowledge about the uses and value of those species is also lost, and so eventually the species themselves and many related technologies disappear as the plants and animals are no longer recognized, valued, cultivated, or propagated, eventually falling into neglect or being lost altogether. Such knowledge also has monetary value as many of the species in an environment produce substances that might have pharmaceutical uses. Often local people know of those uses but the knowledge gets lost as the language that has traditionally encoded that knowledge is not transmitted to the next generation.

Whether or not the relationship between linguistic diversity and biodiversity is causal (in either direction), it is the case that many minority language communities possess highly developed bodies of knowledge about their physical environment and have elaborated technologies to adapt and make use of their environment that are transmitted through equally highly developed linguistic forms in their languages. With the loss of those languages and cultures entire areas of human knowledge are also at risk and at the same time biological diversity is also threatened.

> **Point to ponder**
>
> "The greatest biolinguistic diversity is found in areas inhabited by indigenous peoples who represent around 4 percent of the world's population but speak at least 60 percent of its languages and control or manage some of the ecosystems richest in biodiversity." (Nettle and Romaine 2000:13)

2.5.4 The academic rationale

Linguists and anthropologists depend on the diversity of human languages and cultures as the data for their understanding of how language and culture works. Theories develop as more and more data are tested against hypotheses. To the extent that linguistic and cultural diversity is diminished, the data for theory building and testing are also diminished, limiting the scope of knowledge and impoverishing theory. Local communities often are the sources of data which may prove or disprove a hypothesis. As those sources disappear and the data become scarcer, the development of better linguistic and cultural theories is impeded.

Not only is contemporary knowledge lost with the demise of local languages, but the ability of linguists to reconstruct linguistic prehistory is also affected. Some features of language structure can only be known through the comparison of related languages and the reconstruction of earlier forms of those related languages. The identification of linguistic universals—characteristics of how all languages tend to be structured—is also limited if all languages cannot be examined and analyzed. Even going beyond language itself, it is often possible to reconstruct the social and political history of peoples as their languages reflect their history of contact, conquest, and survival. Even when there are no written historical records, the linguistic features of local languages can give clues to who conquered whom or how much contact two groups might have had in the past. While all of this may seem abstract and distant from the realities of day-to-day life, good solutions to everyday problems rely heavily on good theory. To the extent that theory is wrong or incomplete, its application to problem-solving will also be inadequate.

2.5.5 The ideological rationale

A final, and in some ways the most significant, rationale encompasses the previous arguments in that it recognizes the central importance of ideology—fundamental beliefs and values—in determining what the participants in language development consider to be good and beneficial outcomes. For example, the positive evaluation of diversity that we have described above is an ideological orientation. It stands in contrast to an ideology which views diversity as harmful or burdensome. All participants in language development, whether they acknowledge it or not, approach the issue of language and identity endangerment with ideological perspectives. Those perspectives shape decisions and influence actions.

It is important for community activists, practitioners from outside of the community, and those who evaluate the activities of language development participants and beneficiaries to consciously identify and clarify their ideological orientations. This will allow for a better understanding of the desired outcomes of language development activities and for a consensus among all actors in language development projects about what is aimed for and why it is deemed to be beneficial. Even when participants start from different ideological positions, they may be able to find a common (or complementary) set of values that they can agree upon to guide their actions.

Looking more deeply at philosophical foundations, we include here a brief summary of a further ideological stance—a theological one in the Abrahamic tradition—which also serves as the motivation for the authors' concern for local language communities. Other practitioners, coming from a different perspective, may find ideological grounds of their own to motivate them either from some alternative view of the world or from one or more of the other motivations listed above.

Our concern for the preservation and development of local language communities and the languages they speak is rooted specifically in the perspective of the Judeo-Christian Scriptures where diversity of peoples, languages, and cultures is a cornerstone of God's creation. Further, we understand that the Creator's intent for humankind and all of creation was that it exist in a state of *shalom*–completeness, wholeness, peace, and well-being. As we read the biblical creation narrative (Genesis 1–2) and as we look at the created order itself, we see the Creator's delight in diversity and abundance. Further, we see the responsibility given to humankind to "name" the diversity of creation as a divine endorsement of language expansion. We do not see the biblical narrative of the confusion of tongues at Babel (Genesis 11) so much as placing a curse on humanity but as restoring the Creator's original intent for diversity to fill the earth. And we are inspired by the apocalyptic visions of both the Hebrew Bible (Daniel 7:14) and the Christian New Testament (Revelation 7:9) that reveal an uncountable throng of worshippers that includes every people and nation and language. At the same time, the Judeo-Christian ethic of loving one's neighbor and serving the marginalized compels us to assist local language communities who are struggling to sustain their language and identity as part of their quest for well-being and wholeness.

Given this foundational ideological stance, the following are some general principles that we affirm:

- Diversity of species, identities, cultures, and languages reflects the Creator's original intent that the created order be "fruitful and multiply."

- All human beings, as part of the creation, are valuable, worthy of dignity in their own right, and their creativity in language and culture is to be valued as part of the diversity of creation. This also requires us to treat members of local communities with respect as the primary agents and decision makers in their own language development planning and implementation.

- The maintenance and restoration of each language and culture is an activity that mankind can participate in and is a worthwhile goal in re-establishing *shalom*.

- While human solutions often rely on scientific and technological efforts ("let us build a tower that will reach to heaven"), there is ample evidence both in the biblical text and all around us that such solutions often do damage to the creation in ways that are unforeseen and unexpected. Therefore, we approach language development interventions with a great deal of caution and humility, recognizing that our methods, technologies, and theories are, at best, merely imperfect tools and not "solutions."

2.6 Going deeper

Any technical discussion has to make sure that the terminology that is used is defined clearly and consistently. Otherwise, a great deal of confusion may ensue. In this volume we make use of terms that often have a generally accepted meaning but which, because we or others have chosen to use them in a novel way, may be understood differently by different readers. Some commonly used terms are considered offensive by some. Others do not convey the precise meaning that we intend. In the sub-sections that follow, we discuss some of these. We would also direct readers who desire to go deeper into the terminological background to Grenoble and Whaley (2006:13–16) for a helpful overview of the issues surrounding various terminological choices especially in regard to the references to local communities. Also see Skutnabb-Kangas 1984, 2000, and 2008 for a helpful discussion of the terms mother-tongue, first-language, etc.

2.6.1 What is a local community?

We have chosen to use the term "local" (following Grenoble and Whaley 2006) to characterize these communities in the discussion above as a more generic label and one that has fewer additional connotations.

The status of a language—its desirability and perceived usefulness—is much more related to ideology and cultural mythology than to any inherent feature of the language itself or the population size of those who use the language. Hornberger (2006) asserts that ideology, ecology, and agency must be considered in the evaluation of both the current status of languages and in the formation of language policies. Where sociolinguistic descriptions of communities in the past have taken socioeconomic status (class) and the correlations of that status with language use and language attitudes as a given, increasingly, the disparities in power and the inequalities present in most societies are being understood not only as the context of language planning but as part of the problem that language planning should address. When these dimensions of disparity are in focus, local communities are often identified as minority communities even when they are not numerically in the minority. When an observer wishes to emphasize that the disparity is an imposed one, they may use the term minoritized to describe a local community. While we generally use the term local community, there are occasions in this volume where, in context, the terms minority or minoritized and sometimes also dominant or non-dominant language or community seem to be the better choice.

2.6.2 Language

This volume refers to the concept of language without defining it precisely. As might be expected the phenomenon of human languages is complex. One important longstanding distinction that has served as a foundational concept in the development of structural approaches to linguistics is the difference between *langue* and *parole* (Saussure 1966). The former refers to the grammatical system of a language. One of the premises of structural linguistics following Saussure is that the grammatical rules and structures of a language can be described and are consistent and homogeneous. Though there may be some variation, all varieties of

2.6 Going deeper

the same language will be characterized by the same or very similar grammatical rules. In contrast, *parole* describes the social usage of language where in some cases and for some purposes grammatical norms may be violated or unexpected forms may be innovated. For linguists, who more often focus on the structure of language itself, it has generally been the case that what is of most interest is *langue* and it has been noted that *langue* can be studied and described even in the absence of a community of speakers. This has been done in various ways, using the notion of an "ideal speaker-hearer" (more on this below) or by depending on the intuitions of native speakers regarding the grammaticality of sample utterances created by the linguist to test particular hypotheses about the internal system of the language being studied. In contrast, by definition *parole* requires the existence of a community. The study of *parole* requires the observation of language in use in context (i.e., in daily life). These concepts align closely with Chomsky's (1965) notions of competence and performance. For many sociolinguists, it is language as *parole* or performance that most attracts their attention and analysis.

Another important distinction as to what people may be referring to by the term language was observed by Haugen (1966a; cited from Paulston and Tucker 2003:414). After reviewing the literature on how the terms language and dialect have been used, he notes there are two fundamentally distinct traditions of use: the structural and the functional. The structural approach is descriptive of the language itself (that is, its grammar, vocabulary, and sounds)—"the overriding consideration is genetic relationships." This is the view most commonly taken by linguists in which a language is a grouping of related dialects that are intelligible to each other. Standardization does not enter into the definition of language. By contrast, the functional approach is descriptive of the language in daily communication—"the overriding consideration is the uses the speakers make of the codes they master." In this view, a language has a standardized written form, while a dialect is an unstandardized oral variety. A language is thus seen as the medium of communication between speakers of different dialects. This is the view of 'language' versus 'dialect' that is most commonly held by the public at large.

The *Ethnologue* (Lewis, Simons, and Fennig 2016) is the most widely cited reference work for enumerating the known languages of the world. The issue of defining what makes a language distinctly identifiable in contrast to others is clearly a foundational concern for such a research effort and some of the general issues related to language identification are discussed in the introduction to that publication. *Ethnologue* follows the ISO 639-3 standard (ISO 2007) in deciding what to list as a language. For languages in which standardization is well-established (EGIDS level 4 and higher), ISO 639-3 follows the functional view in assigning codes to languages. For the remaining cases in which standardization is not yet established across the community (EGIDS level 5 and lower), it follows the structural approach in using intelligibility between varieties as the main criterion for grouping dialects into languages. We discuss the EGIDS at length in chapter 5.

Much of the discussion and controversy around the identification of a language centers on how to deal with variation and variability in language forms and use. When taken to an extreme, structural approaches to language rely on the concept of an idealized speaker/hearer who produces and processes language in an environment with no distractions, no errors, and nothing else at work other than the grammatical rules needed to produce utterances. When confronted with the great deal of variation between speakers and hearers in the real world, many linguists have felt the need to find another way to approach the definition and description of "a language" in a way that could account for that variation. So it is that long-held views of languages are being called into question. Traditional understandings of a language as a code that is a discrete and identifiable system of signs (i.e., *langue*) are being abandoned by many current scholars. Instead, these scholars are tending to view language almost exclusively as *parole*. Hopper 1998 (cited in Ricento 2006) proposes that rather than understanding a language as a systematic set of structures and forms, it should be understood as the result of a process of "sedimentation of frequently used forms into temporary subsystems." Harris 1990 (cited in Ricento 2006) goes so far as to observe:

> Linguistics does not need to postulate the existence of languages as part of its theoretical apparatus.... If there is no such object, it is difficult to evade the conclusion that modern linguistics has been based upon a myth.

This view of language represents a significant trend in which rather than speak of *languages,* scholars are coming to refer to *discourses*—the sedimented ways of verbal behavior that are associated with a particular identity or body of knowledge and re-enforced by speakers as they create and maintain that identity.

It has been the practice to identify a specific language as a unit that is countable and definable in its own right. However, languages vary over time and across both geographical and social space. Increasingly, at least some linguists and sociolinguists understand language to be dynamic and are raising objections to counting languages as though they were static objects (Moore, Pietikainen, and Blommaert 2010; Muehlmann 2012; Hill 2002). While a language can be understood as a centered set with a core of generally shared features but an increasing amount of variation the farther one gets from that core, some linguists are adopting the view that rather than a centered set of structures and forms, a language is a centered set of behaviors—utterances which represent the person producing them. Language is understood to be not so much a noun, as a verb. Labov's insight that the variation we observe in linguistic behavior represents "sound change in progress" (Labov 1972a, 1972b) could thus be understood from this perspective as "linguistic (re-)sedimentation in progress" with each successive production of a variant representing one more grain of sand set in place.

In spite of this significant paradigm shift, it is still useful to deal with languages as identifiable discrete units. Haugen (1966a) observes: "We may simply state that the 'particle' theory of language as a unified structure is a fruitful hypothesis, making it possible to produce an exhaustive self-consistent description."

In this volume, as might be expected with our focus on community-based language development, we tend more toward the *parole*/performance/functional perspective, but acknowledge that when we make reference to "a language" we assume a significant amount of structural similarity among the varieties that might be included within the notion of a single language. This issue will arise again in chapter 3 when we distinguish between the language community and the speech community.

2.6.3 Life-crucial knowledge

Trainum (2012) uses the term life crucial information and describes how "shellbooks"—pre-formatted, easily produced booklets on a variety of topics—can be used to transmit helpful and essential knowledge:

> Minority language communities use the Shellbook method to localize literacy, education, and development information of all types. Government and other public and private agencies have provided shellbooks for localization on such life-crucial topics as HIV-AIDS, clean water, sanitation, and enhanced & sustainable agriculture, as well as Primary school curriculum and reading material for neo-literates.

UNESCO has focused on the significant distinction between information societies and knowledge societies. "The idea of the information society is based on technological breakthroughs. The concept of knowledge societies encompasses much broader social, ethical and political dimensions" (UNESCO 2005b:17). While advances in science and technology have greatly increased the amount of information that people can access, UNESCO focuses on the evaluation, interpretation, and integration of that information into usable and beneficial knowledge. "While information is a knowledge-generating tool, it is not knowledge itself" (UNESCO 2005b:19). The creation of a just and fair global social order, in their view, requires much greater equality in access to knowledge. "Every society has its own knowledge assets. It is therefore necessary to work towards connecting the forms of knowledge that societies already possess and the new forms of development, acquisition and spread of knowledge valued by the knowledge economy model" (UNESCO 2005b:17). UNESCO further recognizes the distinction we have made here between language, form (or modality), and content: "It is impossible to separate fully the issue of contents from that of languages and different forms of knowledge" (UNESCO 2005b:18); and, "An analysis of knowledge societies cannot avoid seriously thinking about the future of linguistic diversity and ways to preserve it in a world where the informational revolution may lead to the risks of standardization and generalized formatting" (UNESCO 2005b:26).

The argument for the preservation of local knowledge is quite fully explicated by Nettle and Romaine 2000, who provide multiple examples of societies where the loss of traditional knowledge has had disastrous effects not only for the minority language communities themselves but for outsiders and the natural environment as well. Similar arguments are made by Crystal (2000), Harrison (2007), and others.

In addition, we frame the community's discussion of the transmission of life-crucial knowledge as a practical way to deal with the issue that language preservation *per se* is often too far abstracted from the day-to-day life of most community members to be seen as an urgent priority. Knowledge transmission hits a bit closer to home. Henderson, Rohloff, and Henderson (2014) raise similar concerns regarding efforts primarily focused on reversing language shift.

2.6.4 Multiple identities, languages, and bodies of knowledge

Increased contact between members of different communities has made the dynamics of language change as a result of that contact a much more important area of investigation. What's more, as described above, the linguistic representation of a chosen identity is continuously being constructed and revised as one group stresses its internal commonalities and reinforces its differences from outsiders. This kind of identity construction and maintenance also occurs, albeit somewhat less starkly, within ethnic or community groups as well as between them. Old folks don't speak the same way as young people (diachronic variation over time) nor do they want to. Northerners don't speak the same way as southerners (diatopic variation across geographic space) and upper class people don't speak the same way as lower class (diastratic variation across social space). When one of these identities is perceived to be more desirable than another, those who are "outside" of that prestigious identity group may make attempts to begin to talk as though they were "inside." A language changes over time as the linguistic markers of a particularly valued identity gain in usage (and become more and more sedimented into common practice), while the markers of less desirable identities fade away and are forgotten. In earlier work on language usage, particularly in regard to politeness (Brown and Gilman 1960), it was felt that these evaluations, especially between individuals, were at root based on the strong effects of the human need for both solidarity with others (the unifying function of language) and for power to be able to do what one wanted (the contrastive function of language).

Different linguistic varieties are affected along any of these dimensions (time, geography, social space) by contacts between speakers of other varieties in their environment and the positive or negative evaluation of those others (and the way they speak). Linguistic varieties take on specific roles and functions associated with the identified characteristics of those speakers and are customarily used for different purposes and in different situations. The choice of a linguistic code in any given setting, in itself, communicates a particular message regarding the speaker, the hearer, their relationship to each other, and the content of the communication itself. These choices have been characterized as "acts of identity" (LePage and Tabouret-Keller 1985). In an analysis of community language use that considers all use of language from an acts of identity perspective, it can be seen that power and solidarity are similarly at work (Lewis 2000). One ongoing discussion is whether it is identity that emanates from linguistic differences or is it that linguistic differences are in fact the realizations of differences in identity? The latter view postulates that linguistic features are manipulated to reinforce and dynamically construct an identity. Where a particular identity has been longstanding, the linguistic markers of that identity have become sedimented, are widely known (and unconsciously learned) and form the core of the linguistic system for representing that identity. Alternative or additional identity associations are then signaled by using different linguistic features.

2.6.5 Community

We have defined community primarily in terms of the construction of a shared identity. "Community suggests a dimension of shared knowledge, possessions or behaviours" (Mesthrie et al. 2000:37). In general, however, our usage of the term is quite a bit closer to the notion of speech community proposed by Gumperz (1968). In our usage, we have added the level of interaction of individuals with each other to the shared features which constitute a speech community as described by Gumperz and later by Hymes (Hymes 1972). This will be discussed more extensively in chapter 3.

2.6.6 Why does it matter?

Many before us have published on the topic of why the large-scale loss of languages should concern us. In his chapter on "Why should we care?", Crystal (2000) summarizes his answer in terms of five arguments: (1) because we need diversity, (2) because languages express identity, (3) because languages are repositories of history, (4) because languages contribute to the sum of human knowledge, and (5) because languages are interesting in themselves. Grenoble and Whaley (2006:2–3) make reference to the loss of linguistic diversity, the recognition of human rights, and the reaction of local communities to the pressures of globalization as reasons that language revitalization efforts have proliferated. Harrison (2007) emphasizes the portion of the immense human knowledge base that has been painstakingly assembled over millennia and which will vanish when the languages in which that knowledge is encoded cease to be used. Romaine (2008) explicitly appeals to the ecological rationale linking linguistic diversity directly to biological diversity, building on an extensive set of examples of that connection in Nettle and Romaine 2000. Fishman (1991:2) uses the humanitarian rationale as the primary motivation for his writing of his now-classic work on reversing language shift.

    The rationales that motivate us to care about sustaining language use are not mutually exclusive but often overlap with and corroborate each other. As mentioned above, each of these rationales reflects an underlying set of ideologies that frame the preservation of diversity, both linguistic and biological, the treatment of humanitarian issues, the academic investigation and documentation of language, and the recognition of human rights, as "good things to do" and that frame how different approaches to diversity and language and identity maintenance are to be understood. Hornberger's (1988, 2002) and Hornberger and Skilton-Sylvester's (2000) work on ideological perspectives on language policy are a good place to begin exploring the importance of awareness of ideology in language development work. Other case studies can be found in Ricento 2000 and, though the term ideology isn't used in her discussion of ideological shifts in Guatemala, in Warren (1998:Chap. 1).

3

Community-Based Language Development

Community-based language development empowers and builds capacity in local language communities by assisting them in identifying their own holistic development goals taking into account the relationship of identity and language to the transmission of life-crucial knowledge.

3.1 Introduction

In chapter 2, we introduced the concept of the local community and described some of the salient features of such a community. We described the situation of those communities in light of increasing globalization and how many local communities have been described using the terms minority or minoritized. We discussed the role of language and its importance in both defining a community and in helping a community meet its ongoing needs in all areas of life through the transmission of life-crucial knowledge.

In this chapter we propose that community-based language development can provide a useful conceptual framework for local language communities as they evaluate the status of life-crucial knowledge transmission and as they develop strategies for language and identity maintenance. It is the development—by the community itself—of these strategies for the ongoing management of the different bodies of knowledge communicated by means of the community's entire linguistic repertoire that we are calling community-based language development.

As described in chapter 1, the Sustainable Use Model (SUM) begins, not with language, but with the concept of life-crucial knowledge and its transmission as a key marker of a community's identity. The SUM proposes that local communities must concern themselves with the preservation and transmission of that knowledge if they are to survive as a distinct group. On the one hand, by starting with the community and its knowledge transmission needs rather than with a single language, the SUM provides a perspective on language development that aligns it with other general approaches to development. On the other hand, by including language as a core part of the model, the SUM distinguishes community-based language development from those general approaches which often either ignore local languages to a large extent or assume that the dominant language is adequate for community development purposes.

By starting with the community, the SUM aligns community-based language development with the general domain of community development. Community-based language development is a holistic approach that concerns itself with all areas of life, especially as they relate to the maintenance of community identity. On the other hand, the SUM differs considerably from traditional community development approaches, which often tend to focus on communities but without much awareness of their communication (and knowledge) patterns and needs. While these community development projects do not ignore language entirely, they often are linguistically naive in assuming that a national language or a language of wider communication will adequately serve a local community. Often the communities in focus in such efforts are defined by geographic or geopolitical locations. The coverage of such a project most often seems to be determined by geographic proximity of the community members who live in the same villages or towns or who share access to a central distribution or transportation hub, such as a market town or governmental center. While these very practical factors are significant, they should not be taken as the only—nor even as the primary—factors in defining the focus of efforts to ensure the transmission of life-crucial knowledge.

By defining the focus of language development work as the transmission of life-crucial knowledge, the SUM also departs significantly from traditional language development approaches which tend to focus on a single language rather than on the entire linguistic repertoire of a multilingual community. Such a monolingual perspective defines the scope of a project in terms of linguistically distinguishable varieties present in the region. Multilingualism in such situations is often viewed by this single-language-centric approach as either irrelevant or as an obstacle or even a threat to the (single, isolated) language development work.

The explanation of these shifts in perspective will form the bulk of our discussion in this chapter. In order to do that we need to revisit in greater depth the concept of community that we introduced in chapter 2.

3.2 Community

So far, we have used the term community to describe a definable group of people who recognize themselves as being distinct from other groups because of a shared identity. More precisely, this shared identity is both defined and reinforced by three components: shared knowledge, shared cultural and material possessions, and shared behaviors.

3.2.1 Shared knowledge

In chapter 2 we introduced the notion of bodies of knowledge and described how knowledge which is held by a particular group of people, what we called "internal knowledge," is one of the defining features of their distinctive identity. Knowledge is more than information or data because it is invested with significance by the shared geographical, social, cultural, and historical contexts of the group which possesses it. Internal knowledge consists, in part, of beliefs about the world and how it is structured. It includes ideas about how the community came into existence and what its place is in the world around it. It may also include technological knowledge encompassing productive skills and artistic techniques. It includes historical lore and religious, spiritual, and cosmological concepts. Much of this kind of knowledge is "life-crucial" because it is foundational to the maintenance of the community's way of life and understanding of the world. It is internal knowledge because it belongs to the community alone and is not shared by outsiders.

This internal knowledge, the knowledge that defines a community and makes it distinctive, is passed down from one generation to another. In many cases, this transmission is through oral modalities such as stories, poems, songs, chants, or physical re-enactments involving the performing arts such as music and dance.

A community's identity is almost always closely associated with a particular language or language variety, though the community may use more than one language in daily life. Very often the internal bodies of knowledge will be most closely associated with the language of identity. In order to access and use specialized internal knowledge, community members may need to have proficiency in their language of identity that goes well beyond normal conversational ability. The ability to recite the lore in the proper way, to sing the songs, perform the chants, dance the dances, may require the use of registers, genres, and styles of language that can only be learned through imitation, practice, and apprenticeship. Even where the body of knowledge is largely focused on knowing terminology, much learning may be required for an individual to be able to name the plants and animals and other objects that have special significance for the community.

Outsiders may acquire some of this knowledge, but it is a "native-like" mastery of this knowledge that marks one as a member of the group. In some cases, group boundaries are open and permeable and outsiders are readily welcomed into these internal knowledge domains. In other cases, boundaries are hardened and nearly impassable and few if any outsiders become adequately proficient in the internal knowledge. For some communities their language is part of the internal knowledge which they guard from outsiders. Linguists and others who wish to study the language may be prevented from doing so. If an outsider is given access and permission to learn the language, they may be required not to disclose what they have learned to others.

3.2.2 Shared cultural and material possessions

A community is also distinguished from other communities by its shared cultural and material possessions. Material possessions are the tangible artifacts which represent the way of life of the community in very practical ways. Physical objects are the clearest examples of these shared possessions: homes, tools, clothing, or food. People from the same community may build houses of a certain kind and in a certain way. They may use tools of a particular kind to do the specialized work that they alone do. They may distinguish themselves from people from other communities by the clothing they wear and the way in which they wear it and by the food they eat and the ways in which they prepare it.

A community not only shares physical objects but cultural objects as well. The meaning of physical items in the world comes from this shared cultural understanding. In part, this comes from the shared knowledge described above. The mountain, river valley, plain, or jungle in which they live is not just any mountain, river, plain, or jungle. There is a history, a lore that invests the geographic location with meaning. In most Western societies, an evergreen tree is not simply a tree but has the potential at least to become a Christmas tree. There is a shared cultural understanding of what an evergreen represents, how it can be decorated, and at what times of year it is appropriate to do so. Hammers and sickles, swords and plowshares all have cultural meanings that go far beyond their apparent objective characteristics as tools or weapons.

Such cultural objects have a history and are infused with meaning based on the community's shared knowledge. Tools are designed in a particular way not simply for utilitarian and pragmatic reasons, but often because of a tradition or legend that gives a tool a particular significance that is not shared by any other community in quite the same way. The aesthetics of design is often based on this history and tradition. Clothing identifies the person as being from a certain place or as having a certain social or economic status. Often particular items of clothing or colors and decorative patterns have a historical significance and are worn not so much for any utilitarian purpose but as a marker of identity and status.

Sleeves in Benin

In the mid-1990s in Cotonou, Benin, women's sleeves served as a marker of ethnic identity or ethnic association. Women who went to tailors or seamstresses who spoke Ede languages (languages related to Yoruba) wore tops or dresses with cap sleeves or simple inset sleeves such as Westerners are used to seeing on women's blouses. Women who went to tailors who spoke Gbè languages (such as Gen, Fon or Gun) wore tops or dresses with very elaborate sleeves: often heavily lined or starched, sometimes puffed, and sometimes with details such as braided strips of cloth. An American worker there asked her Fon seamstress for simple sleeves, and she responded by begging that she be allowed to make the sleeves "pretty." The result was puff sleeves, lined with multiple layers of material. (Bonnie Henson, personal communication)

Similarly, food has a meaning. For Americans, roasted turkey is closely associated with special holidays such as Thanksgiving or Christmas. In some parts of Asia, moon cakes and oranges or tangerines have similar festive connotations. Certain foods may only be eaten on certain days or prepared in special ways for certain people. In Guatemala, *fiambre,* a salad-like dish containing red beets (beet root), is only prepared and eaten on All Saints Day. Colored hard-boiled eggs are part of the Easter tradition for many Americans. There may be lore that attributes special powers or characteristics to certain kinds of foods, such as maize for Mayans or rice for many groups in Asia. Outsiders don't share these deeply held emotional associations. They won't know the special names of the foods. They won't know the proper ways to prepare them. Many a cultural faux pas occurs because an outsider handles a culturally significant food item improperly.

> **Guatemala: A flying disc fiasco**
>
> During a gathering of expatriates in Guatemala, it was decided that some recreational activities were called for. Not having any sports equipment available, the participants improvised by using tortillas, one of the local staple foods, as "flying discs" which they tossed back and forth. Guatemalans who observed this behavior were offended since for many of them the tortilla is not simply a kind of food, but represents the essence of who they are, maize being the source of life itself. Treating maize tortillas with such disrespect was unthinkable for them. (M. Paul Lewis, personal experience)

All of the tangible and intangible objects that serve as markers and reinforcers of identity are named and identified using language. The words and phrases used for these identifications become themselves cultural objects because of this close association with both the tangible and intangible aspects of the culture.

3.2.3 Shared behaviors

As described above, physical and cultural objects are used and manipulated in particular ways based on the shared knowledge and understanding of their significance. Community members engage in these shared behaviors because of these shared understandings. They know how a particular tool should be used. They build their houses, prepare their food, wear their clothes, grow their crops, and engage in all of their daily behaviors in the ways that are customary for their community. Often these behaviors become stylized and frozen so that they are simply "the way it is done" and contemporary members of a community may not be able to explain the reason that a certain tool is held in a certain way or certain gestures or movements are required as part of the "proper" way to engage in a particular activity. These behaviors are simply part of their heritage and a way of indicating their participation in their heritage identity.

Language use is also a shared behavior that is deeply rooted in shared identity and shared cultural knowledge. Linguistic behavior follows the same sorts of patterns as do other behaviors with a community consensus imbuing words and phrases with meaning and defining and reinforcing acceptable ways of saying things. Language is identity-based behavior that unifies and separates—that is, defines a community—in the same way that other kinds of behavior do.

Spelling behavior/behaviour

The differences between British and American spelling demonstrate the use of specific linguistic behaviors to mark identity. The distinctive spellings for words like *color/colour*, *check/cheque*, and *advertize/advertise* are not related to differences in pronunciation but are now identity markers that reinforce the users' distinctive identities.

3.2.4 More on language communities

The identity-based description of community that we've used above and in chapter 2, is relatively simplistic and far too general. It gives us a basic understanding of what we are talking about when we say community. In practice though, few communities are so neatly and clearly defined and there are some significant distinctions in the kinds of communities that exist. We describe these in this and the following sections.

The term language community, as described in the previous chapter, has frequently been used to refer to the population of users of a particular language (i.e., *langue*, see chapter 2, Going Deeper), no matter where they are. In the identity-based community that we've described, the concept of there being a set of linguistic structures most closely associated with an identity is an important foundational idea for defining and delimiting the community both for its members and for outsiders. The use of a single language (or of a range of varieties that are perceived as being a single language) is a kind of shared behavior that defines this particular kind of community. Language is an immensely important component of shared knowledge. Its vocabulary, forms, and structures also function as shared cultural objects that unify and separate a community. And it can be argued that language is the most widely shared and pervasive behavior that can characterize a community.

The association of language with identity is a bit more complex than that, however, in that the forms of language that people use often vary across multiple dimensions. There are two perspectives on language variation that need to be kept in mind. First, what is often referred to as dialect variation can occur across geographic space. Within this continuum of variation, specific varieties may come to be associated with a distinctive identity in their own right. Though users of all of the different varieties may agree that they all speak the same language, they may also be strongly aware of their distinctive identities and thus be unwilling to recognize that they are members of the same community. In some cases, these distinctive identity affiliations may be so strong that members of the different communities are unwilling to recognize that they use the same language, in spite of the fact that they can, in large measure, understand each other in face-to-face conversation. The challenge for language development in such settings is to determine the extent to which attempts at developing standardized materials (both oral and written) will be deemed acceptable by as many of the separate communities as possible.

3.2 Community

In situations where a community is relatively small or confined to a single or, at least, a clearly delimited, geographic location, the alignment of identity and language can be quite straightforward. In such cases, the language community, all those who speak a particular language (as identified by its structural coherence), coincides almost completely with the geographical location of the community as a whole. Where there is a great deal of variation and strong identity distinctions among users of those varieties, it may be more difficult to gain a consensus as to how to arrive at an acceptable norm for wider use.

This kind of variation has been dealt with by language developers in very different ways. One approach is to develop a single standard variety that all are expected to learn and use. Sometimes the most prestigious of the local varieties is chosen to play this unifying role. In other cases, a somewhat artificial variety, sometimes called a "pan-dialect" is created by selecting from among the different varieties a standard set of terms, grammatical constructions, and other forms that represent the way no one group uses the language but overall covers the range of usage among the different varieties. A third option is to simply accept variation as normal and acceptable with no single variety being promoted over any other. Where a writing system needs to be developed, it may be designed so as to accommodate the variation with alternate ways of spelling considered acceptable.

There are advantages and risks with any of these approaches. Promoting a single prestigious variety may not be acceptable to users of the less prestigious varieties and they may opt out of the development process. On the other hand, developing and promoting a "pan-dialect" variety as the standard may fail to attract the loyalty of a sufficient number of users, since what is promoted as being "everybody's" language may be perceived to be "nobody's" (and certainly, not "mine"). And, in the third case, allowing free variation may not be acceptable if there is a strongly held sense that it is important to "do something" and it is widely assumed that standardization is the best thing to do. Often, languages with no clear standardized way of being written (or spoken) are compared unfavorably to more prestigious dominant languages with longstanding and widely accepted traditions of standardization.

A very practical issue for local-community language developers is that it is generally more advantageous for a community that wishes to sustain their language and culture to have larger numbers. Any approach that divides an already dwindling population into even smaller groups may be counterproductive. That gives weight to the view that a single standard variety that unifies all segments of the language community is, in principle, the better choice, provided that standardized variety gains acceptance. Nevertheless, broad acceptance of one of the other approaches can be as effective in unifying a community and should not be dismissed out of hand.

As we pointed out in chapter 2, it is increasingly the case that speakers of a language (i.e., members of a particular language community) are in frequent contact with and make significant use of other languages as well. This represents the second perspective on language variation that should be considered. In chapter 2, we discussed the fact that most local communities are significantly affected by other, more dominant communities with whom they are in contact. In many cases these contacts are not casual and rare but are frequent, pervasive, and powerful. This increased contact and the resulting multilingualism can also cause the close association of languages with identities to be less straightforward and much more complex even within a single, well-defined geographic location. Some members of a local community may participate in larger, more extensive social networks and may represent that more cosmopolitan orientation in their linguistic repertoire. Language variation not only extends across geographic space but also extends across social space, with an individual's status and prestige being marked by their language use. And variation can also extend temporally with different forms of language being used by different generations or age cohorts. (More on this below.) Even in local communities that are not widely dispersed geographically, this kind of variation needs to be taken into account in language development in ways that have not generally been considered in the past.

Especially in local communities where contact with others is frequent, speakers of what we would generally identify as the same language share multiple identities and participate in multiple communities. As a result, they are also using multiple languages. That multilingualism in turn has an effect on each of the languages being used as speakers switch more-or-less freely between languages, borrow words, or use innovative grammatical constructions that are borrowed from one of the other languages in their repertoire. Any approach to community-based language development needs to keep this complexity in mind and needs to account for the fact that multi-identitied communities will be characterized by multilingualism (and vice versa). Language development practitioners must expand their concept of community to include the role of multiple languages in managing and representing these complex identities. They must not confine their understanding of the local community to only those who speak the same language. Any multi-identitied multilingual community is, by definition, simultaneously characterized by multiple *language community* affiliations as well.

Since language development by definition will involve activities to solve community problems by using at least one language, many of the products and results of the development of any single language in a particular setting may be of interest and of use in the broader community of speakers of that language (the broader language community). That potential for extensibility needs to be kept in mind and maximized where possible. However, the approach which we are promoting, community-based language development, does not make extensibility to the entire language community the primary focus. It is not the language per se that is in focus. It is the speech community, a concept to which we now turn.

3.2.5 What is a speech community?

Where multilingual communities are managing multiple identities, the concept of a language community isn't entirely adequate. The common feature of such a community may not be the strong association with a single language of identity, but may be more diffuse, encompassing multiple languages. It is, therefore, helpful to make use of another concept, speech community, which resembles more closely the kinds of situations in which many local communities find themselves. Historically, language communities have been the unit of operation for language development work. That is, language developers have tended to focus on (a single) language. However, for the purposes of community-based language development it is the speech community that more properly should be the focus of language development work. In other words, community-based language development programs should operate within and on behalf of speech communities which are characterized by a shared linguistic repertoire, shared norms of language use, and significant levels of internal interaction.

A shared linguistic repertoire

Communities are defined by their shared knowledge, shared possessions, and shared behaviors. An important component of those shared features is language. A speech community, like a language community, is characterized by shared linguistic knowledge (language structures and codes), shared linguistic possessions (words and terminology) and shared linguistic behavior (ways of speaking, norms of use). However, in a speech community those shared linguistic components may not be confined to a single language. Rather, as community members negotiate and manipulate their multiple identities they may also negotiate and manipulate an equally complex set of distinct linguistic codes. Thus, a speech community is not so much defined by its single shared language as by its shared repertoire of linguistic varieties.

In its simplest and most straightforward form, a speech community may be comprised of a single language community. That is, everybody in the community speaks a single common language. It is more commonly the case, however, that speech communities have multiple languages within their repertoire. They use these languages for different activities on a daily basis and children may acquire some of them naturally in those settings. Others may be acquired formally in school or other educational settings, and may not be learned until a child is of a certain age or reaches a certain stage in her life. Not all members of the community may have equal proficiency in all of the languages in the community repertoire, but they know when one language is more appropriate than another and who should use which language in which setting.

Even if a community has only one language in its repertoire, it is very likely that there are different registers or styles of the language, each used in a particular setting, for particular purposes, by a particular group of people. These settings may be defined by age groups or bodies of knowledge or by particular venues or participants. Members of the speech community are aware of them, learn them, and use them as needed, and recognize them as being part of what defines their community identity. Proficiency in these languages or varieties is very closely related to the functions that the languages serve in the community's social, economic, political, and spiritual life and an individual's participation in the activities associated with those domains.

A shared set of norms

In addition to the existence of multiple linguistic varieties, whether genres and registers of a single language or multiple languages, a speech community is characterized by a shared set of norms regarding when each variety is appropriate and what each should be used for and by whom. Here, as described above in our discussion of variation, there are two kinds of norms that are in view.

Linguistic variation, that is, differences in linguistic structure (e.g., grammar and vocabulary), that exist in a community facilitate the use of a language for particular functions. People gain proficiency in those structures to the degree that they need them to communicate the body of knowledge with which they are most closely associated. A specialist in a particular body of knowledge will have a larger, more developed set of linguistic tools at their disposal suitable for dealing with that body of knowledge appropriately. Some linguistic forms are clearly reserved for specific settings and uses. For example, a husband and wife, even if both were lawyers, would not carry on a conversation in their home in which they would refer to themselves as "the party of the first part" and "the party of the second part." However, if they were being referred to in a legal contract, that more elaborate and formal terminology might be called for. While this example demonstrates the functional role of linguistic structural norms, it also exemplifies social norms of language use, where there is a clear differentiation between language use for domestic functions and language use for legal purposes. Where there are multiple linguistic varieties to choose from, those varieties may be closely associated with particular functions, (bodies of knowledge), settings, and users. A child growing up in that community acquires not only the proficiencies needed to use each variety appropriately, but also subconsciously acquires an awareness of the settings in which each variety is appropriate.

In this sense, not all languages are on an equal footing. The norms of use that are arrived at informally and unconsciously by community consensus, establish categories of appropriateness for each variety. A member of the community knows which variety to use when and where. Certain people should be spoken to in a particular way. In many cases, this includes using a different language than one would use with other people. Certain bodies of knowledge are most appropriately discussed in one language and not in another. Public settings may require one language variety while private settings would permit the use of another. The presence or absence of outsiders may also affect the choice of language depending on whether the outsider is to be included or excluded as a participant in the conversation. Outsiders' attitudes towards the language may also have a significant effect on language choice as speakers avoid using language forms that might be evaluated negatively in the presence of certain persons.

Members of the community may not always be consciously aware of these norms, having acquired them unconsciously as they have grown up in much the same way they acquired language itself. Only a few may be able to talk about them in abstract terms. However, they will know how to navigate the norms and will also know how to manipulate them at times for specific purposes such as to make fun or to shame, to include or exclude, or to express approval or disapproval. Even if a particular individual is unable to use all of the varieties that form part of the community repertoire, she will be able to recognize the significance of a particular choice of linguistic code when it occurs. We will consider this issue more fully when we discuss the concepts of Functions and Differentiation in chapter 7.

Significant levels of interaction

Because they are characterized by significant levels of interaction among the community members, speech communities are a particular kind of social network.

3.2 Community

Individuals within a speech community interact with each other in a variety of ways. The greater the number of interactions, the stronger the network ties will be. The stronger the network ties, the more likely that a sense of shared identity exists or is being reinforced. The nature of a network also is such that it provides a better way of understanding a speech community. Communities, like languages, are in fact not unitary. They are complex and overlapping networks of interaction and contact. Planners of language development must follow the lines of interaction and communication and develop the communicative tools that participants in the network must have in order to meet their needs for the transmission of life-crucial knowledge.

For the purposes of community-based language development, it is the speech community that constitutes the most appropriate unit of focus for language development work. Speech communities are often multilingual and multi-identitied. They are characterized by high levels of interaction among community members. And community members call upon and manipulate the components of the community's linguistic repertoire based on the functions assigned to those components. The functions for which any particular language is used and the modalities (oral, written, digital) in which it is produced in each speech community will differ. The opportunities and challenges for language development in each setting will also differ. If language development is the result of a speech community taking actions to deal with its own needs in every area of life, then the language dynamics (both repertoire and norms) of the speech community need to be in view.

Promoters of language development need to recognize the dynamics of this multifaceted language use as an essential aspect of the nature of the speech community. Dealing with "a language" in isolation (i.e., treating a complex speech community as a single language community) in such settings will fail to adequately recognize the true nature of the larger speech community. Though a more narrow focus on the speakers of a single language, a language community, may be an operational and practical necessity where the dynamics of a speech community are especially complex, language development work that ignores such a complex context will inevitably prove to be inadequate.

As a speech community envisions its own language development goals, it is helpful for these concepts to be kept in mind and for community/network identity and boundaries to be continuously clarified and defined. The shared knowledge, possessions, and behaviors of those in a community are in continuous dynamic flux. Just as a language is continuously changing, so is the identity of the community of its speakers. Both the linguistic relationships that exist between varieties within a language community and the social relationships that exist between speakers of different languages that interact regularly with each other must be continuously assessed.

The Majangir case in Ethiopia, given as an example in chapter 2, also demonstrates the distinction between a language community, all those who speak Majangir, and multiple speech communities, namely the speech community in the northwest that uses Majangir and Anuak in its linguistic repertoire, versus the speech community in the northeast that uses Majangir and Oromo, and so on for the other second languages. In other cases, a rural community may have one linguistic repertoire but speakers of the local language who reside in urban areas may have a very different repertoire. In still other cases, speakers of a language who reside in different countries may have different national languages as a component of their respective repertoires. Their variety of the local language may also reflect that contact in its vocabulary of borrowed terms, but perhaps more significantly, in the roles the different languages play within those differing contexts.

Spanish: One language in multiple speech communities

The language community of Spanish speakers is very large and widespread covering not only the territory of Spain in Europe, but also most of Central and South America, as well as Equatorial Guinea in Africa, and in most of the larger cities generally and many rural areas across the United States. A community of Spanish speakers remains in the Philippines as well. However, the significance of "being a Spanish speaker" differs widely among those regions. The norms of use of Spanish in the United States, for example, are quite distinct from the norms of use in many of the countries in Latin America with large indigenous populations. Whereas in Mexico or Guatemala or Peru, being a member of the Spanish language community is prestigious and advantageous socially, economically and politically, in the United States, that identity and language community membership is more likely to be seen as less prestigious and less advantageous. Because of these differences in the norms of use, the single language community made up of Spanish speakers, may be simultaneously viewed as overlapping with multiple speech communities.

While the concepts of language community and of speech community are different from each other, they are not mutually exclusive concepts and the two types of communities interact with and overlap each other in multiple ways as we have described.

Even though there may be a large, widely spread, language community, not all of the members of that particular language community are necessarily members of the same speech community because they may not have frequent opportunity for interaction with each other, the forms of the language (usually vocabulary and phonological features, but grammatical structures as well) and the norms of use of the language may differ significantly from location to location. Their linguistic repertoires may be quite different. Because they live and use their languages in very different contexts, they do not necessarily share the same linguistic knowledge, linguistic objects, nor the same norms of use which characterize a single speech community.

With the fuller discussions of language and community as a foundation, we can now turn to a more complete description of community-based language development.

3.3 What is community-based language development?

3.3.1 Language development

We have chosen to use the term language development, and to define it in a particular way that helps to address some of the problems associated with other terminology that has been used as we describe below and in the Going deeper section of this chapter.

> **Language development: A definition**
>
> **language development** 1. the process starting early in life by which a person acquires language. 2. the process by which a language takes on new functions within a society. 3. activities undertaken within a language community specifically for the purpose of developing new functions for its language or for restoring lost functions. (Simons 2011)

As can be seen in the definition, an initial source of confusion that arises is that the term language development is commonly used among linguists to refer to the phenomenon of first-language acquisition (how infants and children develop the ability to speak and use language). As with other sociolinguistic phenomena, the difference here is between the micro-sociolinguistic focus on language development in the individual and the macro-sociolinguistic focus on language development at the level of society.

We understand language development to be both the *result* of language planning and the entire range of activities engaged in to achieve the desired results.

3.3.2 Community-based language development and language planning

We should note here that language planning is an area of applied linguistics which in many respects parallels the concerns and activities that we are including within our definition of language development. Though there are many different ways of describing and defining language planning, we offer our own definition here as a way to identify some of the more relevant aspects of language planning for community-based language development practitioners.

> Language planning is overt, directed, purposeful, change of language use, language structure, or both in order to solve some identified problem.

Most often the problems being addressed by language planners are political, economic, or social, but those making language policy decisions believe that part of the solution to those problems requires a change in the way language is used. For example, a government may develop and promote a standardized form of a particular language as a way to foster national unity and a shared identification with the nation state. This may be understood as the best way to deal with diversity and strong local allegiances. In such a case, the use of the national language will be promoted and the development, and in extreme cases even the use of other languages, may be discouraged or prohibited. The "problem" of diversity is thus addressed through language policy.

While there is a whole range of definitions of language planning which focus on different important aspects of the work and activities of language planners, we use our definition because it is focused not so much on the content of language planning as on the agency and power dimensions of directed language change. In the context of local speech communities, as defined above, it is the agency and empowerment of the communities themselves that is a critical factor.

Our definition recognizes that language planning is an effort to change the usage patterns (the functions), the actual structures of language, or the skills and behaviors of language users, or all of the above. Of course, language change happens naturally as communities of speakers adapt to their changing environments. What distinguishes language planning from natural language change, however, is that it is not only a response to those external changes by speakers in their daily contexts but that it is "overt, directed, and purposeful." We can explain those modifiers best if we examine them in reverse order:

Purposeful

Language planning is purposeful in that it is attempting to provide a solution to some identified problem. The problem may be any of the features of a minority language community described previously: lack of participation in the economy or political system, inadequate access to education, loss of culture or identity, lack of sustainability. More frequently, the identified problem is one that is not so easily or directly associated with language, for example, efficiency in the operation of the apparatus of governance. Someone analyzes the situation, identifies a problem, and attempts to solve that problem through language-focused solutions.

Directed

Language planning is directed in that it is guided by some agent who is given or takes on responsibility to solve the identified problem. That agent decides what the solution to the problem will be and works to plan the language changes that will be part of that solution. Frequently the language planner is an arm of government but other organizations and agencies can also take on a semi-official or grassroots role in changing language behavior. In some cases, changes are initiated by an individual, a champion, who sets about to solve a problem and uses language as a means to accomplish goals. There are several well-known cases, for example, Cherokee in North America, Vai in Africa, and Korean in Asia, where orthographies which gained wide use and acceptance were designed and promoted by individuals. Even in those cases, however, the individual was already recognized as an authority or took on a position of authority. Unlike the natural process of language change where individuals spontaneously change their language use patterns in response to changes in the external environment, including the perceived prestige of an innovation, changes in language use that are the result of language planning are directed by an agent of change with the aim of achieving specific purposes.

Overt

Language planning is overt in that it is most often consciously thought out and publicly implemented. Natural language change, in contrast, is covert. That is, it most frequently happens so gradually that most speakers of the language are not aware it is taking place. Natural language change is often remarked on (either positively or negatively) after it has happened. By then, the changes may be so far along that reversal would be unlikely or extremely difficult. Some language planning may also seem covert if planned changes are implemented very gradually so as not to attract too much attention or to avoid opposition. Almost by definition, however, language planning involves very public efforts to promote and implement specific new ways of using language. Even when the implementation of a planned language change may be gradual and incremental, those planned changes will be publicly promoted and overtly implemented. Generally, language planning involves highly visible publicity campaigns and efforts to change attitudes and behaviors. Implementation methods may involve legislation and civil and legal rewards and penalties aimed at promoting compliance. These more coercive means might also be accompanied by or be replaced by gentler more persuasive public relations efforts.

As mentioned above, these directed, purposeful, overt efforts are focused on changes in the functions, changes in the structures, and changes in the skills of language users. These three areas of focus have been labeled as "status planning," "corpus planning," and "acquisition planning" in one well-known description of what language planners do. (See the Going Deeper section for more on this). Status planning focuses on the functions, or uses, of language. It answers the question: What will this language be used for? Corpus planning focuses on the language itself and answers the question: "What forms or structures does the language need in order to be able to serve the functions assigned to it by the status planners? Finally, acquisition planning focuses on the users of the language and answers the question: What language skills do the users need to be able to use the language for its assigned functions?

Status planning

Status decisions have political implications (who will have easier access to political discourse?), judicial implications (who will have an easier time representing themselves or being represented in the courts?), as well as social, economic and other kinds of implications. This being the case, it is easy to see why status decisions and the resulting policies are often the tools by which social, economic, and political problems are addressed.

Status planning

Traditionally, status planning has been conceived of as dealing with decisions about whether a particular language will be used for literary functions (reading, writing, literary production) or for education (as a language of instruction or as a language to be taught). A typical example: governments or education authorities making decisions about which languages will be used for official purposes (in the legislature, in government offices, as languages of instruction, etc.).

For the purposes of community-based language development,, it is helpful to think of status planning more in terms of decisions about which bodies of knowledge should be associated most closely with which language(s). The consideration of a language's status is fundamentally a set of decisions that a community needs to make about bodies of life-crucial knowledge and how they will be most effectively and sustainably transmitted to the next generation. As we develop further our explanation of the SUM we will make explicit our understanding that bodies of knowledge, domains of use, and the notion of "functions" of languages are interrelated and overlapping concepts.

Corpus planning

Corpus planning has to do with the language itself. The "corpus" being referred to is the "body" of the language. This shouldn't be confused with other ways in which the word "corpus" is used or understood. It does not, for example, refer to a corpus of literature or a corpus of text materials.

Decisions and activities which are needed in order to fit a language to the functions assigned to it by the makers of status planning decisions constitute corpus planning. Again, for the purposes of community-based language development these decisions depend significantly on the community's decisions regarding life-crucial knowledge transmission. In addition, as we will discuss in chapter 6, corpus planning decisions also depend to a great extent on the community's choice of a desired sustainable level of language use. Decisions regarding the nature of an orthography (script choice, degree of similarity to other orthographies in the region, etc.), standardization, lexical elaboration, and the like are corpus planning activities. The status decision to use a language as the means of transmission of a particular body of life-crucial knowledge along with the choice of a desired level of sustainable use of the language, will result in corpus planning outcomes regarding whether that knowledge will be transmitted orally or in writing, using local terms or borrowed terminology, and so on.

Corpus planning is often described as consisting of two major activities. Codification includes the development of a system of writing for the language where none exists, including standardization, the establishment of norms for spelling, punctuation, and usage. The second major area of corpus planning is elaboration which most often involves the development of the vocabulary, and sometimes grammatical structures, needed to expand the capacity of the language to be used for functions assigned to it by the status planners.

Corpus planning

When Hebrew was being revived in Israel, a lot of corpus planning activity was engaged in as liturgical Hebrew needed to be elaborated to be used for modern innovations in technology and science. As more and more people began to use Hebrew on a daily basis, some of that elaboration occurred spontaneously with technical terms, for example, being borrowed from other languages. This resulted in a lot of variation in those terms as each user adopted vocabulary from their own heritage languages. As a result, speakers of different first-languages often didn't understand each other even though they were both ostensibly using Hebrew. Language planners directed elaboration efforts in order to provide official lists of terms in order to standardize usage. One of these projects was the elaboration of official Hebrew terms for parts of the car (Alloni-Feinberg 1974).

Acquisition planning

Where status planning focuses on the uses (functions, bodies of knowledge) of the language, and corpus planning focuses on the language itself, acquisition planning focuses on the users of the language and their capacity to use the developed linguistic corpus for the desired functions. For example, if the status planning decision is made to use a particular language for arithmetic, and the corpus planning decisions are made to develop a set of terms for all of the needed mathematical operations, a plan must also be developed to train teachers to teach those terms, to develop materials that incorporate them, to distribute that teacher training and the instructional materials, and to deploy those trained teachers to the places where they can make use of their training. At the same time, members of the language community must be made aware of the new terminology, must come to accept it (see prestige planning below), and must be willing to learn it and to have it taught to their children. All of these activities come under the label of acquisition planning.

Acquisition planning

The introduction of the written use of a language requires first of all the status decision that the language should be used for written functions. That is followed by the corpus planning activities of codification and standardization. But literacy skills must be learned so it is necessary for reading and writing pedagogical materials to be developed, tested, and put into use. Beyond that, other literature, at varying levels of difficulty, must also be produced so that new readers have opportunity to practice and perfect their skills. And all of those materials must be distributed and made accessible to the general population. Teachers must be trained and administrative and logistical systems must be developed for the delivery of literacy instruction.

Prestige planning

Prestige planning focuses not only on the prestige of the language being planned but also on the prestige of those involved in the planning process, and the prestige of the products of their planning. In traditional language planning efforts, the prestige of the planners is often derived from the position of authority given to them by legislation or by some recognized (and thereby prestigious) agency. Language academies are often made up of prestigious experts and therefore their decisions are accepted on the basis of that prestige. Local languages are often not generally perceived as being very prestigious, often even by the members of the local communities themselves. Often the products of language planning are designed to emulate the prestigious features of the dominant language, though this need not always be so. Prestige planning needs to address all of these aspects by carefully and consciously identifying the issues and making decisions about how to address them.

Prestige planning focuses on the motivations of community members to use the language and might be described as answering the question: Why should one want to be identified with and use the language? Prestige planning activities frequently do not directly require corpus planning activities, but more often are part of an overall acquisition plan. They help to create an atmosphere which is conducive to ongoing language use and to the acceptance and adoption of the results of status, corpus and acquisition planning. We describe prestige planning in greater depth in the Going Deeper section of this chapter, and in regard to motivation, in chapter 7. We provide some examples in the Appendix.

> **Prestige planning**
>
> It is often the case that a local language is not seen as being as useful or as valuable as a more dominant language. Language development practitioners will need to engage in activities aimed at re-enforcing the perceived benefits (economic, social, religious, etc.) of using the local language. The use of a language for recordings, broadcast, or in film is one way to build the prestige of a language. There are an increasing number of such productions, e.g., the "telenovela" *Baktun* broadcast in the Maya [yua] language of Mexico. (Fox News Latino 2013)

While community-based language development involves the same kinds and categories of issues and activities as language planning (status planning, corpus planning, acquisition planning, and prestige planning discussed in more detail in the Going Deeper section of this chapter) it involves local communities from the start in both the identification of the outcomes that they desire and in the creation of their own capacity and processes to achieve those desired outcomes. Rather than starting at the level of the nation-state and the needs of government or some other higher-level agency, as most language planning efforts have, community-based language development begins at the level of the local community itself and identifies aspirations and desires from the community's perspective.

In addition, the approach we are proposing more clearly recognizes the importance of both the decision-making (planning) processes and the development of as much capacity within the community as possible to carry out and implement the decisions that are made. Community-based language development recognizes the importance of the users and their participation in all of the major areas of focus in traditional language planning.

It also identifies areas in which advocacy may be needed in order to bring a greater alignment between national policy, more local language policy, and the aspirations of the local communities. Advocacy for the development of better language policy at higher levels broadens the understanding of what acquisition planning and prestige planning are about by including within the scope of language planning not only the proficiencies and attitudes of language users in the community but also the attitudes and ideologies of policy makers and authorities.

3.3.3 Characteristics of community-based language development

Based on this background, we can identify the significant characteristics of community-based language development: it is holistic; it is results based; it works from the inside out and from the bottom up; it is language-aware; and it is empowering.

Community-based language development is holistic

Community-based language development recognizes that local communities have more concerns, needs, aspirations, and desires than language alone. It recognizes that these concerns may be in any area of life. The focus is on people, the community, not on *the language* and not solely on language-related products or activities. Most language planning initiatives are intended to solve a social, economic, or political problem by bringing about some change in the way people use language. In community-based language development, the community makes decisions about how their linguistic repertoire can help them meet their needs in all areas of life. We discuss this primarily in terms of the ongoing transmission of life-crucial knowledge. By focusing on knowledge transmission rather than on addressing the defects in language structures or usage patterns, the community can much more clearly see how language matters in addressing all areas of life. The focus shifts from being prescriptive about language forms and functions, to being facilitative in building the capacity of the language to serve the functions that the community finds beneficial. The difference between language planning and community-based language development is in the agency given by community-based language development to the local community in making and implementing these language change decisions that will move the community towards their own desired outcomes in contrast to the outcomes desired by outsiders.

Community-Based Language Development Is Language-Aware

In the context of holism and collaboration, community-based language development recognizes that language is important because it is at the core of the transmission of life-crucial knowledge. Other approaches to development frequently have taken language for granted or ignore it all together, although more recently some development workers have addressed this lapse by calling attention to "language-based community development." Many (non-language-based) development plans naively overlook the so-called "language barrier." Traditional language planning often focuses, almost exclusively, on language but addresses problems in a piecemeal fashion and does not directly address the whole range of social, cultural, political, economic, and spiritual contexts in which language is used. Community-based language development, starting with a speech community as its focus, recognizes the important interrelationships and interactions between language choice (local language(s), language(s) of wider communication), mode of access (oral, written, digital modalities) and content (internal or external knowledge).

Community-based language development works from the inside out and from the bottom up

Community-based language development recognizes the broader scope of community aspirations and focuses on working with others to achieve them. Key stakeholders in the design and implementation of community-based language development projects are first the community itself, including various coalitions and movements within the community; then national and regional agencies, both governmental and non-governmental; and finally, international organizations outside of the community who provide assistance as needed. While there are important national and international policy implications that arise and must be addressed as part of community-based language development efforts, governmental policy concerns are not the starting point. Rather, the development or reform of governmental policy becomes an important advocacy component of the language development plan.

Community-based language development is empowering

The focus of community-based language development is not so much on the solution of immediately visible problems as on the development of capacity within the community to address ongoing needs and aspirations in all areas of life. It involves the community not only in identifying what they would like to sustain and what they would like to change, but also in the design and implementation of the means to bring about sustainability or implement those changes or both. This focus on capacity building is discussed at somewhat greater length in chapter 10.

Community-based language development is results oriented

Language planning, as traditionally implemented, is largely problem oriented. Language planners identify a problem and attempt to solve it through status planning, corpus planning, acquisition planning, and prestige planning decisions and activities. In contrast, community-based language development attempts to focus more on results—community goals and a desired future—identified by community members themselves. The identification of those goals requires that the local communities be involved from the outset as agents of planning and implementation and not as passive recipients of a plan produced for them by outsiders. This is what makes community-based language development empowering.

3.3.4 Community-based language development and the transmission of life-crucial knowledge

By beginning at the level of the local speech community, community-based language development is able to respond more immediately and appropriately to the specific needs of each community. It empowers community members themselves to identify the life-crucial knowledge that they wish to preserve, access, introduce, and transmit across geographic space, through social space, and over time. It then identifies what capacities need to be developed and what policies need to be advocated for in order to achieve those goals.

Across geographic space

Community-based language development needs to take into account the geographic distribution of the people who consider themselves to be members of any given local speech community. Because of geographic barriers (rivers, mountains, deserts, etc.), some parts of the community may have less frequent contact with the rest of the group. Some members may also be displaced from their homeland as refugees or emigrants. There may be some degree of linguistic variation that results from this less-frequent contact (and from other causes as well). At the same time, many of these physical barriers to interaction are being overcome via the use of digital communications. Existing assumptions about who is speaking to whom, when, and where need to be re-examined in light of these developments. Community-based language development, because it is "language aware," will take this dispersion and linguistic variation into account and look for ways to accommodate it. It will also carefully consider how widely language-development goals and activities can be shared and coordinated, not limiting itself to a single language but looking instead at transcending variation across as broad a cross-section of the speech community as possible.

Across social space

Community-based language development projects will also take into account the social variation that exists within local speech communities. Communities are not entirely homogeneous. Even in the most egalitarian of societies, there will be some degree of social stratification. Each community will have its own mechanisms by which individuals gain prestige, power, and influence. There may be important language, modality, or content related features which accompany social status and prestige (or lack of it). There will also be similar features that mark community identity. Because community-based language development is holistic and empowering, it will look for the life-crucial knowledge that members of the community need in order to function well within their social system. Well-designed community-based language development projects won't ignore these important language use patterns and linguistic features nor will they dismiss them as unimportant. Those working in community-based language development projects will want to identify the whole range of life-crucial knowledge, lore, and history that is part of the community's cultural patrimony as well as external knowledge that the community may wish to access and transmit.

Across temporal space

Community-based language development projects also need to take into account the need for communities to be able to pass on their life-crucial knowledge from one generation to the next. This requires the preservation of the knowledge itself through documentation of content, skills, and technologies. It also requires that the skills and technologies not only be documented but actually transmitted from one person to another, generation after generation. The issue of sustainability is an important concern for well-designed community-based language development projects.

3.3.5 Community-based language development and the Sustainable Use model

The preceding sections have provided a general description of the defining features of community-based language development but have not laid out in any clear way how a community would actually proceed to design and carry out its own language development. For that, we must turn to the general theoretical framework of the SUM which not only gives us a set of concepts and perspectives on life-crucial knowledge transmission, but also defines a process by which a community can begin to design its own knowledge management plan. The remainder of this volume describes the concepts and the process of the Sustainable Use Model which were graphically displayed in figure 1.1.

In general terms, the SUM process involves, first, an analysis of the current language ecology of a speech community. What languages form part of the community's linguistic repertoire? What associations exist between those languages and specific bodies of knowledge? In part, the number of functions (bodies of knowledge) associated with a language is a measure of the language's vitality. Vitality can be measured using an evaluative scale such as the Expanded Graded Intergenerational Disruption Scale (EGIDS) which we describe in chapter 5. That scale also helps the community identify whether the current status of any language in their repertoire is a sustainable one (described in chapter 6). The evaluation of the current status(es) allows the community to make a decision about the desired level of sustainable use for each of the languages in their repertoire. Generally, local communities will focus primarily on the local language(s) in making these decisions, but the functional assignments of the other languages present in the language ecology need to be kept in mind as well. At that point, the community can then engage in a more detailed analysis of the language use patterns in their community using the FAMED conditions which we describe in chapter 7. That analysis will then provide the basis for the development of a plan of action which we describe in chapters 8, 9, and 10.

3.4 Going deeper

3.4.1 Community

As mentioned in chapter 2, we have largely followed Mesthrie et al. 2000 in our definition of the term "community". The concept of a speech community (Gumperz 1968) has been variously described in the sociolinguistic literature (see, for example, Patrick 2002) and, though abandoned by some, serves, we believe, as a useful starting point in defining the working scope of a language development project. We primarily follow Gumperz' use of the term, emphasizing the high degree of interaction between members of a speech community, making it, in many ways, akin to a social network.

3.4.2 Community development

Chambers 1983 is one of the earliest sources for more information on the dynamics of power and inequality, and insider and outsider roles in community development work generally. He notes, for example, that "Outsiders are people concerned with rural development who are themselves neither rural nor poor" (1983:2). As a result, the nature of life in a local community may never be fully seen or understood by outsiders.

Chambers also identifies the phenomena of cores and peripheries of knowledge. The way we distinguish between internal and external knowledge, paradoxically, inverts his categorization as he uses the outsiders' perspective to identify the continuum of outsider-valued and reinforced "core" knowledge in contrast to insider-valued and transmitted knowledge which is considered peripheral by those on the outside.

Community agency

A current focus of discussion among both applied linguists and community development workers is the concept of agency, the roles that different stakeholders can or should be permitted to play in community-based development activities. A case study of three different situations in the African context can be found in Trudell 2006. Other examples of regional and national level movements taking agency over their own language development are found throughout the literature. Just a few examples from Latin America include: Hornberger 1988, 1993/1994; King 2001; and Lewis 1993.

In addition, some very helpful and practical applications of community-based development principles in the implementation of multilingual education programs can be found in Kosonen, Young, and Malone 2006, Malone 2004, and UNESCO 2007.

Chambers' perspectives (1983, 1994, 1995) are foundational to the approach taken in this volume. Chambers' work in large measure provides the basis for many of the contemporary approaches to community-based development work and even to participatory research methods. Results Based Management is one development planning framework that has grown out of the experience of development workers engaged in such community-based work. Some references for further reading on approaches to community-work that are inclusive and participatory are: Asian Development Bank 2006, Baldwin and Easthouse 2005, Cox et al. 2004, Cox 2005, Cooperrider 2004.

3.4.3 Language planning

Language planning uses language policy and its implementation to address social, economic, political, and other "problems." As we described above, those problems generally are not in themselves issues of language *per se* but policy makers believe that they can be remedied by making some change in the way language is used. In this section, we provide more depth and references to the literature on the major components of language planning as well as a discussion of some of the shortcomings and grounds for criticism. This provides more background and a set of foundational concepts for our use of the term language development and for our definition of community-based language development and how community-based language development both builds upon and differs from language planning. The steps taken to implement community-based language development projects are discussed in later chapters. In our description of language planning, we synthesize the models described in Cooper 1971 and Haarman 1990.

Cooper (1971:30–31) lists a dozen different definitions of language planning from the literature and adds to those one of his own. Each definition focuses on one or more of the concerns of language planners, on different ways of categorizing the activities engaged in by language planners, or on different ideological interpretations of the language planner's task. More recent work adds the perspective of a critical approach, (i.e., an understanding of language planning as the exercise of power). For this, see for example, Ricento 2006.

3.4.4 Major components of language planning

We begin our model of language planning with Cooper's (1971) model, which identifies three major components of language planning:

- Status planning—decisions and activities regarding the functions or uses (bodies of knowledge) that languages will be associated with in the community.

- Corpus planning—decisions and activities required to fit the forms and structures of language to the assigned functions.

- Acquisition planning—decisions and activities required to enable current or potential *users* of the language to implement the status and corpus decisions.

Each of these categories includes both the making of decisions as well as the activities that are needed to implement those decisions. Status planning includes not only the decisions about what bodies of knowledge a language will be associated with, but also the activities needed to implement that decision, such as enacting legislation or changing written policy statements, disseminating the decisions and putting in place the mechanisms needed to carry out the decisions. This means that there is always some overlap between the three components of language planning. The implementation of either status or corpus planning decisions may often involve activities that are primarily aimed at building the capacity of the language users (acquisition planning) to use the new forms (corpus planning) for the new functions (status planning). The three components are helpful ways to think about language planning but they should not be understood as entirely mutually exclusive categories.

Haarman (1990) identifies prestige planning as an additional component of language planning. He argues that "any kind of planning has to attract positive values, that is, planning activities must have such prestige as to guarantee a favorable engagement on the part of the planners and, moreover, on the part of those who are supposed to use the planned language" (Haarman 1990:104). This prestige factor plays a crucial role in winning acceptance of planned changes. Within Cooper's model this would be considered an aspect of acquisition planning but Haarman argues that it is significant enough to be considered separately. We agree and discuss prestige planning, specifically in chapter 7, in relation to the Motivation condition of sustainable use.

3.4.5 What's wrong with language planning?

The major criticism of language planning is that it tends to be carried out by governments and powerful authorities who are not always aware of, or primarily concerned about, the local communities which will be most affected by the policies being created and implemented. These powerful outsiders decide what problems are to be solved and what the solutions should be. No matter how well-intentioned, often the language planning solutions proposed do not favor minority language communities and may further disempower those communities. Most frequently, language planning objectives are addressed in terms of policy creation or change which is intended to motivate the preferred kinds of language behaviors and discourage (and sometimes punish) non-preferred behaviors. There are also more subtle ways in which attitudes and values can be shaped so as to motivate or discourage certain kinds of linguistic behavior. Further, language planning solutions frequently do not build capacity in the minority language communities so that those communities are able to solve their own problems sustainably into the future. As a result, many instances of language planning fail to adequately address the needs of minority language communities.

Because of these criticisms, the term language planning is not well-accepted in some quarters. One critical analyst of language planning has labeled it "planning for inequality" (Tollefson 1991). Synonyms for language planning such as language (or social) engineering share these negative connotations. Early on, as described above, the more favorable term language development was used and we continue to use it here. Another more positive label is language cultivation. Both of these terms align language development activities with the field of community development which also attempts to solve problems in communities through the introduction of (usually technological) innovations. Community development, however, has also been criticized as being top-down and outsider-in in its orientation as we've described above. Some dislike the word "development" as it implies that there is something wrong with the communities that are "underdeveloped" when in fact external agents or circumstances may be the causes of the lack of capacity, opportunity, or resources. And as mentioned earlier, community development, as typically implemented, also tends not to be adequately aware of the important role of language in bringing about the desired changes.

In principle, the criticisms that solutions created by outsiders, no matter how well-intentioned, almost always benefit those outsiders and do not necessarily provide the benefits that members of minority language communities most desire, can be addressed if the local speech communities take on this central role. Additionally, the crucial issues of the multiplex nature of identity, language, and knowledge are best accounted for if those who are living in that complex milieu are the decision makers and primary implementers.

> **A point to ponder**
>
> "The links of modern scientific knowledge with wealth, power and prestige condition outsiders to despise and ignore rural people's own knowledge. Priorities…reflect biases against what matters to rural people. Rural people's knowledge is often superior to that of outsiders…. Rural people's knowledge and modern scientific knowledge are complementary in their strengths and weaknesses. Combined they may achieve what neither would alone. For such combinations, outsider professionals have to step down off their pedestals, and sit down, listen and learn." (Chambers 1983:75)

3.4.6 Ideological orientations in language planning

Ruiz (1984) describes the ideological orientations that have characterized language planning and language policy over the years. The post-colonial ideology can be seen to have dealt largely with linguistic diversity as a problem which made effective governance of emerging nation-states more difficult. More recently, the ideological perspective has shifted to view linguistic (and cultural) diversity as a resource. In the same way that natural resources can be developed to produce economic wealth for a nation, linguistic resources can be seen as a source of cultural and social well-being. The development of these linguistic resources can enable a nation to engage more effectively with the outside world and to enhance its own identity and internal richness. Policy guided by this ideology will attempt to shape status and corpus planning decisions in order to maximize the benefits of linguistic diversity. A third, more recent, ideology is that of viewing linguistic and cultural diversity as a basic human right. This view obliges governments and authorities to protect and preserve diversity.

Works which expand on these concepts include the article by Hornberger (2006) and the edited volumes by Ricento (2006), already mentioned above, as well as Spolsky 2004. A summary description of the issues related to diversity policy more broadly conceived can also be found in Lewis and Trudell 2008.

3.4.7 Language development

As described earlier in this chapter, the issues which motivated some to criticize language planning have motivated a search for a more neutral term. We, along with others, have used the term "language development." The choice of that term, however, is not a recent innovation. Haugen (1966a) as early as 1966 (reprinted in Paulston and Tucker 2003) referred to some languages as being "underdeveloped" and identified codification and elaboration as major components of the development of such languages. Charles Ferguson introduced the term in reference to the societal use and change of language functions (Ferguson 1968). The expansion and development of the concepts of what we now call language development differ little from the core framework that Ferguson described. Language development as a sphere of activity more recently has been much influenced by the perspectives of Chambers and others, as described above, so that the important role of communities in participating in their own language planning has come to be part of the core conceptual framework among practitioners.

Language development more broadly needs to be understood primarily as the result of a whole series of activities that are aimed at increasing the number of functions (bodies of knowledge) with which a particular language is associated. Language development, then, can refer to the desired outcome as well as to actions that are being taken. The key shifts in perspective that we are emphasizing in this volume are: (1) community agency as being essential for sustainable language development outcomes, and (2) the need for the activities of language developers to be focused on remediating the key conditions that are undermining sustainable use (see chapter 7).

3.4.8 Community-based language development

The distinctions we've made here between language planning, community development broadly understood, language-based community development (briefly mentioned above), and community-based language development are largely the result of a synthesis of the thought and work of many others. We see community-based language development as a sub-field of community development that accounts for the importance of language in development work and that takes the agency of local communities seriously. It uses the general conceptual framework of language planning but starts from a very different place in the application of those conceptual tools and methods.

4

Local Languages in Ecological Perspective

> One cannot properly address the development of a local language without first understanding how it fits into its language ecology.

4.1 Introduction

In the preceding chapters we identified the speech community, a social network that shares a common linguistic repertoire (and norms of use of that repertoire), as the most appropriate focus of community-based language development work. In this chapter we explore how the configuration of multiple language varieties in a speech community forms a language ecology. In the same way that each of the organisms in an environmental ecology fills a specific niche, so do the languages in a language ecology. The niche of a language is identified in terms of the functions that it has within the life of the community. These functions are directly related to the specific bodies of knowledge a language is used to transmit and in what communication genres that transmission takes place. One cannot properly address the development of a local language without first understanding how it fits into its language ecology since development efforts will both affect that ecology and be affected by it.

In the best of circumstances, this distribution of functions to the languages used within a speech community (or as sociolinguists call it, the "functional distribution" of the languages) is such that a given function is assigned to just one language so that the languages and what they are used for are clearly differentiated as opposed to being in competition with each other. When this happens the result is stable multilingualism that, in turn, produces sustainable use of the languages for their respective functions. However, the circumstances are typically less than ideal; the characteristics of local communities which we described in chapter 2 often result in situations where multiple languages are competing for the same function. These circumstances act as significant ecological factors affecting the stability of multilingualism in those communities and reducing the sustainability of the local languages.

Community-based language development, with its holistic orientation (as described in chapter 3), starts not with an individual language but with the community as a whole and its need to maintain (and enhance) the transmission of life-crucial knowledge. The existing functional distribution of the languages in the community's linguistic repertoire must be understood as a starting point for any language development work. The desired outcome of language development in a community represents a (re)configuration of the functions associated with each of the languages in the repertoire based on the decisions made by community members regarding the transmission of life-crucial knowledge. Community-based language development includes the planned actions that a community takes to (re-)assign those functions in order to achieve the community's knowledge transmission goals. We propose that in order to be sustainable, any such reconfiguration of functions must aim at the attainment of stable multilingualism.

4.2 Multiple languages for multiple topics, participants, and locations

Most speech communities, especially local speech communities, are multilingual. Generally, however, it is not the case that a multilingual person, no matter how proficient they might be in their multiple languages, is *equally* proficient in all of the languages in their linguistic repertoire. Most multilingual people find themselves using one language more often for certain topics, or with particular individuals, or in particular locations. Often, if asked to do so, a multilingual person will find it difficult to talk about certain topics in a language which is not customarily associated with that subject matter. Or they may find it embarrassing or uncomfortable to use a particular language variety with some groups of people or in a location where that language is not commonly used. These habitual patterns of language use are frequently not noticed by multilingual individuals, but upon reflection they may quickly recognize that their entire community shares these behaviors and the accompanying levels of language proficiency. In many cases, a member of a speech community can tell you that with certain people in certain places they speak one language and with other people in other locations, they would feel more comfortable using a different language. More often these unconsciously held norms of use only come to the fore when an outsider or a language learner violates the rules and uses the wrong variety in the wrong location or with the wrong people. Sometimes when one additional participant joins the conversation, the entire group of speakers will switch to a different language in order to accommodate the new arrival. That accommodation may be based on the new arrival's lack of proficiency in the language being used, but it may also reflect the social status of the newly arrived participant. Similarly, participants may feel more comfortable using a particular language in one location, but if they change locations, it may seem more appropriate to them to switch to a different language. A third possibility is that as the topic of conversation changes, the language of the

4.2 Multiple languages for multiple topics, participants, and locations

conversation may change as well with certain topics discussed in one language and other topics discussed in another (or multiple others).

This phenomenon has been well-known and documented (see the Going Deeper section below) and provides the basis for our description of speech communities not only as social networks but as language ecologies. When there are multiple language varieties present in a local setting, the general tendency is for each of those languages to find a niche in the language ecology and for the patterns of use of each variety to become established and predictable. As in a biological ecology, each variety in the system has a role or function to play. Each combination of participants, location, and topic (e.g., children in the street playing games, customers and merchants in the market haggling over prices, etc.) constitutes a domain of use. Generally, there is a particular linguistic variety that comes to be associated with that domain. The total system of domains of use is subject to the same dynamics as other ecological systems.

A common statement among linguists and others is that all languages are equal. From the linguist's perspective, every language has the ability to express any concept that needs to be expressed and no language is "defective" structurally. Potentially, it is possible to say anything one needs to say in any language. Not all languages will express those ideas in the same way, however. In some societies, concepts may be conceived of quite differently than in others, so the ability to translate from one language to another can often be challenging and may require some deliberation. However, the linguistic structures of any language are capable, with some effort, of a complete range of expressions and concepts. Where no established linguistic structures are already present, speakers are very capable of borrowing from another language or adapting existing structures from their own language, or creating completely new ones to meet their communicative needs. Were this not so, the possibility of language development itself would be in doubt.

On the other hand, the perspective which we are emphasizing in this volume and recognizing in the Sustainable Use Model is that while all languages are theoretically equal, in practice and actual use, they seldom are. Each language in the ecology of a speech community is used for an identifiable set of activities and the linguistic forms and structures are adapted by their users for those activities. Both the vocabulary and the grammatical features of the language expand to provide users with the linguistic tools they need for those associated functions. In turn, users acquire the necessary proficiency in those linguistic structures in order to engage in those different kinds of activities. Speakers will find that each of the languages in their repertoire serves them quite well to talk about particular topics in particular places with particular people, but does not serve them so well in other settings with other participants to talk about other topics. It isn't so much that the language could not be made to serve those other additional functions; it is just not customary to do so. In many cases, the needed vocabulary and grammatical structures have not been developed because the language has never been called upon for that domain of use. In other cases, the vocabulary and structures have atrophied, that is, users of the language are no longer familiar with them, as the domains associated with the language have been reduced. The terminology and structures associated with those bodies of knowledge are not learned and called into use. This process of reduction of domains of use leads to the linguistic features associated with those domains not being passed on to succeeding generations and thus falling out of use completely.

Based on this understanding of domains of use and the association of languages with specific domains, we can restate our definition of language development as follows:

> Language development begins as the overt directed purposeful reconfiguration of the functional assignments of the languages in a speech community's linguistic repertoire.

What is described in this statement is status planning. All that follows from that, corpus planning, acquisition planning, and prestige planning, are necessary results of status planning decisions.

Because of heightened language contact as described in chapters 1 and 2, established domains of use are encroached upon by larger, more dominant languages. These pressures in turn alter the linguistic ecology (the configuration of the functional assignments of the languages in a speech community) as the dominant language becomes associated with more and more domains (topics, participants, locations) and the local language gradually loses its close associations with those domains. Language development as we envision it in the SUM is the intentional altering of the linguistic ecology in order to re-establish and preserve domains of use (bodies of knowledge, functions) for the local language. As with any intervention in an ecological system, change must be introduced with great caution and based on as thorough an understanding of the current state of the ecology as possible.

Among sociolinguists it is common for domains of use to be identified in terms of the location component. As a result they are talked about frequently as if they were the geographic or social spaces in which talk takes place. The Home, Community, Market, and School are a few of the frequently used labels for commonly identified domains of use. Such shorthand labels are useful and efficient because, as described above, a domain is a configuration or constellation of location, participants, and topics. Certain topics are typically talked about in the home. And the participants in those conversations, family members, are generally quite predictable as well. Similarly, any of the other commonly known domain labels can be quickly seen as summary labels that assume the predictability of topics and participants in the specified locations.

Domains could alternatively be identified by referring to the different kinds of participants (adult men, young men, adult women, young women, children) and many descriptions of language use break down populations by age and gender in order to identify such patterns of use. Gender-based studies of language often approach language use from this perspective. This is a less common approach to describing domains, however, because people of any age and any gender often find themselves in different locations talking about different topics (though they may talk differently from each other in those settings). While the study of age-related language use patterns can be very helpful and revealing, it doesn't provide the same sort of summary understanding of the domain patterns.

In contrast to these approaches, we have chosen to frame the analysis of language use patterns by starting with the third component of a domain of use, the topic.

4.3 Functions, topics, and bodies of knowledge

Our reason for choosing to talk about the transmission of life-crucial knowledge, as we do in this volume is because in most cases the preservation of a community's identity has been approached by language developers "language first." That seems like an obvious place to start if the concern is the preservation of language transmission and the revitalization of an endangered language. The difficulty, however, is that most people are relatively unaware of their language(s) and how they manage their linguistic repertoire. Language is so much a part of our everyday life and so embedded in all areas of life and activity that it becomes like the air we breathe. We barely notice it even though we use it constantly. As a result, it is often only when a language is very far along in the process of losing functions that people begin to take notice of the loss. It suddenly becomes apparent that the linguistic air is getting thin. And often by then, a more dominant language has taken hold in most of the domains of life. At that point, the possibility of reversing the process of local language attrition seems daunting indeed.

The process of language shift and death is very gradual and few people notice what is happening in time to do anything about it. In any case, most don't know what to do. As this language shift progresses, more and more community members come to believe that the local language doesn't provide them with enough benefits to be worth saving, or they may even come to believe that the local language itself is what is holding them back and so needs to be abandoned. The linguistic ecology of the speech community has changed and the stability of that ecological system is being lost.

Because it is frequently difficult for community members to think about language as an abstract concept, and because it is the local language that is often seen as "the problem," a more concrete place for community members to begin thinking about their language use patterns is by looking at the bodies of knowledge that they possess (or wish to acquire) and then to examine the language(s) associated with those bodies of knowledge. When posed with the question of how they will maintain the transmission of life-crucial knowledge, community members are more likely to grasp quickly the need to develop strategies that will address that issue. The question of which language to use for each body of life-crucial knowledge that they identify then follows naturally. From this perspective, a domain of use could be just as easily labeled with the name of its topic—a particular body of knowledge. That body of knowledge (traditional lore, health and healing, agricultural methods, flora and fauna identification, or whatever it may be) is associated with a particular set of participants and is typically talked about in a particular location, using a particular set of communication genres. The linguistic ecology of any speech community consists of the combined configurations of all of the bodies of knowledge, both inside knowledge and outside knowledge (see chapter 2) that are in use within that speech community and the communication genres that are associated with them.

In the chapters that follow, when we are speaking of the ways in which communication genres are associated with topics or bodies of knowledge we will often use the term *functions*. We have already mentioned that stable multilingualism occurs when there is a clearly defined functional assignment of the languages in an ecology. The aim of the SUM is to achieve stable multilingualism by encouraging each speech community to engage in a discussion regarding their life-crucial knowledge and how they will transmit it to future generations. As the local speech community comes to a consensus around this issue, they will begin to see how their linguistic ecology needs to be altered in order to achieve a desirable and clearly differentiated functional assignment of the language varieties in their repertoire.

4.4 Categorizing functions

We have already mentioned the distinction between internal knowledge and external knowledge as one way of categorizing the bodies of knowledge that a speech community possesses. There are other ways to think about these functions.

4.4.1 Formal and informal functions

In general terms, functions can be categorized by their level of formality. Other terms for this distinction are private vs. public or intimate vs. non-intimate and sociolinguists often refer to High vs. Low languages (or domains) when referring to this distinction (see Going Deeper below).

> **My Fair Lady**
>
> George Bernard Shaw's play, "Pygmalion," brought to film as "My Fair Lady," provides a good example of conscious efforts to modify a person's speech in order to achieve social acceptability. The main character, Eliza Doolittle, is taken off the streets of London and taught to speak in the variety of the British educated upper class of the era. While she was able to master the phonetics of that higher register, she did not adequately learn the norms of use. Her violations of the social norms form the basis for the comedy that follows.

The modalities of language use (oral, signed, written, digital) and art forms (poetry, song, dance, etc.), which together constitute communication genres, often coincide with the level of formality of the functions associated with the language. Languages used for more formal functions often have standardized orthographies and are written. Languages associated with informal functions are less frequently standardized and may be associated with oral modalities. Certain art forms may be considered inappropriate for formal functions. Often, users of the languages associated with informal functions feel that the languages are incapable of being written or that it would be inappropriate to do so. These perceptions, though widely held, are not absolutes and can be changed. Part of the work of language development is to provide the needed perspective and awareness so that users of informal varieties can make decisions about how particular bodies of knowledge will be expressed both in terms of the choice of language and the choice of modality and art forms.

Another aspect of this distinction is the means by which community members acquire proficiency in the different language varieties. In general, they learn the more informal varieties informally. That is, they learn them in the home or in the community ("on the street") and from friends and family without much overt instruction. The more formal varieties often require a formal teaching and learning process and are often learned in a classroom setting or through overt instruction of some sort. For this reason, formal varieties are generally considered to be the proper forms or the language of the educated. They are often more overtly prestigious. Informal varieties are frequently less overtly prestigious, and often are deprecated as being faulty or an improper use of the language. Sometimes they aren't considered to be "a language" at all and are considered to be mere "dialects". There is often a social stigma attached to being proficient only in the informal variety. It is this stigma that works so powerfully against local languages when they are cast in the role of the "Low" language in the linguistic ecology of a speech community.

> **The case of body parts**
>
> A common example of the differences between formal and informal language varieties is how the body and its functions are discussed by different participants in different settings. Frequently the anatomical terms that are used among intimates are not considered suitable for public usage. Nor are the scientifically accurate, more formal, terms considered appropriate in more intimate settings. The informal terms are learned in the home or on the street while the less stigmatized terminology is taught and learned more formally.

4.4.2 Sentimental and instrumental functions

Another way to categorize the functions is in terms of their sentimental vs. instrumental nature. Some functions are considered sentimental in that they serve more to reinforce a person's feelings and sense of community membership. Others are more instrumental in their focus on a person's need to be able to act independently, be competent, and in today's globalizing world, become more socially and economically mobile. Another related set of terms that has been used for this distinction are solidarity vs. power. In many ways the distinction between functions that serve more to promote solidarity and those that serve more to promote power (independence) aligns with the distinction between inside knowledge and outside knowledge that we have already discussed.

Sentimental functions also are associated with the local language. It is the language of the home and community, the language learned in one's childhood, that is often associated most closely with inside knowledge and with one's sense of identity as a member of a particular community. Sentimental functions are often those that would be categorized as informal or intimate, though not all informal functions are necessarily sentimental.

Similarly, instrumental functions are often associated with a dominant language or a language of wider communication. This language may be perceived as offering the greatest opportunities for advancement, social mobility, or economic success. Often bodies of outside knowledge serve instrumental functions and the focus of social network ties for these functions is outside of the local community or includes speakers of the dominant language within the speech community. Instrumental functions often coincide with the more formal functions in that the language varieties used are more often learned formally outside of the home and the immediate neighborhood.

4.5 The quest for stable multilingualism

In most speech communities these different categories of functions overlap and are intertwined in complex ways. Some functions associated with the local language may be categorized as both sentimental and formal. Informal topics may be written about (whether or not there is a standardized way to do so). Other functions may be instrumental in terms of the inside knowledge they are associated with but may be acquired informally. Art forms may be adapted and modified for use in unexpected and non-traditional ways. The categories are neither completely separate nor completely mutually exclusive and in communities with hybridized identities the norms of use may represent a mix of inside and outside usage patterns. The concepts, however, can be useful as a community considers the bodies of life-crucial knowledge that it wishes to manage and identifies where those bodies of knowledge fit in the overall linguistic ecology of the speech community. The important thing is that the community be able to recognize the important connections among functions (topics, bodies of knowledge) and the settings (participants, locations) where those topics most often are in focus, and the communication genres most closely associated with those functions. An understanding of the overall configuration of the linguistic ecology gives those engaged in community-based language development a starting point for setting their language development goals.

The SUM does not encourage wholesale efforts to resist language shift by attempting to replace an encroaching language in every domain of use. We are not proposing that the only safe setting for an endangered language is where that language and only that language is in use (i.e., the initiation or restoration of local language monolingualism). Our goal is to identify the life-crucial bodies of knowledge and associate them most appropriately and sustainably with each language in the linguistic ecology, that is, to achieve stable multilingualism. The existing configuration of languages and functions in a speech community may not be optimal for the preservation and transmission of life-crucial knowledge. Language development interventions may be called for in order to realign the functional distribution of the languages. Interventions that are based on a good understanding of the existing linguistic ecology and which are targeted to address the transmission of life-crucial knowledge are more likely to be achievable and to be effective in sustaining language use.

4.6 Going deeper

The twin concepts of diglossia and domains of use are central to the approach to language development embodied in the SUM. The concept of diglossia, initially proposed by Ferguson (1959) and further developed and elaborated by Fishman

(1965), established the understanding that languages in a specific ecology tend to be configured in terms of domains of use (Fishman 1965, 1972a, 1972b) which essentially are constellations of participants (users), topics (bodies of knowledge) and locations which become generally associated with a particular language variety. In most societies these dynamic configurations tend to become conventionalized to the extent that they can be categorized and named (most often in terms of the location: home, neighborhood, marketplace, school, etc.) and one can then say that a specific language is used in the home or in the school or in any other identified domain. Where these associations of a language with a domain of use are widely accepted as norms by the community (i.e., they are prevalent), Fishman (1967) asserted that language use would be both persistent and predictable. (We will discuss prevalence, persistence, and predictability as characteristics of sustainability in chapter 6.

The differences between Ferguson's definition of diglossia and Fishman's later elaboration of the term have led to some terminological confusion such that different uses of the term lead some scholars to focus on one aspect of the concept (e.g., the H and L distinction which seems more prominent in Ferguson's conceptualization) while others focus on other components (e.g., the functional compartmentalization which seems to be more in focus in Fishman's treatment of the concept). Because of the potential for misunderstanding and confusion, we have largely avoided using the term diglossia in this volume. We have chosen instead to highlight the stability or persistence of diglossic situations which is a shared feature of both Ferguson's and Fishman's definitions of the concept. And, as will be seen in chapter 7, we take particular note of the compartmentalization of domains of use when we discuss Differentiation. We use the term stable multilingualism to describe those situations where there is diglossia, that is, complementary functional distribution of the languages in a given ecology. This is not to deny that other features of both Ferguson's and Fishman's definitions of diglossia may also apply in these same contexts. Those are referenced in the SUM at various points as appropriate. For a comprehensive overview of the various definitions and the development of the concept, we recommend Fasold's introductory sociolinguistics textbook (Fasold 1984) which dedicates an entire chapter to the topic.

Our emphasis has been that local language communities are, of necessity, increasingly made up of bilingual individuals, and so are characterized, as a community, by multiple languages. Establishing stable multilingualism (a sustainable functional distribution of the languages in use in the speech community) is key to sustaining language use. Thus, we must think about how multiple topics or bodies of knowledge will be distributed among multiple participants, in multiple locations where each language will be used and the communication genres associated with each of these domains of use. It is this compartmentalization of functions that is the key insight encompassed by the term diglossia. It is useful as well to make clear the relationship of individual multilingualism to stable societal multilingualism (diglossia).

4.6.1 Individual and societal multilingualism within the speech community

The process which we have described where a dominant language encroaches more and more on the domains of use of another language is referred to as language shift. Gal (1996:586) describes language shift as a process "in which ever more speakers refrain from using language X and instead use language Y in ever more social functions and situations." As more and more speakers see the value of using "Language Y" for particular functions they increase their level of proficiency in that language to the level needed in order to participate in those functions. Romaine (1989:8) cites Mackey (1968:554) to point out that bilingualism is not so much a matter of language itself, the linguistic codes, as it is a matter of the use of those linguistic codes. This being the case, it is important that community members understand the relationship between bilingualism, both individual and societal, and individual and societal language choice. The contact of two speech communities with each other has a significant effect on their language use patterns. Language shift within a speech community cannot occur if individuals are not bilingual. It is the aggregation of all of the choices that individuals make about which language they will use for which domains of use that leads to either language maintenance or shift at the community level. We most frequently use the term functions and, alternately, bodies of knowledge to describe these established language use choices also identified as domains of use (see also chapter 7).

The acquisition of a second language can be seen as the acquisition of domains of use (functions) for that language by an individual. This represents not only a change in the linguistic competence of the individual but also a change in the social meaning of the use of that language for that individual in that speech community. Individuals make use of all of the varieties of language within their linguistic repertoire in very intricate and complex ways which are determined by a number of interrelated and overlapping factors. Fasold (1984:213) makes the observation that "language shift and, the other side of the coin, language maintenance are really the long-term, collective results of [individual] language choice." Thus, societal bilingualism is very much related to bilingualism in the individual and societal choices of language can be seen to be influenced by many of the same factors which affect individual language choice.

Looking at the negative consequences for many local languages resulting from contact between different language communities and the resulting increase in bilingualism, Fasold (1984:216) also notes that "bilingualism is not a sufficient condition for [language] shift, although it may be a necessary one." We argue here that a necessary condition for sustainable language use where bilingualism is present, is the relatively unambiguous and clearly defined functional distribution of the languages that comprise the linguistic repertoire of the speech community, that is, stable multilingualism.

4.6.2 The interaction of diglossia and bilingualism

Societal bilingualism is present whenever two different languages are in common use within a speech community. Diglossia refers to the special case in which they are not competing because there are societal norms as to when one language rather than another should be used. Though the term had been used previously, Ferguson made the term diglossia part of the working vocabulary of sociolinguists in his seminal work on the topic (Ferguson 1959). Ferguson carefully laid out what he considered to be the defining characteristics of High and Low languages in a diglossic relationship to each other. Ferguson's defining features include:

4.6 Going deeper

- Specialization—High and Low languages are used for different functions.
- Prestige—High and Low languages have different levels of prestige.
- Literary Heritage—High language is written and has a literary heritage; Low language may not be written and has no literary heritage or only a minimal body of literature.
- Acquisition—The High language is learned formally, usually at school; the Low language is learned at home or in the community.
- Standardization—The High language has a standardized form for writing and often for speaking; the Low language has not been standardized.
- Stability—The differentiation between the High and Low varieties is stable and "persists at least several centuries".
- Grammar—The High language has a "fuller" grammar; the Low language tends to have less elaborated grammatical forms.
- Lexicon—High and Low languages share a lot of vocabulary, but the High language tends to have more technical terms and expressions that must be learned.
- Phonology—Both High and Low languages share a single phonological system with the Low language phonology being the basic system, appearing more often in oral use.

The distinctions we have described above in the section on Categorizing functions coincide in large measure with Ferguson's defining features. Ferguson's conceptualization of diglossia was highly constrained as evidenced by the degree of specificity and elaboration in his definition:

> Diglossia is a relatively stable language situation in which, in addition to the primary dialects of the language there is a very divergent, highly codified (often grammatically more complex) superposed variety, the vehicle of a large and respected body of written literature, either of an earlier period or in another speech community, which is learned largely by formal education and is used for most written and formal spoken purposes but is not used by any sector of the community for ordinary conversation. (Ferguson 1959:336)

Ferguson's definition severely limits the number of cases to which the concept can be applied in that his defining cases are all closely related languages. It is often the case that some but not all of the characteristics of diglossia can be observed where the varieties are not closely related. In order to allow for these situations, Fishman (1967) broadened the range of cases to which the term diglossia could be applied by making the distinction between bilingualism, the use of multiple languages by an individual, and diglossia, the stable compartmentalized use of *multiple varieties* within a community. Fishman's description of diglossia differs from Ferguson's by not only admitting the use of multiple languages at the societal level, but more importantly for our purposes, by stressing the centrality of the compartmentalization of roles or functions for each of the languages in use in the speech community (Ferguson's notion of specialization.) From Fishman's perspective most of the other features that distinguish H from L, while often found in diglossic situations, are not as fundamental. To distinguish Fishman's use of the term, which encompassed all of the linguistic varieties in use in a community, from Ferguson's more restricted definition, which described the relationship between two related varieties, Fasold (1984) has suggested that Fishman's broader concept be referred to as broad diglossia. Broad diglossia exists in a society when each of the linguistic varieties, related or not, is assigned a specific role or is used for a delimited set of functions. Fishman proposed that multilingual (i.e., language contact) situations can be characterized by the logical combinations of the presence or absence of bilingualism (an individual phenomenon) and diglossia (a societal phenomenon). Fishman (1967, 1968) recognized that the existence of bilingualism and diglossia is the direct result of a variety of non-linguistic factors. While the non-linguistic factors may vary from situation to situation, individuals and social groups respond to them by assuming a specific socio-psychological orientation, an identity. Though intended primarily as a descriptive framework, Fishman makes predictions about expected language maintenance results for each of the quadrants in the matrix produced by the interplay of bilingualism and diglossia. The four possible combinations are: (1) both diglossia and bilingualism, (2) bilingualism without diglossia, (3) diglossia without bilingualism, and (4) neither diglossia nor bilingualism. For each situation Fishman posits a degree of stability based on the interplay of individual bilingualism (or its absence) and societal diglossia (or its absence). Fishman's description of these four combinations is summarized here.

Bilingualism with diglossia

In situations where there is both diglossia and bilingualism there are individuals who use more than one language or variety and there is societal compartmentalization of the roles for each of the varieties that the members of that society use. It is this fairly tight compartmentalization of roles for the language varieties which maintains the use of each. This sociological perspective complements what investigators of bilingualism have also observed: "Theories of bilingualism thus argue that there must be a series of areas of life in which one language, for bilingual speakers, is the only accepted medium of communication" (McAllister and Mughan 1984:321).

It is not compartmentalization alone, but also access to the various roles assigned to each linguistic variety which characterizes a society in which both diglossia and bilingualism occur. If a large segment of the population is denied access to the roles in society wherein the use of a particular variety is appropriate that segment will not acquire proficiency in the variety associated with those roles. Elwell (1982) includes language proficiency as one of the sociolinguistic factors which affects language use in a multilingual society. A society which does not provide the means for individuals to acquire proficiency in a second language cannot be considered to be a society where there is both diglossia and bilingualism. Thus, compartmentalization characterizes diglossia and access to the means of acquisition is a prerequisite of bilingualism. Fishman asserts that diglossia with bilingualism will be the case "wherever speech communities exist in which speakers (a) engage in a considerable range of roles (as all but the extreme upper and lower levels of complex societies are coming to do); (b) wherever access to several roles is encouraged or facilitated by powerful social institutions and processes; and (c) wherever the roles are clearly differentiated as to when, where, and with whom they are felt to be appropriate" (Fishman 1968:140).

This summarizes clearly the need for both compartmentalization (clearly differentiated roles or functions) and access (access to roles and the means of language acquisition) in order to be able to classify a language contact situation as one where both diglossia and bilingualism occur. From the perspective of the SUM, this configuration results in stable multilingualism, and is the best-case scenario for sustaining local language use.

Diglossia without bilingualism

In the second combinatory possibility, those situations where there is diglossia but not bilingualism, there exist two or more linguistic varieties within the society but relatively few people who speak both. Frequently, this is the kind of situation where two or more ethnolinguistic groups have come to be united within political boundaries but there is little or no opportunity for one group to learn and use the other's language. In terms of compartmentalization and access, this situation represents the existence of clearly defined compartmentalization but low levels or the complete absence of access. Fishman notes that in such situations "at least one of the speech communities involved will be marked by relatively impassable group boundaries and such an emphasis upon ascribed rather than achieved status, that both role and linguistic access is severely restricted for 'outsiders'" (Fishman 1968:141). In these kinds of situations interaction between the groups will largely be by means of interpreters. With access denied to the prestige roles in society, the general population will have neither adequate means nor adequate motivation for bilingualism. Here the compartmentalization of roles is so strong that the boundaries between the groups become impassable. Thus, the factors that ensure diglossia inhibit bilingualism. Fishman predicts that such societies are likely to experience severe strains centered around language as social patterns are altered by the forces of industrialization, universal education and literacy, modernization, and democratization with their emphasis on the increased participation of the general population in more and more areas of society. Many post-colonial nations find themselves confronting this configuration where the legacy colonial language is dominant and prestigious and speakers of local languages have historically had only limited access to the means of acquisition of the prestigious variety. As access to the dominant language increases, the pressures on local communities to shift to the dominant language increase as well.

This linguistic configuration tends to be stable and unchanging so long as the intergroup boundaries remain fixed and impassable as described above. Though stable, this configuration represents stable monolingualism, with each of the speech communities living side by side with only a few bilinguals on each side of the divide. That stability quickly erodes when the social and ethnic boundaries break down as described in the next configuration.

Bilingualism without diglossia

The third possible situation is that of bilingualism without diglossia. It exists where there are individuals who use or can use more than one linguistic variety but where there are no societal norms as to which language is appropriate to use with which interlocutor concerning which topics, under what circumstances. Fishman states that this situation will only occur under circumstances accompanying "rapid social change, great social unrest,...widespread abandonment of earlier norms before the consolidation of new ones" (Fishman 1968:145). Furthermore, it seems that in this kind of situation bilingualism is acquired at an early age and in the home and neighborhood. The variety brought home from work and school is acquired as a second language. In these situations societal institutions tend to promote monolingualism in the second language. Thus, industrialization and modernization will further motivate members of the society to abandon their traditional sociocultural patterns in order to acquire the patterns (and the language) of the institutions which control the means of production. Fishman suggests that under these unstable conditions language interference as well as language shift and language loss should be an expected outcome: "Instead of two or more carefully separated languages each under the eyes of caretaker groups of teachers, preachers and writers, several intervening varieties differing in degree of interpenetration may obtain. The standard varieties of immigrants are given no language maintenance support under these circumstances, yet at the same time the varieties they use may come to be ridiculed as 'debased' or 'broken'" (Fishman 1968:149). The result is that "the language or variety which is fortunate enough to be associated with the predominant drift of social forces tends to displace the others" (Fishman 1968:149). This characterizes the situation of many local language communities in a globalizing world, and is the default circumstance leading to the pressures on local communities to abandon their languages.

Neither diglossia nor bilingualism

The fourth situation described by Fishman's framework is that in which neither diglossia nor bilingualism is present. Such situations are extremely rare, if they exist at all. In order for there to be no role compartmentalization (diglossia) the speech community would have to be one in which no social significance was attached to differences in linguistic varieties. A speech community with neither diglossia nor bilingualism would be a community in which all are monolingual and there is no internal social or geographic variation within the single language that is used. Such a situation is, indeed, hard to imagine.

4.6.3 Formal and informal, sentimental and instrumental functions

Kelman (1971) made the distinction between sentimental and instrumental attachments to language. Writing from the perspective of political science, he discussed the role of language (and identity) as an aid or a barrier to involvement in national economic and political systems. This distinction highlighted the important role of language as a re-enforcer of local identities through the sentimental attachments that users of a language construct by sharing that common behavior. It was Ferguson, however, who made the important distinction between High and

Low languages in diglossic relationship to each other. The defining characteristics of the diglossic varieties laid out by Ferguson make frequent reference to the use of the High language in formal domains and the Low language in informal contexts. These distinctions, in general, can also be described as representations of an individual's need to experience both power and solidarity (Lewis 2000).

5

Assessing the Ecological Profile of a Speech Community

The place of the languages within an ecology can be more readily understood when the status of each is located on the EGIDS, a scale for assessing language development versus decline.

5.1 Introduction

In chapter 1 we defined the concept of sustainable language use and mentioned briefly that there are three sustainable levels of language vitality and one level which represents sustainable documentation of a language. These levels constitute plateaus or thresholds on a larger, more comprehensive scale of language vitality. In this chapter we will describe that larger scale, called the Expanded Graded Intergenerational Disruption Scale (EGIDS), in greater detail. In chapter 6 we will provide a more extensive explanation of the sustainable levels. The EGIDS, as its name states, is an expansion of the Graded Intergenerational Disruption Scale developed by Fishman. The GIDS and other measures of language vitality and the theoretical background of the EGIDS itself are discussed in greater detail in the Going Deeper section of this chapter.

Sustainable language use can be described in terms of both the uses and the users of a language. In chapter 4, we focused on the uses by describing how languages in multilingual settings comprise an ecology. Each language in the setting performs particular roles and functions. We proposed that the sustainable use of a language depends crucially on those functions being clearly identifiable and compartmentalized. The EGIDS, described at length below, looks at both the uses and the users of a language. An adequate understanding of the language ecology of a speech community requires both a description of the functions assigned to a language in that ecology and an assessment of the number and age range of the users of that language. The EGIDS provides a means of assessing both major factors (and others) in a relatively straightforward way.

The EGIDS forms the centerpiece of the Sustainable Use Model (SUM) as it is the primary tool within the model that language development facilitators and implementers can use both to identify the current state of vitality of a language and to establish a desired sustainable level of use to be aimed for. In addition, the EGIDS can be used in any speech community as a tool for profiling the roles and relationships of each language within the language ecology (see Chapter 4) of that community.

5.2 The Expanded Graded Intergenerational Disruption Scale (EGIDS)

The EGIDS is made up of 13 levels. Table 5.1 gives the summary definition of each of the levels. The following paragraphs give a brief description of each level.

Table 5.1 Expanded Graded Intergenerational Disruption Scale (Lewis, Simons, and Fennig 2016)

Level	Label	Description
0	International	The language is widely used between nations in trade, knowledge exchange, and international policy.
1	National	The language is used in education, work, mass media, and government at the national level.
2	Provincial	The language is used in education, work, mass media, and government within major administrative subdivisions of a nation.
3	Wider Communication	The language is used in work and mass media without official status to transcend language differences across a region.
4	Educational	The language is in vigorous use, with standardization and literature being sustained through a widespread system of institutionally supported education.
5	Developing	The language is in vigorous use, with literature in a standardized form being used by some, though this is not yet widespread or sustainable.
6a	Vigorous	The language is used for face-to-face communication by all generations and the situation is sustainable.

5.2 The Expanded Graded Intergenerational Disruption Scale (EGIDS)

Level	Label	Description
6b	Threatened	The language is used for face-to-face communication within all generations, but it is losing users.
7	Shifting	The child-bearing generation can use the language among themselves, but it is not being transmitted to children.
8a	Moribund	The only remaining active users of the language are members of the grandparent generation and older.
8b	Nearly Extinct	The only remaining users of the language are members of the grandparent generation or older who have little opportunity to use the language.
9	Dormant	The language serves as a reminder of heritage identity for an ethnic community, but no one has more than symbolic proficiency.
10	Extinct	The language is no longer used and no one retains a sense of ethnic identity associated with the language.

5.2.1 EGIDS level 0 (International)

The relatively few languages that are used internationally are at this level. While few if any local languages will even aspire to this level of safety and use, the level is included in the scale for completeness and to allow a categorization of all the languages of the world. These languages not only have very large L1 user populations but also large numbers of L2 users of the language in many different countries. In addition, an EGIDS 0 language will be given official recognition in multiple countries (i.e., be identified as a national or official language in those countries) but also be given similar recognition as a working or official language by international bodies and agencies. The 6 official languages of the United Nations, Arabic, Chinese, English, French, Russian, and Spanish are at this level.

> **English—An international language**
>
> The spread of English [eng] around the world makes it the primary example of an International (EGIDS 0) language. The spread of English has been compared to the spread of Latin [lat] during the expansion of the Roman empire. Then, the spread of Latin was largely carried out through Roman military expansion. The spread of English has been largely attributed to economic and technological expansion starting first with the colonial trading companies and the expansion of the British empire. More recently, the spread of English can be seen to follow the economic, political, scientific, and technological dominance of the United States.

5.2.2 EGIDS level 1 (National)

This level encompasses languages which function as official languages at the national level and have full face-to-face and, more importantly perhaps, written use that is supported by the apparatus of the nation-state through standardization, use in government documents, compulsory national-level education, and official publishing and dissemination institutions. This status may be formally established in law (de jure), such as in the national constitution. In many cases, however, the status has been established on a de facto basis. For example, the United States has no constitutionally identified national or official language, but English serves those functions in practice. Note that the identification of a language as a "national language" in a constitution is not what makes it a language at Level 1. Many constitutions identify a national language which serves a symbolic function as a language of national identity. Many officially recognized languages serve both functions (identity and governance) but only a language that is used in education, work, mass media, and government at the national level qualifies as EGIDS Level 1.

Bahasa Malaysia / Bahasa Indonesia / Kiswahili—officially recognized languages

Many nations identify one or more languages officially (de jure) as languages of national identity or as recognized languages for official purposes. In the linguistically-diverse nations of Malaysia and Indonesia, a standardized variety of Malay (Bahasa Malaysia [zsm] and Bahasa Indonesia [ind] respectively) has been so identified and promoted as the national language. Similarly, in Kenya and Tanzania, Kiswahili [swh] has been officially recognized as a national language in an effort to unify those nations around a single identity. These standardized national languages are intended to bridge the linguistic diversity within the population and to provide a focus for a sense of identity associated with the nation-state in contrast to more localized and more globalized identities. At the same time, they are used for government functions at the national level.

5.2.3 EGIDS level 2 (Provincial)

This level includes languages which function similarly to national languages, but only within the scope of a major administrative subdivision of a nation (e.g., province, state, territory, department, etc.), as opposed to within the nation as a whole. As with EGIDS Level 1, the status may be established either in law or on a de facto basis. When there are distinct local ethnolinguistic groups within a province, the provincial languages often also serve as languages of intercommunication between them. Within each state these languages function in much the same way as an official language does at the national level, as the recognized language of government functions, education, and business.

Gujarati, Tamil, Kannada, Marathi, etc.—state languages of India

In a highly linguistically and culturally diverse country such as India, national unity and a sense of identity have been promoted through the recognition of a national language, Hindi [hin]. At the same time, for very pragmatic reasons, local identity associations and language loyalties must also be recognized along with the practical issues of enabling communication where proficiency in the national language is low. Along with the national language, India has adopted a system of officially recognized state languages which are used for governance functions at the state level, such as Gujarati [guj], Tamil [tam], Kannada [kan], and Marathi [mar].

5.2.4 EGIDS level 3 (Wider Communication)

This level encompasses languages that do not have official recognition but which are "vehicular" in that they are used as a second language by members of multiple first-language communities and serve important functions for business and intergroup communication. They are generally learned outside of the home either formally or informally and often have a standardized (though perhaps not officially sanctioned) written form. However, many trade languages are unwritten and the existence of a written form is not essential for a language to be identified as a language of wider communication. This violates one of the general characteristics of the EGIDS, scalability. For more discussion of the notion of scalability and other general features of the EGIDS, see the Going Deeper section, below. Suffice it to say here that it seems clear that an unwritten language with significant numbers of second-language users is in a stronger position than a written language with relatively few users. The sustainability of a language of wider communication, however, is subject to some additional observations, for which also see the Going Deeper section.

> **Hausa—A language of wider communication**
>
> Hausa [hau] is a Chadic language of Nigeria. It is the mother tongue of ethnic Hausas and settled Fulanis in northern Nigeria and southern Niger. It is recognized as an official language of northern Nigeria (EGIDS 2) and serves as a trade language (EGIDS 3) in neighboring countries like Benin, Niger, Chad and Cameroon, and beyond (Ghana, Burkina Faso, Togo, Sudan, etc.). Some sources suggest that there are as many as 35 million Hausa speakers, of which approximately 15 million speak Hausa as a second language. Hausa is establishing itself as an urban mother tongue in towns and cities just outside the more historical territory of the ethnic Hausa, (e.g., Potiskum and Gombe in northern Nigeria). Where Hausa is not replacing the indigenous languages, it is being used on a daily basis as a lingua franca. (Lewis, Simons, and Fennig 2016; Newman 2000)

5.2.5 EGIDS level 4 (Educational)

This level includes languages that are used both as a medium of instruction and as a subject of instruction in a system of nstitutionally supported, widely-accepted system of education, but which do not have official recognition beyond that use nor do they serve as vehicular languages like those at EGIDS 3. Such a language may be the first language of literacy for speakers of local languages with eventual acquisition of, and transition to, one of the languages at a higher level on the EGIDS for more extensive written use. This is the stage that is often described as "mother tongue literacy" or "first language literacy." Institutional support for literacy acquisition is often situated within the state-run formal education system, but this is not a requirement. It may be situated primarily in the local community and be provided by more-or-less formally constituted local institutions that are sustainable.

By institutional support we understand "institution" to refer to societal institutions rather than formally constituted organizations or agencies. That is to say that the institutional support for literacy comes about in the form of a community-wide acceptance of L1 literacy as a valued and important set of behaviors that have become part of the social fabric of the community. This acceptance of literacy and literate behavior as a value is reflected in community-based structures (e.g., literacy teacher as an identified social role, literacy acquisition recognized as a legitimate social activity, etc.) that attend to the community's felt need to be a community that is literate in their L1. Thus, "institutionally supported, widely-accepted system of education" should be understood here as a very broad range of activities and behaviors that reflect a literate mindset or community self-image.

We recognize that in many cases the actual implementation and maintenance of literacy acquisition activities and programs may require external resources and may never be feasible without those external resources being available. Nevertheless, in defining this level, we focus primarily on the existence of societal institutional support for education in the local language community in contrast to introduced literacy without such widespread community-based institutional support (EGIDS Level 5).

The EGIDS category of Educational is the topmost level of sustainable language use within the SUM. Other higher, stronger levels also qualify as sustainable as we've defined the term (see chapter 1) but those levels largely go beyond the scope of efforts within the reach of community-based local language development.

Ngbaka—An educational language

Spoken in the Democratic Republic of the Congo and the Republic of the Congo, Ngbaka [nga] is a language with over a million speakers. Literacy has taken root as a societal value with as many as 150,000 readers. The language is taught in primary schools. Thousands of Ngbaka teachers are involved in literacy acquisition programs and many more Ngbaka speakers are learning to read and write. (Lewis, Simons, and Fennig 2016)

5.2.6 EGIDS level 5 (Developing)

This is the level at which literacy is incipient, more often than not through informal educational structures and systems and with only weak or transient societal institutional support as defined above.

Although the introduction of literacy can serve powerfully to improve the prestige of a minority language and may increase its prospects for survival in many cases, the stronger institutional support for literacy acquisition and maintenance found at EGIDS level 4 is required for ongoing transmission of local-language literacy from one generation to the next. The presence of incipient literacy in a speech community is not in itself sufficient to ensure sustainable ongoing use of the language.

Furthermore, the existence of an orthography or the production of some literature are not, in themselves, sufficient to qualify a language as having achieved EGIDS level 5. Reading and writing must actually be used by some segment, albeit a small one, of the overall population. Many communities where preparations for the introduction of literacy have been initiated are effectively at EGIDS 6a

(Vigorous). To qualify as EGIDS level 5, the language must also be in vigorous use as described for level 6a; when the language is losing uses and users, it should not be classified at level 5.

> **Pulaar—A developing language**
>
> Spoken in Senegal and neighboring countries, Pulaar [fuc] is one of many languages where literacy has been introduced. With a population of nearly 4.5 million speakers, the language is written in both the Arabic and Roman scripts. The literacy rate is still quite low, however, and it cannot be said that, even with official recognition in Senegal, literacy in Pulaar has achieved a level of institutional support adequate to make literacy sustainable. (Lewis, Simons, and Fennig 2016)

5.2.7 EGIDS level 6a (Vigorous)

At this level, intergenerational oral or face-to-face transmission of the language is intact and widespread in the community. The language use and transmission situation is stable or gaining strength. At this level, the vast majority of adults, parents, grandparents, and great grandparents are using the language and making it possible for children to acquire and use the language for everyday communication. In most cases intergenerational transmission happens naturally in the home and neighborhood and is not dependent on schools or other more formal mechanisms outside of the "home and hearth." Sign languages constitute a special case in that the acquisition of a sign language most often occurs in Deaf schools, especially when a deaf child has hearing parents.

Languages with vigorous face-to-face use and clearly identified functional assignments within a speech community can remain in use for many generations. As described in chapter 4, stable multilingualism provides the ecological setting for sustainable use.

> **Vincentian Creole English—A vigorous language**
>
> Spoken in Saint Vincent and the Grenadines, Vincentian Creole English [svc] is a language that is widely spoken by all generations and in all domains of use. Standard English is used in the schools and is the de facto language of governance, but Vincentian Creole English serves as the language of identity and is maintained orally. (Lewis, Simons, and Fennig 2014)

5.2.8 EGIDS level 6b (Threatened)

This is the level of face-to-face use that indicates the beginnings of erosion in language use. Level 6a represents a stable multilingual configuration as described in chapter 4 where informal functions are assigned to the Low language and more formal functions are assigned to the High variety. In contrast, Level 6b represents the loss of that stable arrangement with the informal domains being overtaken by another language or languages. At Level 6b, a large number of parents continue to transmit the language to their children even while a significant number do not, so that intergenerational transmission is weakening. With each new generation there will be fewer speakers or fewer domains of use or both. At this level, there may only be barely discernible portents of language shift and few in the community may have any sense of impending danger. EGIDS 6b is the first of the EGIDS levels that is not considered "safe" according to the criteria used by UNESCO.

> **Kwegu—A threatened language**
>
> The Kwegu [xwg] live in villages along the Omo river in southwestern Ethiopia. Their villages are currently threatened by a dam project. They consider themselves "river people" in contrast to the surrounding Mursi [muz] and Bodi dialect speakers of Me'en [mym] (related languages) who consider themselves "cattle people." The Kwegu are substantially outnumbered by the Mursi and Bodi. There are between 200 and 450 Kwegu, and over 3,000 Mursi and approximately 4,000 Bodi. National census figures treat all of these together. These two larger groups operate as "patrons" to the Kwegu, and all three groups consider the Kwegu to be lower in status to the other two groups.
>
> Mursi and Bodi men marry Kwegu women, and it is common for the Kwegu people to be bilingual in Mursi [muz] and/or the Bodi dialect of Me'en [mym], but very few outsiders learn Kwegu [xwg].
>
> "The Kwegu are diminishing in number because of intermarriage, and they are beginning to lose their identity as a separate ethnic group, a fact of which they are very much aware. The domains in which either Kwegu or Mursi or Bodi are spoken are beginning to overlap, a situation abetted by intermarriage. The contexts in which Kwegu is used among adults are decreasing, and the acquisition of Kwegu as a first language becomes less frequent because it strongly depends on the social network of which parents are part." (Muldrow 1976:606, Dimmendaal 1989:17–18)

5.2.9 EGIDS level 7 (Shifting)

This is the level that identifies clear cases of language shift in progress. The fact that parents are not passing the language on to their children is clearly discernible and has become the norm within the language community. Consequently the number of domains where use of the language is dominant are decreasing. Language revitalization through reestablishing home transmission would still be a possibility at this stage since the language is the first language for most of the parents and is in use among people in that generation and older. The language could be transmitted to at least some of the children if parents could be made aware of the need to do so.

> **Kwakiutl—A shifting language in Canada**
>
> Kwakiutl [kwk] is a First Nations language of southwestern Canada, with 170 proficient L1 speakers and around 500 semi-speakers, out of a total ethnic population of over 7,000. Most of the users of the language are 35 years of age or older, and the community is shifting to English as its primary language. (Lewis, Simons, and Fennig 2016)

5.2.10 EGIDS level 8a (Moribund)

At this level only the grandparent generation has any active and frequent users of the language. Though some in the parent generation might be able to use the language with their elders, they do not do so with their peers or their children. When they do use the language, it is likely with limited proficiency and with many borrowed words and frequent code-switching. The language is moribund because when the members of the grandparent generation die, the last fluent users of the language will be gone.

> **Gooniyandi—A moribund language of Australia**
>
> Spoken in Western Australia by only 410 people according to the 2006 Australian census, Gooniyandi [gni] is used only by the elderly. There have been some efforts to document the language with multiple grammatical descriptions and a dictionary. (Lewis, Simons, and Fennig 2016)

5.2.11 EGIDS level 8b (Nearly Extinct)

This level encompasses the stereotypical language loss situation where the only remaining speakers are among the grandparent or great grandparent generation, and those are so few or so scattered that they have little opportunity to use the language with each other.

> **Cayubaba—A nearly extinct language**
>
> Cayubaba [cyb], a language of Bolivia, is reported to have only 4 elderly speakers remaining as of 2007 and a few additional semi-speakers out of an ethnic population of 650. Most of the people now use Spanish (Lewis, Simons, and Fennig 2016)

5.2.12 EGIDS level 9 (Dormant)

This level includes languages which are associated closely with the heritage identity of some group of people but which are no longer used by anyone in that group for anything other than very limited public celebrations of that identity. Some people in the community may remember fragments of the language, perhaps as much as a song, poem, or short story. Some vocabulary items may be retained such as animal names or common expressions, but no one in the community has sufficient proficiency in the language to be able to carry on a conversation of any significant length. The language has no day-to-day communicative functions within the speech community.

This level describes the situation which is increasingly common among languages that have gone out of use fairly recently. Some community members may "remember" some bits and pieces of the language but they can't use the language in their daily life. In some cases revitalization efforts may be underway or at least contemplated. The community may have a strong (and perhaps increasing) sense of identification with their no-longer-spoken heritage language and wish to foster its use as a reinforcement of that identity. Heritage cultural festivals may feature use of the language with recitations and performances by community members as a way of celebrating that identity.

While the use of the language for daily communication will be minimal, the most common use will be ceremonial and symbolic, requiring the support of the community and home for intergenerational transmission of the words and phrases, stories and songs, that are used as markers of identity. Where revitalization efforts are underway, there may be some emerging speakers who are gaining proficiency but until an adequate number of people with language proficiency is achieved, use of the language will of necessity remain confined to only those few limited domains of use closely associated with identity preservation.

EGIDS 9 is the third sustainable level of use within the SUM. While not necessarily the most desirable situation, a language of identity—though dormant—can be retained as an identity marker for many generations. It is another example of how adequate compartmentalization of functions, even very limited functions, provides the kind of ecological stability needed to sustain language use.

> **Klamath-Modoc—A dormant language**
>
> There are no remaining fluent speakers of Klamath-Modoc [kla], a Native American language in the USA. The last native speaker died in 2003. According to the 2000 US Census there were 170 people who identified themselves as Klamath-Modoc at that time. Six adults have some second language proficiency in Klamath-Modoc and revitalization efforts are underway through lessons for children in the local primary school, the Head Start (pre-school) program, and weekly community meetings. The language has been documented with a dictionary and a grammar. (Golla 2007)

5.2.13 EGIDS level 10 (Extinct)

This level accounts for those situations where there are no remaining speakers and no one retains a strong sense of identity associated with the language. To prevent reaching this stage, while a declining language still has fluent speakers, it is important that the community be encouraged and assisted in the documentation of linguistic and sociocultural practices which will be adequate to preserve a record of the language for future generations. With such documentation, revitalization at least to the stage of recovering ethnolinguistic identity (EGIDS Level 9), might be achievable at some point in the future should the community so desire.

Without such documentation, the possibility of the language being totally forgotten and passing irrecoverably into oblivion is very strong. There is no way to know how many languages have already been lost to all memory because the last speaker died before the language could be documented.

Some languages at EGIDS Level 10, those that have been adequately documented, correspond to the fourth level of sustainable use included in the SUM. The label Sustainable History can be applied to those languages because adequate documentation has been produced and made sustainably accessible to future generations of scholars and community members. When that is the case, the historical record of the language is sustainable. While we consider this a sustainable level within the model, it is a bit difficult to call it a sustainable level of *use* since in fact there is no ongoing use of the language at all.

Tillamook—An extinct language

Tillamook [til], a Salish language of the Pacific Northwest in the United States, has been extinct since the last speaker died in 1970. There is some linguistic descriptive material about the language. (Lewis, Simons, and Fennig 2016)

5.3 The EGIDS and language revitalization

Like its predecessor, the GIDS, the EGIDS was created primarily as a measure of the disruption of intergenerational language transmission. By adding and expanding the higher levels of the scale, however, the EGIDS is also a tool that can be used to evaluate the degree of development of a language. With EGIDS 6a (Vigorous) identifying the "normal" state of most of the languages of the world, languages higher on the EGIDS are those which have undergone or are in the process of development while those which are lower on the scale are those which are undergoing decline and loss.

The primary descriptions provided for the lower levels of the scale assume that language loss is the norm. They are framed in terms of which generation remains as proficient users of the language. Clearly, though this is the common state of affairs, this will not always be the case. Where the trend is being reversed and language recovery and revitalization efforts are underway, the nature of the levels 6b–9 is fundamentally different.

5.3 The EGIDS and language revitalization

The normal pattern of language loss is for each succeeding (younger) generation to diminish its use of the language until only the grandparents retain proficiency and, with their passing, the language passes as well. It might be expected, then, that the process of revitalization would simply reverse that pattern with grandparent-aged users of the language being successively joined by adults and then by children over time. Generally, however, when language revitalization efforts are instituted, it is through the instigation and activism of young or middle-aged adults. If older speakers are still present in the community, they may be called upon to teach those activists who will then become the teachers of their children in their homes, until full intergenerational transmission is recovered. This may not always be the pattern that is followed, however.

Where no elders remain who speak the language, revitalization efforts may initially focus on children while not excluding adults if there is interest. Thus, the intergenerational transmission of a language may not be re-introduced following any set generational order. In some cases adults will be the emerging speakers (using their heritage language as a second language). In other cases, children may be taught the heritage language as a second-language by first-language speaking elders. In yet other situations, there may be no L1 speakers remaining and reintroduction of the language to any generation may be entirely through archival materials. Where language use partially remains in all generations, revitalization efforts may focus on expanding the domains of use and on increasing the number of speakers in all generations simultaneously. In all cases, however, it is adults who are aware of the need for revitalization and who participate in the development and implementation of the language re-acquisition effort.

Because the revitalization process is not nearly as predictable as the process of language loss, this is an area of continuing development for the EGIDS as an evaluative tool. The application of the EGIDS in these situations needs to be more nuanced and thoughtful. The evaluation of a community's place on the successive levels moving back up the scale should take into account both the increase in users, generation by generation where applicable, and an increase in the functions of the heritage language among those users. It will often be the case that the more salient feature for understanding the situation of the language will be the change the community is bringing about in moving *between* the EGIDS levels. In such cases, more process-oriented labels may be warranted—for example, reawakening, revitalizing, reestablishing, and so on.

As mentioned above, an important distinction to be noted about the revitalization process is that it changes the focus of the evaluation from first-language users to the emerging language users, most of whom will be learning and using the heritage language as their second language. The progression of language use described moving up the scale (from 8b to 8a to 7 to 6b) will necessarily focus on the shift from use of the heritage language predominantly as a second language to a fully re-integrated first-language used in the home or community by all generations at EGIDS 6a. In essence, evaluators will want to measure the loss of functions for the dominant language as the heritage language gains functions and proficient users. That sort of evaluation may be more usefully done using the FAMED conditions (see chapter 7) rather than the EGIDS scale with its focus on degree of endangerment. While the endangerment categories of the EGIDS still apply and may accurately reflect the level of risk for a language that is being revitalized, they do not, on their face, accurately reflect the changes in the underlying conditions that are taking place. For that, the FAMED conditions are more likely to describe the dynamics of the situation more precisely.

5.4 Assessment of EGIDS levels

The EGIDS was designed to provide a useful framework for assessing the vitality of any language in the world. The scale itself does not presume any particular methodology for making that assessment. There are a variety of ways in which the place of a particular language on the scale can be determined.

5.4.1 Best guess

One method for assessing the vitality of a language is to simply look at the definitions of the EGIDS levels in table 5.1 and, based on one's general knowledge of the situation of a language, assign an EGIDS level to that language according to the criteria in the EGIDS level descriptions.

The EGIDS levels are intended to be general characterizations of vitality and not detailed descriptions of all of the factors that contribute to the strength or weakness of language use—for example, the number of users, attitudes, and the numerous other complexities that contribute to ethnolinguistic vitality generally. In many cases a simple "best guess" based on general knowledge is all that is needed and may be entirely adequate for at least an early evaluation of the status of a language in a particular context.

In complex situations where the patterns of language use are unclear or where trends are mixed or contradictory, more quantitative methods may be called for, but the EGIDS does not require precise quantitative analyses in order to be usefully applied.

5.4.2 Four diagnostic questions

Another method for determining the EGIDS level of a language is to use a set of four diagnostic questions. The diagnostic questions form a decision tree such that the response to the first question determines which other question needs to be answered. That process enables a user to make an EGIDS determination by answering no more than two questions. The following tables (5.2 through 5.5) present the four questions and the logic of the decision tree. The first question (given in the header of the first column in table 5.2) is "How is the language used?" The answer to that question narrows the choice to one of the EGIDS levels listed in the second column. The exact EGIDS level is determined by asking the follow-up question given in the third column and then referring to the subsequent table as directed.

5.4 Assessment of EGIDS levels

Table 5.2 EGIDS decision tree based on four diagnostic questions

How is the language used?	EGIDS Levels	Follow-up question
It is a *vehicular* language—it is widely used, not only within its native community but by other language communities as well.	0, 1, 2, 3	What is the level of official use? (Go to table 5.3.)
It is a home language—it is used by people of all generations within its native community in the home, family, neighborhood, and community.	4, 5, 6a, 6b	What is the sustainability status? (Go to table 5.4.)
It is a heritage language—it retains an identificational function for its native community but is no longer used fluently by all generations.	7, 8a, 8b, 9	What is the youngest generation of proficient speakers? (Go to table 5.5.)
It is an extinct language—it retains no function for any living ethnic community.	10	

Table 5.3 What is the level of official use?

When it is a vehicular language, if...	Then the EGIDS level is...
The language is widely used between nations in trade, knowledge exchange, and international policy.	0 (International)
The language is used in education, work, mass media, and government at the nationwide level.	1 (National)
The language is used in education, work, mass media, and government within officially recognized subdivisions of a nation.	2 (Provincial)
The language is used in work and mass media without official status in order to transcend language differences across a region.	3 (Wider communication)

Table 5.4 What is the sustainability status?

When it is a home language, if...	Then the EGIDS level is...
The language is used for face-to-face communication by all generations and this is being reinforced by sustainable literacy.	4 (Educational)
The language is used for face-to-face communication by all generations and is being used in written form in parts of the community though literacy is not yet sustainable.	5 (Developing)
The language is used for face-to-face communication by all generations and the situation is sustainable.	6a (Vigorous)
The language is used for face-to-face communication within all generations but at least one of the conditions for sustainable oral use is lacking.	6b (Threatened)

Table 5.5 What is the youngest generation of proficient speakers?

When it is a heritage language, if...	Then the EGIDS level is...
The youngest proficient speakers are members of the child-bearing generation.	7 (Shifting)
The only remaining active speakers of the language are members of the grandparent generation and older.	8a (Moribund)
The only remaining speakers of the language are members of the great-grandparent generation.	8b (Nearly Extinct)
There are no fully proficient speakers, but symbolic use may remain as a marker of heritage identity for an ethnic community.	9 (Dormant)

The questions examine language use in terms of some key concepts related to language development (how the language is used) and intergenerational transmission (which generations use the language). In particular, the *vehicularity* of the language—how widely it is used by others as their second language—and the scope of official recognition at the national or regional levels—are key factors used in this evaluation. These are discussed at greater length in the Going Deeper section of this chapter.

The diagnostic questions serve primarily as a guide for evaluation and provide a bit more guidance for the evaluator who may not feel qualified to provide a "best guess" evaluation. They are not intended as quantitative research instruments with well-defined criteria and quantifiable thresholds for determining when a particular situation fits into one category or another. For example, the diagnostic questions do not specify how many need to be able to use the language being evaluated in order for it to be described as a vehicular language. Nor do they set thresholds regarding in how many countries a language needs to be used (or recognized) for it to qualify as international.

Both the Best Guess approach and the slightly more structured Diagnostic Questions are global in their perspective. They ask the evaluator to look at the overall circumstances, the big picture, of each language within its particular ecological setting. The major requirement for such an evaluation is that the evaluator have such general knowledge and awareness. If an evaluator cannot provide that broader perspective on the situation, they may wish to consider a different approach to the evaluation process. An alternate approach that uses a more detailed description of the language ecology is described in chapter 7 where we discuss the sustainability conditions which affect the EGIDS level of the language. A tool for using those conditions is described in the next section.

5.4.3 The SUM Assessment Grid

Another approach to evaluating the EGIDS level of a community was developed by Simons and Lewis (2012). It can be downloaded at http://www.sil.org/resources/archives/57632. This tool begins not with an overall evaluation of the EGIDS but with a finer-grained analysis of the conditions which contribute to the dynamics of language use. We discuss this set of five conditions (the FAMED conditions) at greater length in chapter 7.

The grid asks the user to score the situation on each of the five conditions both with respect to sustainable oral use and sustainable written use by selecting the descriptor that best fits the language community's current status or practice. The user of the tool reads all of the descriptions in a row of the grid; then selects the description that best fits the situation for the language community in focus. The SUM Assessment Grid is designed to be used by someone with more in-depth knowledge of the community.

5.4.4 A Guide for Planning the Future of Our Language

Another tool is *A Guide for Planning the Future of Our Language* (Hanawalt et al. 2015). This tool is designed for use in community settings by a trained local facilitator. It guides the community through the EGIDS evaluation using participatory research activities. It also presents the sustainable levels of use and facilitates the community's identification of the level of sustainable use that it desires to achieve. The major strength of the Guide is that it is a participatory process which involves community members in the evaluation as well as in subsequent decisions regarding their own language development.

5.5 Going deeper

5.5.1 Language endangerment, language vitality, and sustainable use

Language endangerment has already been alluded to in our discussion thus far under the rubric of the preservation (and loss) of local knowledge and the preservation of diversity in chapter 2. The literature on the topic is extensive and growing. The concept of vitality is closely related and has a similarly large and proliferating academic literature. There are numerous approaches to describing what is variously called language vitality, ethnolinguistic vitality, and somewhat less frequently, language viability as a theoretical construct, only some of which we will describe briefly below: Bourhis, Giles, and Lambert 1975; Bourhis and Giles 1976; Lamy 1979; Bourhis, Giles, and Rosenthal 1981; Husband and Khan 1982; Johnson et al. 1983; Bourhis and Sachdev 1984; Allard and Landry 1986; Landry and Allard 1991; Paulston 2000.

There is also an extensive literature on approaches to assessing vitality which apply those theories and others: Landweer 1991, 2012; Kindell 1991; Kindell and Lewis 2000; Karan 2011. And there are multiple frameworks and evaluations of those frameworks for categorizing the results of such assessments: Fishman 1991; Krauss 2007; Brenzinger et al. 2003; Lewis 2006, 2008; Lewis and Simons 2010; Obiero 2010.

More general reference works on language maintenance, language shift, and language death abound. The following represent just a few of the early and more recent treatments of the topic: Campbell and Muntzel 1989; Crystal 2000; Dimmendal 1989; Dorian, 1973, 1977, 1978, 1980a, 1980b, 1981, 1986, 1987, 1989; Fishman 1964, 1964/1978, 1965, 1986, 1991, 2000, 2001; Grenoble and Whaley 1998, 2006; Harrison 2007; King 2001; Nettle and Romaine 2000; Tabouret-Keller 1968.

5.5.2 The roots of the EGIDS: The GIDS

The EGIDS, as its name suggests, is an expanded version of the Graded Intergenerational Disruption Scale (GIDS) created by Joshua Fishman and most widely made known in his now classic volume *Reversing Language Shift* (Fishman 1991). The GIDS was developed by Fishman as a way to evaluate the level of disruption of the transmission of language proficiency from one generation to the next. Fishman focused on languages that were undergoing shift and death—those at weaker levels of language use and vitality.

Fishman's foundational notion is that language shift and loss occur over time (and across geographical and social spaces) in a progressive fashion. As language shift progresses the situation worsens. The affected language loses both users and uses. These two dimensions (users and uses) are often reciprocal: as a language becomes used for fewer functions, there are fewer people who feel the need or have opportunity to use it; and conversely, as a language loses users, it is used for fewer and fewer functions. In addition, as a language loses ground in this way, its links to the identity of the community of users weaken and that further erodes the perceived value of the language. Thus, it is that a language that is undergoing shift enters a downward spiral leading to oblivion if nothing is done to halt or reverse the process.

5.5 Going deeper

Fishman identified stages in this downward progression and placed them on a scale as summarized in table 5.6 below. Each level on the scale represents a characteristic configuration of language use with each higher number on the scale representing a progressively weaker or more disrupted pattern of language use. These levels or grades can be used diagnostically to assess the extent of language shift.

Table 5.6 Fishman's Graded Intergenerational Disruption Scale (GIDS)

Level	Description
1	The language is used in education, work, mass media, government at the national level.
2	The language is used for local and regional mass media and governmental services.
3	The language is used for local and regional work by both insiders and outsiders.
4	Literacy in the language is transmitted through education.
5	The language is used orally by all generations and is effectively used in written form throughout the community.
6	The language is used orally by all generations and is being learned by children as their first language.
7	The child-bearing generation knows the language well enough to use it with their elders but is not transmitting it to their children.
8	The only remaining speakers of the language are members of the grandparent generation.

The GIDS measures the degree of disruption in intergenerational language transmission. That is, it focuses on the loss of users and uses from one generation to the next. Higher numbers on the scale represent greater degrees of disruption in intergenerational language transmission. Lower numbers represent less disruption or higher levels of intergenerational transmission. Thus, somewhat counter-intuitively, a lower number on the GIDS identifies a stronger level of language use. A higher number represents greater disruption and weaker levels of language use.

The GIDS is focused primarily on the assessment of intergenerational transmission of language. It measures the degree to which older generations are failing to pass on the language being evaluated (or conversely, the degree to which younger generations are failing to acquire the language being evaluated). The division of Fishman's GIDS level 6 into EGIDS 6a and 6b that we have introduced follows from the observation that level 6 straddles the line of diglossia (King 2001). As we've described earlier, the normal pattern for language transmission is in the home and from parent to child. The beginnings of the loss of intergenerational transmission can generally be traced to the loss of the stable multilingualism that characterizes EGIDS 6a as the language is used for the transmission of fewer and fewer bodies of knowledge. The progressive nature of language shift can then be traced to the failure in transmission and acquisition over time by looking at the average age of the youngest first language users of a particular language. It would be expected that the extent and seriousness of language shift could correlate almost directly to that statistic (Lewis 2008).

The pattern of loss of uses and users, viewed schematically, proceeds generationally with the youngest generation being the first to lose proficiency. As that generation grows up and becomes parents, they are then unable to pass the language on to their children resulting in two generations without speakers. Finally, as the second generation grows up and becomes parents, their children in turn fail to acquire the language and the cycle of shift completes itself with no living, fully proficient speakers (except perhaps some isolated surviving members of the great-grandparent generation).

However, except in very small communities or in cases where catastrophic loss of life has occurred, it isn't likely that everyone in an entire generation will stop using the language at the same time. Rather, like most language change, the pattern of language shift begins as an innovation with only a relatively small number of early adopters who begin acquiring and using a second language for the transmission of some bodies of knowledge at the expense of their first language. Eventually, some of those innovators fail to pass the heritage language on to their children. If that innovation is perceived to be rewarding or beneficial in some way, others will begin to emulate it. As more and more members of each succeeding generation adopt the same pattern of language use, the norms of language use spread throughout the community in a self-re-enforcing pattern. While the idealized generational model of language shift that we've just described as typical represents the shift as potentially occurring in only three generations, more often the shift happens at a slower pace with each succeeding generation showing more and more disruption in intergenerational transmission. It is usually only towards the very end of the cycle that there is a precipitous change, sometimes described as the tipping point or "the tip" (Dorian 1986, 1989). Preceding that sudden shift there is almost always an extended period of gradual, almost imperceptible erosion of use. In many cases the process is so gradual that members of the community are unaware of what is happening. The process is only recognized when it is very far along and often when it is too late or extremely costly to engage in effective remedial action.

While the GIDS provided the seminal set of categories for categorizing language shift in progress, at the extreme lower end of the scale, the GIDS does not address those situations where no intergenerational transmission at all is taking place (below GIDS level 8). And the basic set of 8 categories are not fine-grained enough to account adequately for the stages of loss of intergenerational transmission.

5.5.3 Language shift in ecological perspective

While the notion of language ecology was present in the academic environment at the time of the development of the GIDS, the primary perspective of the GIDS is to focus on a single endangered language and to look at what needs to be done to reverse the pattern of shift for that language alone. The focus is primarily on the loss of intergenerational language transmission and its reinvigoration. Certainly other languages, especially the "threatening" languages are considered, but only as background for or as obstacles to the goal of rescuing, reviving, and strengthening the position of a single minority or minoritized language.

Since 1991, when Fishman published the GIDS, language ecology has become a much more influential perspective and has reshaped the way in which we understand language use. As we've emphasized in earlier chapters, languages cannot be dealt with in isolation and interventions on behalf of one language must be planned and implemented taking into account the current roles and relationships among all of the languages within a speech community.

While there is a certain amount of contestation and potential for conflict in any social situation where the speakers of one language variety (and its associated identity) are vying for social space with the speakers of another language (and its associated identity), the original formulation of GIDS did not pay a great deal of attention to this as a factor to be considered. The agenda of Reversing Language Shift, as Fishman termed it, in its single-minded focus on reversing the downward spiral of use and users, was to strengthen the endangered language at all costs. The implication of the GIDS seemed to be that a language was only truly safe when it reached the very highest levels on the scale. In practice, attempts to achieve such an outcome would inevitably put the endangered language in direct competition with the dominant national and regional languages. Adopting a more ecological perspective leads us to think in less dichotomous and adversarial terms. The goal of reversing language shift need not necessarily be to wrest dominance away from the currently powerful and more widely used language(s). A more beneficial approach for all concerned is to find an equitable distribution of functions for the languages in the ecology, taking into account both instrumental and sentimental motivations for their use.

This shift from a single-language-in-isolation perspective to a more ecological perspective serves as a fundamental mindset of the Sustainable Use Model and is reflected in the way the EGIDS is intended to be used within the SUM. Some examples of this higher level approach to assessing the language ecology of an entire country using the EGIDS can be found in (Lewis and Simons 2015). This view also underlies the notion of *levels of sustainable language use* that we describe in chapter 6.

5.5.4 Language revitalization and reversing language shift (RLS)

Fishman's GIDS focuses largely on intergenerational transmission. His prescription for reversing language shift was to reinstitute and strengthen intergenerational transmission by all means possible. This principle forms the central core of the GIDS and remains a well-accepted premise that no serious practitioners of language revitalization can argue with. Many language revitalization programs address this concern centrally and directly. Community language classes for adults and children, language camps, language nests, the use of the language in formal and non-formal education, and master-apprentice programs, all represent efforts to get people to once again use the language. Most centrally for practitioners interested in reversing language shift (RLS), these efforts are attempts to get people to use the language with the next generation (either older or younger). These methods, techniques, and activities are described at greater length in chapter 9 and in the Appendix.

Many of these efforts have seen some success in bringing little-used languages back into use although often the new speakers of the language are not fully proficient. As a result, a category of language, the emergent language (Grinevald 1998) has been identified to describe languages that are reawakening after a period of dormancy. The profile of the users of emergent languages is in some ways similar to that of the semi-speaker but the difference is in the trajectory of their proficiency. Where semi-speakers are those who have only partial proficiency and are seeing their language skills erode over time, users of emergent languages are those who have only partial proficiency but are acquiring more and more skills as their proficiency, and the language itself, expands rather than retracts.

In addition to the proficiency of the speakers in each case, the functions of the languages in society and the capacity of the languages to fulfill those functions are also on different trajectories. In the case of language loss, as the number of users decreases so too does the functional utility of the language decrease. This results in fewer uses for the language, and accompanying that decreasing use is a gradual attrition of the features of the language itself. Where language revitalization is occurring, the growing association of the language with particular domains of use requires increasing proficiency of the speakers enabling them to use the language for those functions. With that increased use of the language comes an expansion of the language itself with new vocabulary and more complex grammatical constructions emerging over time.

Fishman clearly recognized that the addition of new uses and functions for a language that is being lost are helpful and could be supportive of the reversal of language shift. He also recognized that the introduction of literacy can in some cases, but not always, also strengthen the position of the language. Fishman's repeated refrain, however, was and continues to be that any new use that does not foster and support greater levels of intergenerational transmission must be considered as a lower priority.

There also is a growing body of evidence that literacy, per se, can be a double-edged sword. While it can represent a significant expansion of potential new functions for a language, unless literacy is built on a solid foundation of identity maintenance and ongoing face-to-face intergenerational transmission and day-to-day use, it may very well undermine the vitality of a minority language due to the lack of resources, materials, and opportunities that we described in chapter 2. Lee and McLaughlin (2001) make the distinction at GIDS level 4 between institutions which are primarily under local control (what they label as Level 4a) and those which are under the control of outsiders (their Level 4b). That distinction may well be useful in many contexts as it reflects the importance of literacy acquisition becoming a community valued behavior in contrast to an externally offered "solution" to a problem. A weak language placed in direct competition with a stronger language, in any domain of use, is very likely going to become weaker. Experience is teaching us that the way to rebuild a failing language is by strengthening the identity of its users and cementing its face-to-face use. The SUM describes this as the hierarchy of sustainable use which we will describe at greater length in chapter 6. This may represent a small philosophical departure from Fishman. Where intergenerational transmission has been disrupted, it is indeed crucial that it be re-established. However, from the perspective of the SUM, the re-establishment of a foundational level of Sustainable Identity through the identification of relevant bodies of life-crucial knowledge is key to achieving that goal. The EGIDS provides a richer set of levels to measure progress both up and down the scale of vitality versus disruption and the sustainable levels of use delineate important plateaus of pervasive, prevalent, and predictable use (see our discussion of these characteristics in chapter 6) on the path towards ongoing use of the language for the transmission of life-crucial knowledge.

5.5.5 Language documentation and conservation

Another major advance in our learning since the GIDS was first introduced is the development of a far richer understanding of the importance of efforts to preserve and document a language. The field of language documentation and conservation, or documentary linguistics, has emerged as a new subfield of linguistics with an online, open access journal by the same name (see http://www.nflrc.hawaii.edu/ldc/). Documentary linguistics has come to be distinguished technically from descriptive linguistics and incorporates many of the concerns of sociolinguists. For example, it takes into account that adequate documentation requires not only sufficient data to serve analysis of language structure but also sufficient data to be able to preserve patterns of language use and the genres, styles, and registers used in different social settings and for different functions (Himmelmann 1998). Having such a rich and varied sample of the language is essential for the reconstruction and reintroduction of the language by future generations, should they so desire.

The role of language documentation as part of the reversing language shift process is hardly in view at all in the GIDS. The GIDS seems to assume that the lowest point on the scale from which that reversal of the decline of language use could be implemented is at GIDS Level 8 (the lowest on the scale overall) where only a few remaining elderly speakers are living and able to be used as resources for the recovery of the language. Since 1991 (when Fishman's RLS book was published), many communities which retain only a sense of identity, and in some cases, only a very weak linkage to that identity, have made efforts to recover their heritage culture, including the revival of their language (e.g., Hobson 2004, several case studies in Ostler and Rudes 2000, and Warner 2001). These efforts have made the importance of rigorous and comprehensive language documentation abundantly clear. The GIDS was premised on the idea that unless there were at least some speakers using the language for some few functions (or at least remembering how to use the language for those purposes), all was lost. Even in the most well known and oft-cited case of language resurrection, Hebrew, there was still oral and written liturgical use of the language and a considerable body of written text in the religious domain that could serve as a foundation for more prosaic contemporary uses.

While the overall prospects for success of revitalization efforts remain uncertain where the only extant record of the language is in archival materials, our model for evaluating the degree of disruption needs to go beyond intergenerational transmission alone to include levels of disruption that take into account the possibility of documentary transmission of the knowledge of the language.

5.5.6 Expanding the GIDS

Fishman's GIDS has been widely referenced and used. It is arguably the best known evaluative tool available for the purposes of identifying relative language vitality. The Expanded Graded Intergenerational Disruption Scale (EGIDS) (Lewis and Simons 2010) is an attempt to build on that foundation, to evaluate endangered languages with a finer-grained scale, and to provide a tool for a similar evaluation of languages that are being developed. This broader scope includes languages that are strong and widely used, such as international and national or provincial languages, as well as those where language shift has run its full course and the language is no longer used at all.

Why expand?

With the broad acceptance and use of Fishman's GIDS, the question must be asked why another scale is needed. We've already mentioned that the GIDS and its alternatives have some weaknesses that can be addressed in an expanded and updated framework. In addition, as more has come to be known about the process and progress of language shift and death (and its reversal), there is room for improvement in some aspects of the scale. Also, the scope of what Fishman originally called "reversing language shift" as an overall endeavor has broadened and expanded beyond what Fishman had originally considered it to encompass, not only revitalization, but language development.

In the following sections we present a brief rationale for that expansion by looking at the additional factors that comprise the EGIDS.

The numbering of the EGIDS levels has been designed to maintain correspondence with Fishman's GIDS. Expansions in the EGIDS are designated either by the assignment of new numbers or by the addition of a letter to an existing number. Thus, Levels 6a and 6b in the EGIDS together correspond to what is described in Fishman's GIDS as Level 6. Similarly 8a and 8b correspond to the original Level 8. EGIDS levels 0, 9, and 10 are entirely new descriptive categories that allow the EGIDS to be applied to all languages of the world. In addition, for convenience, each numbered level is also assigned a short one or two word label that identifies the major functional category of that level.

The multi-scalar nature of the EGIDS

The EGIDS takes into account different dimensions at different levels on the overall scale. Figure 5.1 identifies the dimensions that are in focus at the different levels of the EGIDS.

5.5 Going deeper

EGIDS 0-2	Official Recognition
EGIDS 3	Vehicularity
EGIDS 4-5	Educational Use
EGIDS 6a-8b	Intergenerational Transmission
EGIDS 9	Identity
EGIDS 10	Documentation

Figure 5.1 Multi-scalar nature of the EGIDS.

At the lower end of the EGIDS, the focus of the scale is on not only the loss of speakers but also the loss of any identity associations with the language. A language which is no longer spoken and which is not associated closely with any community's identity is considered extinct. Secondary to this state of affairs is a consideration of the amount and quality of documentation of the language. As mentioned above, an undocumented language will pass into oblivion. The language's existence and a description of the range of use and the structures of the language must be adequately documented if its history is to be sustainable. We discuss this and other sustainable levels of language vitality further in chapter 6.

Above EGIDS 10, the EGIDS focuses its attention on the existence of an associated identity with the language. Following Leonard 2008, a language with no fluent speakers which is associated with an extant community's identity, is more properly considered to be "sleeping" or dormant rather than extinct. The distinction between EGIDS 10 (Extinct with or without adequate documentation) and EGIDS 9 (Dormant) depends on the association of the language with a group identity.

Intergenerational Transmission is the dimension that is the core of the EGIDS and is derived with only minor modifications from Fishman's GIDS. The key to language maintenance is the achievement of EGIDS 6a, the widespread use of the language in day-to-day life by all generations. The levels between that "vigorous" level and dormancy (EGIDS 9) or extinction (EGIDS 10) are characterized by increasing degrees of disruption in the intergenerational chain of transmission.

Educational Use of the language (that is, its development as a written means of communication) is the next dimension that the EGIDS focuses on as we move up the scale beyond widespread vigorous oral use. EGIDS level 5 describes the early stages of that development and EGIDS 4 describes its establishment as a societal norm. The use of a language for literate functions in any given language ecology, generally, should be considered a good thing. The caveat is that in order for that assertion to hold, the language must have already achieved sustainable oral use at EGIDS 6a. Fishman's maxim holds true: Intergenerational transmission of the language is an *a priori* condition for sustainable oral use. We would go further and assert that the hierarchical nature of the EGIDS makes it clear that without the foundation of an associated identity and sustainable oral use, the introduction of the written use of a language cannot by itself contribute to the overall vitality of the language and may in fact undermine that vitality significantly (cf. UNESCO 2005b). Keeping that in mind, we can confidently assert that a language at EGIDS 6a which is beginning to be used for written functions (at or moving through EGIDS 5 to EGIDS 4) is more vital than a language which is not being used for reading and writing at all.

Vehicularity refers to the degree to which a language is used not only by the group of people who associate it most closely with their identity, but also by others who find that the language provides them with rewards and benefits that can't be as easily derived by using any other language. Putting it simply, if a language has a large number of people who see value in learning and using it as a second language, it is in a more sustainable position than a language which has few or no second language learners. This dimension is called Vehicularity since the language serves as a vehicle of communication that can take a user beyond the spheres of activity in which they could operate without it.

Vehicularity comes into focus at EGIDS 3. The widespread use of a language as a second language is an additional indicator of its vitality. EGIDS 3 in particular focuses on the use of the language as a trade language. At this point the overall hierarchical nature of the EGIDS is violated to a certain degree in that the use of the language for writing is considered less salient than the fact that it is vehicular. This anomaly is discussed by Kim (2015) who discusses the question of "how widely a language had to be used as an L2 in order to be considered vehicular"? She notes that several of the vehicular languages she identified in Bangladesh did not meet the criteria to be considered EGIDS 4, and were they to lose their vehicularity (widespread use as an L2 by others), would necessarily have to be classified as EGIDS 5 at best, but more likely EGIDS 6a. Thus, some languages at EGIDS 3 would not qualify as languages of education (EGIDS 4), or in some cases, even as a developing language (EGIDS 5). However, if the number of first-language speakers of any language is decreasing, that is, if a language is no longer at EGIDS 6a among its first-language users, the use of the language as a second language for trade or interethnic contacts may prove to be but a hollow victory, as the foundational identity associations needed to support ongoing language transmission may be lacking. This is precisely the situation of constructed languages, such as Esperanto, which though widely promoted as potential languages of wider communication, lack sustainability because there is no speech community which links its core identity with the language. Such languages must always be on artificial life support as a result.

Official Recognition refers to the extent to which a language is recognized by governments at the international, national, and sub-national levels for legal and juridical purposes and in different types of policy documents and statements. The scope and quality of these recognitions also contribute to the overall vitality of a language. An officially recognized language generally has more resources available to support its ongoing use, transmission, and development. Though there is often a significant gap between policy rhetoric and policy implementation, the general principle is that more positive policies tend to strengthen vitality while more negative policies work against it.

At the highest levels of the EGIDS, official recognition is in view, with statutory or even de facto official use for governance at either the provincial (EGIDS 2) or the national (EGIDS 1) levels indicating a high degree of institutional support and prestige for the language. Languages which are recognized for significant international uses (e.g., the official languages of the United Nations and other international bodies) are assigned EGIDS 0.

Those working in community-based language development projects, engaged as they are most frequently with local language communities, often don't contemplate ever needing to, or having the possibility of, affecting national and international language policies. Nevertheless, the overall policy environment is a significant factor which needs to be kept in mind and engaged with when necessary. The policy environment will be discussed at greater length in chapter 7 when we discuss the FAMED conditions.

The multi-scalar approach of the EGIDS provides for a richer analysis of the vitality of each language to which it is applied and fits the assessment of the languages into a theoretical model which practitioners can use to help them establish priorities and next steps in language development activities. It has many similarities to the UNESCO LVE (discussed below) in its theoretical breadth. In addition, the SUM has been found to provide reflective practitioners of community-based language development with a "more precise vocabulary and framework for description, analysis and planning" (Quakenbush 2015:122).

5.5.7 Other theoretical approaches to ethnolinguistic vitality

Ethnolinguistic Identity Theory

The broad framework around which much of the evaluation of ethnolinguistic vitality revolves is variously known as Ethnolinguistic Identity Theory or Ethnolinguistic Vitality Theory.

Ethnolinguistic vitality is a broad concept which includes social, cultural, economic, political, and linguistic factors as a means of estimating the relative robustness of an ethnic group's identity in situations where the group is in frequent contact with another group or groups. Implicit in this, of course, is the assumption that there is a scale of increasing (or decreasing) ethnic strength which can be used to measure the sociocultural health of ethnic groups. It also recognizes the multiple group memberships which are possible for an individual and is an attempt to measure the relative strength of an individual's attachment to those competing identities and to identify the most salient group focus.

Objective ethnolinguistic vitality factors

Three general categories of objective vitality factors have been identified: demographic factors, institutional support factors, and status factors. Not surprisingly these correspond rather well with the areas of dislocation that Fishman (1991)] has described as producing language shift: physical/demographic, cultural, and social. These broad categories take into account socio-structural factors relating to group size and distribution, political and economic dominance, institutional support, boundary maintenance, and relative status and prestige. The relationship of these categories to language maintenance and shift is fairly obvious, but institutional support requires some additional discussion since it is specifically called upon in the EGIDS as one of the distinguishing characteristics of EGIDS 4 (Educational) in contrast to EGIDS 5 (Developing).

Institutional support factors are those which relate to the kind of recognition and use given to a language or variety in education, media, government, religion, and other societal institutions. Giles, Bourhis and Taylor (1977:315–316)] observe that institutional support can be either formal or informal, where informal support refers to the extent to which a community has organized itself in terms of advocacy movements, and formal support is that built into the institutional structure itself. The kinds of institutions are many and diverse. It would seem likely that some (e.g., education) are more influential than others. The use and support of a language in education at all levels is not only an objective indicator of vitality but also plays an important role in shaping subjective perceptions of ethnolinguistic vitality. The language of religion is an indicator that also should be considered carefully.

The relative prestige of the institution can be influential upon the perceived status of the language variety associated with that particular situational and topical context and may influence its acceptability for a specific function. The roles assigned to a language may be affected by ideological pressures, as is the case in many bilingual education programs with assimilationist ideologies or in vernacular language schools where the purpose is language and identity maintenance. In most cases institutional support is both a reflection of and a reinforcer of status.

Subjective ethnolinguistic vitality factors

A group's own perception of its vitality apart from the objective indicators can be analyzed as subjective vitality factors. Groups which perceive themselves to be successful tend to behave in ways which reinforce that success. Groups which perceive themselves to be failing may react by engaging in language and identity maintenance efforts or by shifting to behaviors which conform more to the norms of outsiders.

Multiple identities and boundary maintenance

An additional factor is the sharpness of focus of an individual or group on a single, most salient identity from among the multiple allegiances which exert their influence on the individual or group. If the in-group is relatively homogeneous and there is a considerable focus on a single ethnic identity and allegiance to that identity, the adoption and maintenance of those linguistic norms is more likely. If, however, group members feel multiple allegiances to other group identities, their identity associations will be more diffuse, less focused, and they will be less likely to respond to the norm enforcement mechanisms of any single group.

Giles and Johnson (1987) explain that groups not only have a core identity but they also have boundaries which they attempt to maintain. Individuals must cross these group boundaries when they pass from one group identity to another.

Perceptions of hard and impermeable boundaries make identification with a single ethnicity easier and make the in-group membership more focused. Even though individuals may have multiple group memberships, the development of certain inter-group boundaries into hard and impassable ones makes the group membership associated with those particular boundaries more salient. Other group memberships still exist but become less salient because the core group distinctives are more in focus.

Boundary maintenance factors include the relative hardness or softness of group boundaries as measured by the degree of access to the full range of roles within the society. Both diglossia (compartmentalization) and access (bilingualism) are important contributors to stability in language contact situations. Just as compartmentalization is an important status factor, so access is an important reflection of the nature of boundary maintenance. Where group boundaries are rigid and unyielding, there is likely to be greater language maintenance. However, pressures for social change will tend to break down those boundaries and that accounts for the rapid changes in language maintenance when diglossia without bilingualism (discussed in the Going Deeper section of chapter 4) is lost.

Giles and Johnson (1987:72) sum up Ethnolinguistic Identity Theory by listing five factors which affect the degree to which an individual (and the number of individuals) in the in-group diverges from members of the out-group (i.e., engages in language maintenance behaviors). These controlling factors are the following:

- The degree to which the individual identifies himself with, and the strength of his identification with, a group identity which is strongly associated with a particular language.
- The degree to which the individual or group makes insecure social comparisons of themselves with the out-group.
- The degree to which the group members perceive their own group's vitality to be high.
- The degree to which the group perceives its own boundaries to be hard and impassable.
- The degree to which the group has strong feelings of identification with few other social groups.

5.5.8 Other scales and evaluative tools

The GIDS is not the only evaluative tool that has been used, although it is probably the most widely known. Beginning with the 8th edition, the *Ethnologue* (Grimes 1974) began using a very general set of categories (Living, Nearly Extinct, Extinct). The lack of precision of these categories made them largely unsuitable for the evaluation of ethnolinguistic vitality and that led to the development of the EGIDS and its introduction into the 16th edition of the *Ethnologue* (Lewis 2009). Other more comprehensive evaluation systems bear mentioning, however.

Krauss' ten level scale

Notable among these is an early proposal by Krauss (republished in 2007) where a 10-level graded scale based on the ages of the speaker population is proposed. Krauss not only proposes the age-based classification scheme but suggests some terminology for those different levels. Early on, this proposal identified factors that are significant in the assessment of language vitality but it has not been widely used.

UNESCO's Language Vitality and Endangerment (LVE) framework

In 2003 UNESCO launched the *Language Vitality and Endangerment (LVE)* framework which was the result of the deliberations of a UNESCO-convened group of experts (Brenzinger et al. 2003). The LVE provides an inventory of factors that must be taken into account in order to arrive at an evaluation of the vitality and overall endangerment status of any given language. This framework was endorsed by UNESCO and offered as a state of the art or best practice approach to the evaluation of language endangerment.

The LVE document and the methodology it describes is a rich and theoretically well-founded instrument. It outlines a theory of language endangerment which takes into account many of the factors that we have already mentioned under the rubrics of the number of users and the kinds of uses of a language. In addition, it attempts to evaluate the adequacy of the existing documentary materials for those languages that are seriously endangered. Since it is not directly related to the actual vitality of a language, the adequacy of the linguistic documentation is a factor not included in the GIDS as we've discussed above. However, it has been incorporated in the SUM in the notion of Sustainable History.

The LVE uses the following nine factors to evaluate language vitality:

1. Intergenerational language transmission
2. Absolute number of speakers
3. Proportion of speakers within the total population
4. Loss of existing language domains
5. Response to new domains and media
6. Materials for language education and literacy
7. Governmental and institutional language attitudes and policies
8. Community members' attitudes towards their own language
9. Amount and quality of documentation

When using the instrument to assess a particular language, a score based on a six-level scale is assigned to each of the nine factors. The scores for the factors are then weighted and combined to provide an overall measure of the level of endangerment and a sense of the level of urgency for documentation and revitalization efforts to be undertaken. The six levels of vitality in the LVE scale are listed in table 5.7. The developers of the LVE have emphasized that no single factor should be considered in isolation since a language that seems relatively secure in terms

5.5 Going deeper

of one factor may require "immediate and urgent attention due to other factors" (Brenzinger et al. 2003:10).

Table 5.7 UNESCO's Language Vitality and Endangerment framework

Level	Description
Safe	The language is spoken by all generations; intergenerational transmission is uninterrupted.
Vulnerable	Most children speak the language, but it may be restricted to certain domains (e.g., the home).
Definitely Endangered	Children no longer learn the language as mother tongue in the home.
Severely Endangered	The language is spoken by grandparents and older generations; while the parent generation may understand it, they do not speak it to children or among themselves.
Critically Endangered	The youngest speakers are grandparents and older, and they speak the language partially and infrequently.
Extinct	There are no speakers left.

The LVE, like the EGIDS, accounts for languages that have no remaining speakers (below GIDS 8), but defines the large, unspecified group of languages with strong vitality only as Safe. For many purposes, it is helpful, when assessing a particular language ecology as a whole, to be able to more precisely distinguish the roles and functions of these stronger languages in relationship to other languages in the same context.

The broader theoretical perspective and the combination of the 9 factors measured at six levels results in a fairly complex instrument. That complexity has made its widespread use and implementation somewhat difficult and time consuming. The UNESCO LVE's complexity provides precision but at the cost of feasibility in its implementation. The LVE instrument has been used to provide quite fine-grained and detailed evaluations of relatively few languages. The general category labels of the LVE (*Safe*, *Vulnerable*, etc.), however, have found broad use and acceptance.

Grenoble and Whaley's levels of vitality

Grenoble and Whaley (2006, chapter 2), in a very useful volume on language revitalization, provide an excellent overview of other vitality scales that have been proposed, including one of their own. Their proposal identifies, "as a minimum," six levels of vitality: Safe, At Risk, Disappearing, Moribund, Nearly Extinct, and Extinct (Grenoble and Whaley 2006:18).

Schlie-Landweer Indicators of Ethnolinguistic Vitality

Schlie and Landweer (1991; Landweer 1998) developed the Indicators of Ethnolinguistic Vitality (IEV) especially to address what they considered to be the unique nature of ethnolinguistic vitality in Papua New Guinea. They argued that much of the description of language maintenance and shift had been based on research in other parts of the world and that the context in which they worked had been neglected and omitted from most of the theoretical models.

The eight indicators which make up the IEV are the factors that have been documented in the sociolinguistic literature and found to be particularly applicable in the context of Papua New Guinea. Briefly, the eight indicators consist of the following:

1. Potential for contact
2. Domains of use
3. Frequency and type of code-switching
4. Population and group dynamics
5. Social network strength
6. Social outlook
7. Language prestige
8. Access to a stable and acceptable economic base

These factors are used to infer the probable direction a speech community will go relative to the maintenance of, or shift from, its traditional language. Thus, much like the UNESCO LVE, the instrument explores a broad range of factors in several categories and provides an overall rating on a "continuum of vitality" (Landweer 2012).

6

Sustainable Levels of Language Use

Community-based language development must focus on helping local language communities identify and achieve a sustainable level of language use for their heritage language.

6.1 Introduction

In chapter 5 we described the EGIDS which can be used to evaluate language vitality. We have already noted that the goal of the Sustainable Use Model (SUM) is to assist a local community in achieving a sustainable level of language use and we noted that not all of the levels of vitality identified in the EGIDS can be sustained over a long period of time. There is a strong tendency for language use to decline under the pressures of globalization and increased contact. That process will lead to the eventual loss of the local language all together. It is essential that local language communities identify a sustainable level of language use and engage in language development activities that will help them to achieve it. In this chapter we will examine more closely the sustainable levels of language use.

The increase in global multilingualism, as described earlier, leads us to assert that the most significant issue confronting local language communities in the 21st century is the transmission of life-crucial knowledge. As the primary means of knowledge transmission, the sustained use of the languages most closely associated with specific bodies of knowledge becomes an important area of focus as communities consider their strategies for sustainable knowledge transmission. Therefore, language development interventions must recognize and address the issue of language and identity maintenance or management.

Increased access to larger networks of interaction through electronic and other means tends to add perceived value to the languages that allow the greatest ease of navigation and participation within those networks. The obvious corollary to that statement is that languages that provide only limited participation, and which facilitate only limited navigation of the larger networks are frequently perceived to be less valuable and less desirable. The instrumental values, prevalent in the global economy, place strong pressures on local languages. Unless members of a speech community can see how their local languages provide them with some benefit, they are not likely to retain the language in their repertoire by passing it on to future generations.

The value of a language is not entirely measured in terms of its practical or economic benefits as a means of communication, however. For many local language communities, their heritage identity is precious and highly valued by at least some significant segment of the population. While the globalizing forces around them emphasize the purely utilitarian value of different linguistic varieties (and especially the dominant, more-widely-used global languages) there is an important social and psychological role for local languages in affirming the distinctiveness and diversity that local language communities contribute to the world scene.

6.1.1 Vitality

By identifying levels of language vitality using the EGIDS and asserting that only three of those levels of use are sustainable or stable, we propose that not only can any language be characterized in terms of its vitality status but that a sustainable level of use (which we will describe below) can be identified as a target or goal for language development efforts.

The SUM, using the EGIDS as its measure, provides a way for a speech community to evaluate the current vitality status of each language in its linguistic repertoire. Inevitably, those languages will be at different levels on the scale. Not all of them may be at one of the sustainable levels and it will then fall to the community to decide how they wish to respond. The current vitality status of a language serves as a baseline for making those language development decisions. That status and its distance on the scale from one of the sustainable levels also serves as an indicator of what will be required, either moving up or down the scale, for the community to achieve stable multilingualism.

The prospects for maintenance of a language have largely to do with the notion of sustainable levels of language use. Ideally, it would be comforting to think that a language with very low vitality could, through dint of effort, financial investment, and enthusiastic hard work, be brought back to a higher sustainable level of use. In practice, however, the costs and investment required to bring that about are not insignificant and are sometimes insurmountable. Most local language communities lack the needed resources and expertise, so undertaking a very ambitious language development program may, in the end, be more demoralizing than ameliorative if clear strategies are not in view from the outset.

The notion of vitality which underlies the SUM is one which stresses that vitality can be re-established most effectively in an incremental fashion by moving languages up (or sometimes down) the vitality scale to a level of use that is sustainable. While longer range desired outcomes may nurture the hope of a full, strongly vital level of language use, in the most dire cases where a language is on the brink of extinction, a community may do well to consider how to re-establish a sustainable configuration of language use that is far less grandiose in its scope, at least as a first step. The practical implications of this idea will be explored further in chapter 9.

6.1 Introduction

6.1.2 Sustainability

Since Sustainability is a key concept in the SUM, we should define the concept a bit more clearly. We understand sustainable language use in terms of three important characteristics: persistence, prevalence, and predictability.

Persistence

A sustainable level of language vitality is one that persists or is likely to persist over a relatively long period of time. All things being equal, if a language is being used sustainably, the current configuration of language use is unlikely to change. Where sustainability is present, the patterns of language use are not succumbing to the external or internal societal pressures to decline. In many cases, this configuration of language use has been in place for generations.

In general, persistence is achieved or can be observed when there are no clearly identifiable forces or trends within a community that are reconfiguring the hierarchy of perceived benefits relative to each language currently in place in the community's linguistic ecology.

> **Swiss—German an example of persistence**
>
> The continued use of Swiss German in Switzerland is a commonly cited example of persistence. The Swiss German varieties, which have no widely accepted standardized written form, have been used for face-to-face communication in the valleys and villages of Switzerland without interruption for generations. Though Standard German is learned by all in schools and is used for public, formal, and nearly all written functions, Swiss German continues as the language of day-to-day interchange in the home and community.

Prevalence

In addition to the temporal dimension, sustainability has to do with the prevalence and distribution of language-use norms within the community. While few communities are entirely homogeneous, the essence of the SUM's approach to community-based language development is the idea that higher levels of interaction within an identifiable social network lead to widespread adoption and conformity to accepted patterns of language use. The community social network serves both as the locus of shared behaviors, as the means of distribution or spread of shared behaviors, and as the re-enforcer of those behaviors. Failure to conform to the norms has a social cost, that is, it relegates one to the fringes of the network. Conformity provides social rewards and benefits, that is, it draws one into more and more close-knit relationships. As a result, the norms of use spread via person-to-person interaction and are widely evident within the community.

A sustainable level of language use is one in which the behaviors associated with that level of use are widespread within the community, broadly accepted, and consensually enforced. Moreover, the majority of the members of the community share the values assigned to those linguistic behaviors and so perceive the benefits and rewards that accrue from conformity. While there will always be some variation within any given population, such variations are marked behaviors and recognized by the community as such. Where a community is losing its attachment to a coherent identity (and the rewards and benefits associated with that identity) or where identity attachments are diffusing and hybridizing, the forces that re-enforce conformity will be weakened. To the degree that a norm of language use permeates the network, greater sustainability is achieved. Linguistic behaviors and patterns of use which are sporadic or randomly distributed in the network, are likely to be passing and transitory.

Guaraní—An example of prevalence

Guaraní [grn] in Paraguay is an example of the prevalence of a sustainable language. Though the majority of the citizens of Paraguay would consider themselves to be first-language speakers of Spanish, and standard Spanish is used not only in the home but taught in the schools, a great many Paraguayans also learn and speak Guaraní in the home, community, and in school. Guaraní use and proficiency is so widespread in Paraguayan society that the language is considered a marker of national identity.

Predictability

Closely associated with both of the previous aspects of sustainability is the idea that where a sustainable configuration of language vitality exists, language use is relatively predictable. Because certain norms of language use are widely prevalent in a speech community, they will tend to be more-or-less self-re-enforcing. Aberrations from the prevalent patterns of use will be noted, remarked on, censured (by some) or emulated (by others). In general, the tendency is for the status quo to prevail. That is, where there is sustainable use, the established norms are likely to persist over time.

In addition to persistence, however, an important feature of sustainability is that individuals in a speech community know what to expect and what is expected of them. There is little sociolinguistic insecurity in such situations. Speakers know which language (or variety of a language) to speak to whom in what contexts. We have referred to this state of affairs as "stable multilingualism." The predictability of the functional association of a language with a specific body of knowledge contributes to sustainability. This is a situation where a community may have multiple languages in their repertoire but individuals know which of those languages to use when, where, and with whom.

Language development interventions should be understood to include all efforts aimed at assisting a local speech community to (re-)establish persistent, prevalent, and predictable patterns of language use as a means of securing the ongoing transmission of life-crucial knowledge. This may not always mean an increase in the number of functions for which a particular language is used. In some cases, it may mean assisting a community to move to a lower, but more sustainable, level of language use (i.e., a level with fewer, but persistent, pervasive, and predictable functions for the language).

6.2 Sustainable levels of language use

The SUM has been developed around the notion that there are sustainable (persistent, prevalent, and predictable) configurations of language use. That is, there are only three configurations where functions are clearly defined and compartmentalized and where intergenerational transmission is intact. In addition, we wish to recognize within the SUM that even when intergenerational transmission has been completely disrupted and there are no longer any speakers, the memory of a language and its features can be sustained through adequate documentation. Thus, in addition to three levels of sustainable use there is also a level of Sustainable History. We refer to these configurations as levels because they correspond to levels on the EGIDS and because they build upon each other in an ascending hierarchy starting with no ongoing use at all to the highest level of full face-to-face and literary use of the language.

The following sections describe the four levels in more detail. Figure 6.1 illustrates the sustainable levels of use in terms of the metaphor of plateaus on a mountainside. During the language development journey up the EGIDS scale, the levels of sustainable use are like plateaus where one's position may be sustained without expending great effort. However, when moving between the plateaus, significant exertion is needed to climb to the next level and, in the absence of such effort, the natural forces of gravity pull one back down. We begin our description of the sustainable levels at the foot of the mountain and work our way upwards.

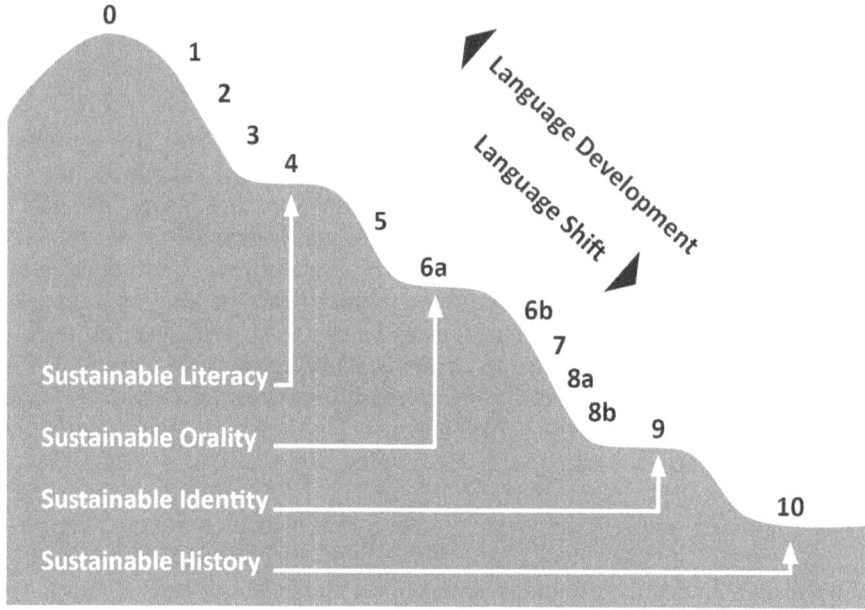

Figure 6.1 Levels of sustainable use: The mountain metaphor

6.2.1 Sustainable History

At the level of Sustainable History, the language is no longer spoken and has no functional use for anyone (except perhaps scholars) in day-to-day life. The key to sustainability at this level is that the language has been documented adequately and that the documentary materials are safely and reliably archived for future access. The most relevant characteristic of sustainability is the persistence of that documentation, though there are certain aspects of prevalence and predictability that apply as well. This level corresponds to EGIDS 10 (Extinct) though not all extinct languages necessarily meet the conditions to be categorized as having achieved Sustainable History. The criterion for achieving Sustainable History is that there be adequate documentation of an EGIDS 10 language.

This configuration is persistent in that the documentary evidence exists in a secure location and is retrievable for use by future users for generations to come. It is prevalent in that there is sufficient documentation both in quantity and in coverage of the language features to provide a basis for ongoing analysis and for potential revitalization efforts. It is predictable in that the documentary materials are organized and structured so as to be adequate for the various uses to which they might be put (analysis, pedagogy, language re-acquisition, cultural revitalization, etc.).

This level of use implies that EGIDS level 10 (Extinct) could be further split into EGIDS 10a representing the well-documented languages that have a sustainable history and EGIDS 10b representing those languages which might be called "Forgotten." Forgotten languages are those which at one time were spoken but

6.2 Sustainable levels of language use

which were never adequately documented before they went out of use or where any existing documentation was lost or destroyed. As a result, the language is irrecoverably lost for all future generations. We cannot know how many languages have gone out of use unremarked by history. There are some tenuous clues of some of these where there are written fragments which remain undecipherable because the language they represent cannot be determined and was never documented. Undocumented extinct languages are lost forever and will eventually be forgotten completely.

We identify Sustainable History as a significant category in the SUM because it is important for communities and linguists to document languages not only for scholarly purposes but also as insurance against the day when some future generation might wish to reconnect with their heritage identity and re-establish that identity using the archived language materials. While such efforts to revitalize a no-longer-spoken language require large investments of will and activity, there are an increasing number of communities worldwide who are engaging in just such activities using whatever resources they can muster. To the extent that adequate documentation is available and accessible the task of revitalization is facilitated.

Language documentation and the archiving of language documentation and linguistic descriptions are extensive (and developing) fields in their own right. We make no attempt to cover them in this volume. However, in the Appendix we discuss some activities that language development workers can engage in if achieving Sustainable History is their goal.

6.2.2 Sustainable Identity

At the level of Sustainable Identity there are no proficient speakers of the language. Some individuals may be considered semi-speakers in that they know some phrases, such as greetings, which they use on occasion. More frequently, most people in the community remember but do not speak the language, identifying it as the language of previous generations. The salient feature of this level is the association of their ethnic or personal identity with the heritage language and related cultural features. Sustainable Identity corresponds to EGIDS 9.

Language is used at this level primarily as a marker of a heritage identity. Another language has taken on the functions of day-to-day communication of life-crucial knowledge and the heritage language is not being learned by anyone as their first language. Only remnants of the language are in use. Children may be taught songs or poems. Adults may remember stories. Other cultural markers of identity are called upon (clothing, food, dance, drama, other performing arts) to re-enforce and pass on the sense of connectedness to the heritage identity. Members of such a community may also use a non-standard form of the dominant language which shows the influence of their heritage language and which may have come to replace the heritage language as their primary language of identity.

While this level represents a kind of stable multilingualism, the heritage language in this case has so few functions and the speakers such low levels of proficiency that the language cannot be sustainably used by anyone for day-to-day communication. Languages that are losing speakers and functions often reach this level but then fall below it to full extinction as speakers abandon their identity and the association of that identity with the language. In some cases, languages reach this level and then undergo a revival as the re-enforcement of identity leads community members to work to at least remain at the level of symbolic use of the language as a marker of that identity. Others may strive to move back to the re-establishment of the language as a means of day-to-day face-to-face communication.

This level is sustainable because the elements of heritage identity that a community deems to be important (life-crucial bodies of knowledge about their heritage) are persistent (transmitted from one generation to the next), prevalent (widely shared by the community) and predictable (clearly identifiable and relatively unchanging).

The EGIDS identifies languages at this level not as extinct but as dormant—sleeping languages that can, with effort, be reawakened and brought back to fuller use. Many languages that are at the level of Sustainable Identity may not be thoroughly documented. Frequently only enough documentation exists so that the language can be used for the symbolic and ceremonial purposes necessary to re-enforce the heritage identity. That documentation needs, at the very least, to be preserved so as to achieve Sustainable History if the downward trajectory continues. More optimistically, knowledge of the language needs to be expanded and made available as a resource for language revitalization. This happens as additional functions come to be associated with the language.

6.2.3 Sustainable Orality

At the level of Sustainable Orality large numbers of people in a community, in fact the vast majority, are highly proficient in the language, having learned it as their first language. They are actively, and usually without conscious thought, passing the language on to their children. Though we use the term orality to describe this level, we explicitly include signed languages which are used for face-to-face interaction. Recall that the levels of sustainable use are hierarchical and build one upon the other, so a language that is at the level of Sustainable Orality is also already at the level of Sustainable Identity. Sustainable Orality corresponds to EGIDS 6a.

The most salient component of Sustainable Orality is the ongoing transmission of the language from one generation to the next by some well-established, and generally (but not always) unconscious, means. Most often this transmission occurs in the home as parents and family members expose a child to the language and the child learns the language naturally as part of her own cognitive development. The means of transmission of signed languages also differ in significant ways from the ways in which oral languages are passed from one generation to the next, but our intention here is to identify this level of sustainable use with the normal means of language transmission, whether in home, community, or school. Sign Language proficiency may be gained from a community of users that is either larger than the family or entirely separate from the home and neighborhood, such as deaf schools or clubs. In highly multilingual communities, a child may be simultaneously acquiring multiple languages, and may achieve, on a personal level, Sustainable Orality in more than one language. As a result, an entire community may have multiple languages within its particular language ecology which could be characterized as being used at this level. The persistence of language use is achieved through this unbroken chain of intergenerational transmission.

A second salient component of Sustainable Orality is the widespread use of the language for most aspects of day-to-day life, particularly in those domains of use which are closely associated with the heritage identity. Because of this strong linkage to identity, a language that is at the level of Sustainable Orality frequently is the unmarked or default language in a community and may well be taken for granted. The prevalence of the language leads many speakers to live their lives assuming that "our language will always be with us" and have no sense of its being threatened or pressured.

This description of Sustainable Orality describes the optimal case. Sustainable Orality does not necessarily mean that the language is the only language used nor that the language is used in all settings and to discuss all topics. In highly multilingual communities not everyone will necessarily have high levels of proficiency in all domains of use in all of the languages in the community's repertoire. Some topics and bodies of knowledge may be dealt with more easily and more frequently in a different language. Frequently these areas may be new domains of use dealing with technologies or sets of concepts brought in from the outside or from contact with the globalizing world. However, in order for a language to have achieved the level of Sustainable Orality, it must be the primary spoken language predictably associated with the transmission of at least some bodies of life-crucial inside knowledge.

6.2.4 Sustainable Literacy

At the level of Sustainable Literacy, not only is the language built upon a strong linkage with a heritage identity and used by every generation as the primary means of face-to-face transmission of life-crucial knowledge, but it is also widely used for reading and writing. Moreover, the literary use of the language is well-established as a norm of language use and there are sustainable institutions within the society (either formally or informally constituted) that engage in the ongoing transmission of literacy skills and the production of pedagogical materials.

In these communities, literacy in the local language is more than a novelty and has passed from being a cultural and technological innovation adopted by a few or sporadically promoted, to being a commonly accepted tool that is considered the norm for most individuals. Parents value literacy enough to see that their children are taught to read and write. There may also be a developing set of functionally defined styles or registers of language that are associated closely with writing. And there is a growing body of such literature being produced by those who are acquiring and using their writing skills for the production of literature in the language. These literary styles and products are taking (or have taken) their place in the linguistic repertoire of the community alongside the oral genres that are already in use.

The transmission of literacy from one generation to the next generally does not occur in the home as is most frequently the case with oral language. Rather, the community may have developed social institutions outside of the home for literacy transmission. These may be formally constituted in the form of schools or classes. These formal institutions may be either publicly or privately funded and resourced, or both. Alternatively, there may be more informal institutions or the by-products of other social institutions (clans, intergenerational initiation rites, etc.) which serve the function of making each new generation literate. As with the other sustainable levels, literate use of the local language is persistently being transmitted intergenerationally, the use of literary materials and literacy skills is prevalent, finding wide use in the community, and that use is predictable with a clearly defined set of norms for written language use in place and widely accepted.

As with oral language use, it is not a prerequisite of Sustainable Literacy that reading and writing occur exclusively in the heritage language. There may be certain bodies of knowledge which are written and read about in a different language. Some bodies of knowledge may be written about in multiple languages that are within the repertoire of the community. The salient feature of Sustainable Literacy, however, is that there are identifiable bodies of knowledge which are considered to be most appropriately and authentically written about in the heritage language.

6.3 Going deeper

Fishman (1991) describes language as being both indexical (i.e., it provides a catalog of the important concepts shared by a community) and symbolic (i.e., it represents and expresses the identity of the community). It is this dual functionality of language that underlies the important distinctions made in this chapter between the levels of sustainable use. Sustainable Identity is more closely related to the symbolic function of language, while Sustainable Literacy is often (but not exclusively) more aligned with the more utilitarian indexical function of language.

6.3.1 Vitality and Sustainability

The primary theoretical construct that underlies the concept of sustainable language use is diglossia which we considered in some detail in chapter 4. The notion that stable functional distribution of the languages in any given ecology is characterized by widespread (prevalent) language use patterns that are persistent and thus predictable, lies at the core of our notion of sustainability.

6.3.2 Sustainable History

The increased awareness of language endangerment among linguists late in the last century and of the possibility that thousands of local languages might be lost by the end of this century has spawned a call to action within the linguistics community. Many linguists have recognized that the urgency of the situation calls for a new strategy of documenting languages before attempting to fully describe them. Documentary linguistics, as distinct from descriptive linguistics, has emerged as a subfield of linguistics largely due to the seminal work of Himmelmann (1998). He draws a contrast between documenting the actual linguistic behavior of a speech community (by compiling, commenting on, and archiving recordings of a representative sample of their language in use) versus describing the language as

6.3 Going deeper

a system of signs (by producing a phonology, grammar, and lexicon). Woodbury 2003 is another influential work on defining documentary linguistics. The leading textbook on the subject has been Gippert, Himmelmann, and Mosel 2006.

Archived language documentation can be drawn upon for later analysis and description, even after a language has fallen silent. More significant for the topic of sustaining language use is that it can provide the foundation for future revitalization efforts (Grenoble and Whaley 2006). Amery (2009) points out the shortcomings of traditional language description as the basis for revitalization and highlights the importance of documenting the full range of speech behaviors.

Along with methodologies for compiling and commenting on language recordings, documentary linguists are also concerned with archiving. Given the relentless degradation of field recordings and the march of innovation that inevitably brings obsolescence to the devices used for storing those recordings, it is imperative that linguists give attention to the issues of archiving lest their field recordings become just as endangered as the languages they document. Bird and Simons (2003) and Simons (2006) identify best practices for long-term usability of digital language documentation. Chang (2010) provides a checklist that linguists can use to evaluate whether an archive is following best practices that would guarantee the long-term preservation of their digital materials.

6.3.3 Sustainable Identity, Orality, and Literacy

The three sustainable levels of language use that we identify draw on a large body of research dealing with the nature and role of identity, special features of face-to-face language use—in particular oral knowledge transmission—the nature of literacy and its effects on societies, and the transmission of knowledge through written and, increasingly, digital technologies. The respective literatures for each of these areas of study are far too large for an adequate overview here. Nevertheless, we suggest a few starting points for further study.

Sustainable Identity

In addition to the literature on Ethnolinguistic Identity Theory mentioned previously, multiple works by Edwards (1977, 1985, 1988) and Edwards and Chisholm (1987) provide an entrance into the discussion of identity. More recently, Joseph 2004 provides an extensive historical and theoretical overview of identity, the complexities of defining the concept (and its various shapes and sizes) as well as the relationship of language to the construction of both individual and group identities.

Sustainable Orality

The oral or face-to-face use of language may seem obvious or as a given, but early investigations into language were primarily focused on the written use of language. Philology used written materials as the basis for its investigations and the earliest grammars developed by linguists were designed to foster a standardized way of producing written language. Some of this historical perspective is discussed in Joseph 2004. An important early investigator of the nature of oral language use is Goody (1968, 1982), who examined the differences in cognitive processes between oral societies and those in which the literary use of language had taken root. The work of the Jesuit scholar Walter Ong (2002) is also foundational in both proposing and examining the distinctions between oral and written language use and knowledge transmission. Numerous other sources examine specific cases of oral language use, the oral transmission of knowledge, and the nature of oral literature (sometimes referred to as *oracy* or *orature*).

Sustainable Literacy

There is a vast literature examining all aspects of the introduction and acquisition of literacy. The literature examines both the pedagogical aspects of literacy acquisition and the sociological and psycho-sociological aspects of the development of literate societies with the accompanying changes in cognitive processes. For the latter, the work of Goody (1968, 1982) is a good starting point though much has been done more recently, particularly in reference to the sociolinguistic issues of the role of written language in multilingual and multi-identitied communities. Hornberger's (2002, 2003) development of the concept of continua of biliteracy addresses the sociological, educational, and policy dimensions of literature-in-use in previously oral but multilingual communities. Her work is of particular interest because it also takes an ecological perspective. Beyond these few hints as to where to start, we dare not wade much deeper into these waters which are vast and deep.

7

Conditions of Sustainable Use

Sustainable language use can only be achieved when certain conditions are met. The labels we use for these conditions spell out the acronym FAMED: Functions, Acquisition, Motivation, Environment, Differentiation.

7.1 Introduction

In chapter 5 we described the EGIDS, which constitutes a major descriptive tool in the Sustainable Use Model (SUM). The EGIDS enables a community to evaluate its current level of language use and the vitality of the language, assigning it to a specific level on the scale. In chapter 6 we described the sustainable levels of language use. The sustainable levels constitute possible goals for language development efforts undertaken by local language communities. In this chapter we turn to the question of how to address the sociolinguistic, sociopolitical, and socioeconomic conditions which affect the EGIDS status of a language. The EGIDS level provides a useful shorthand description of the status of a language. That status, however, encompasses a complex set of factors and conditions that are interrelated. If a community wishes to engage in language development activities that will move it to one of the sustainable levels of use, it must answer the question what conditions need to be in place in order to achieve the desired sustainable level of use? This requires a more detailed analysis of the situation than the EGIDS provides. Though the factors contributing to a language's status are many and are complex, they can be understood in terms of five general conditions, each of which addresses an important component in determining the vitality of a language within a given speech community.

7.1.1 The need for a general set of conditions

The complex set of social variables that are represented by the numbered levels of the EGIDS are too overwhelming for most communities to think about and develop adequate language development responses for. Digging into the details is daunting and may be discouraging. That complexity can be more usefully described within the schema of a set of conditions that are more detailed than the EGIDS but not as academically rigorous and technically oriented as a sociolinguist or linguistic anthropologist might wish to see. (Other attempts at this are described in the Going Deeper section.) That is not to say that rigorous additional research might not be called for in the future, but at the stage of designing a language development agenda, an exhaustive, in-depth analysis may not be what is immediately needed.

In any speech community the complex interactions of the sociolinguistic variables affect attitudes towards the languages in the linguistic repertoire. They create or deny opportunities for use of those languages. They can promote or impede the acquisition of language proficiency. And, more generally, they establish how the languages themselves are perceived as useful or not-so-useful tools of communication and markers of identity. The interaction and interplay among all of the different conditions creates an exceedingly complex system that requires a considerable investment of time and knowledge to analyze and describe fully. What's more, once analyzed, it isn't always clear how to address the different variables in a way that will effectively achieve the language (and other) development goals of a particular community. Because the variables describe the social fabric of the speech community, they are often neither easy to perceive nor readily changed.

For many working in language development, their attempts to reverse language shift or to promote the use of a local language can be aptly characterized as "swimming upstream." As mentioned in chapter 1, in the worst cases, attempts to change language behavior are imposed from the outside and are examples of the imposition of power to engage in social engineering. In other cases, such efforts might be described as "voices crying in the wilderness," tiny flames of community interest that are being fanned in an effort to develop a language rescue or revitalization movement. The complexity of the social, economic, political, and ideological context makes these efforts all the more difficult and frustrating. Often, language development efforts attempt to address all possible causes of loss of vitality and so sometimes misdirect resources towards factors that do not need to be addressed or overlook factors that should be addressed. What is needed is a way to categorize the multiple factors so that resources can be more adequately and efficiently allocated.

7.1.2 Five general conditions

This complexity can be somewhat simplified and generalized into a set of five conditions using the acronym FAMED. In addition, the status of each condition can be described on its own scale which provides a way to describe various combinations of the variables in terms of a profile. Much like how a physician looks at various vital signs such as pulse, respiration, temperature, blood pressure, pallor, and so on to diagnose a patient's condition, the five FAMED conditions can provide a more detailed diagnostic evaluation of each language's vitality status. Where the EGIDS provides us with a descriptive evaluation, telling us in general terms where "the patient" is overall (good condition, fair condition, stable condition, guarded, seriously ill, critically ill), the FAMED conditions provide a more detailed diagnosis of what is contributing to the current status and thus provide helpful guidance as to what needs to be addressed to bring about a change.

Sustainable language use, at any level, can only be achieved if each of the five conditions is at a level which supports it. The FAMED conditions are the following:

- Functions—Functions (uses, bodies of knowledge) associated with the language must exist and be recognized by the community.

- Acquisition—A means of acquiring the needed proficiency to use the language for those functions must be in place and accessible to community members.

- Motivation—Community members must be motivated to use the language for those functions. They must perceive that the use of the language for those functions is beneficial in some way.

- Environment—The policy environment (including at national, regional, and local levels) must not be hostile to the use of the language for those functions.

- Differentiation—Societal norms must clearly delineate the functions assigned to the local language marking them as distinct from the functions for other languages in the speech community's repertoire.

7.2 The FAMED conditions

7.2.1 Functions

Languages are like clothing. People dress appropriately for the place, the event, or the activity that they are engaging in. Work clothes aren't worn for formal ceremonial events. Wedding dresses aren't worn to market. One's "Sunday best" isn't put on for a day of work in the fields. In the same way, languages come to be associated with particular kinds of activities or topics or with particular groups of people or audiences. A language must be seen as being appropriate for a particular setting or for a particular topic or for use with a particular group of people if its use is to be sustained. As we described in chapter 3, for most community members, it will be somewhat easier to identify a body of knowledge and relate that to the choice of language, the participants, and the locations in which that body of knowledge is discussed. The existence of functions associated most closely with a particular language is the evidence of that language's usefulness and value as a communicative tool and as a marker of identity. A language which has no uses is a language which will have no users.

The existence of functions with which a language is closely associated is the primary condition for sustainable use around which the other FAMED conditions form a constellation. In chapter 4 we proposed that a good starting point for community-based language development is the identification of the life-crucial bodies of knowledge that the community wishes to preserve or acquire and pass on to future generations. Those choices, along with the decision regarding a desired level of sustainable use for the local language(s) (described in chapter 6) serve as the overall focus of targeted language development efforts. The process of identifying functions for a language carves out a sociolinguistic space, a niche, within the life of the community where the language is perceived to be useful and can, in fact, be used. As the community makes these choices regarding functions, additional, more detailed, and practical decisions can then be made regarding how to implement those choices.

7.2.2 Acquisition

Whatever the functions are that a language is associated with, at whatever level of sustainable use, a second condition for sustaining that level of use is that there must be a means by which community members can acquire the proficiency they need in order to be able to use the language for the identified functions. Where the means of acquisition do not exist, are not accessible to enough people, or are not adequate, sustainable use will not be achievable.

At the different levels of sustainable use, Acquisition will take quite different forms. At the lowest level, Sustainable History (EGIDS 10), Acquisition refers primarily to the accessibility and usability of archival materials. The documentation of the language must not only be sufficient in terms of quantity of materials, but it must also be adequate in terms of its usability. Will the existing archived materials provide the right kind of data for the purposes of reintroducing and regaining use of the language for the desired functions?

If Sustainable Identity (EGIDS 9) is the goal, there must be acquisition mechanisms that will make it possible for community members to learn the heritage songs, stories, and other identity-related language competencies needed for identity maintenance and re-enforcement. Sometimes this takes the form of formal community-based heritage schools or classes. In other cases, the knowledge and skills may be passed on in the home and family setting.

If Sustainable Orality (EGIDS 6a) is the goal, the primary means of acquisition will very likely be through oral transmission in the home and the community. These may be supplemented by formal education, especially where there is a standardized form of the language or particular registers or oral genres that must be learned.

Where Sustainable Literacy (EGIDS 4) is the goal, formal and informal educational institutions are likely going to be the primary means of acquisition of the technologies of literacy (including digital literacy) and the evaluation of their accessibility and effectiveness comes to the fore.

7.2.3 Motivation

The Motivation condition deals with the perceived benefit that is derived from the use of a language for its associated functions. Community members must perceive that there are benefits that accrue when one speaks the language in the appropriate places to talk about the appropriate topics with the appropriate people. Occasionally, there may also exist costs or penalties that arise if the language is used inappropriately.

These benefits (and penalties) are frequently, but not exclusively, economic. For most local communities the benefits that accrue from using the dominant language are almost always understood in economic or political terms. Probably the most frequent explanation given by parents for their decision to interrupt the intergenerational transmission of the heritage language is their desire to see their children gain access to better education and ultimately economically more rewarding employment. These economic benefits almost always are linked to higher prestige and that can also be a very strong motivator. Sometimes the motivation behind language shift is the desire of a community to be better able to participate in the political system and thus have a greater level of self-determination and self-governance.

Social prestige, economic benefits, and political power are not the only strong motivators. The rather obvious, but sometimes overlooked, need to communicate with those one has frequent contact with can in itself be a motivator that works either for or against heritage language maintenance. Frequently, the preservation of a valued heritage identity can provide motivation for language maintenance and revitalization. The use of a language for identity construction provides rewards in terms of group solidarity (a sense of belonging and of in-group connection). Notable examples of language maintenance which produce sustainable ongoing language use against seemingly overwhelming odds based on the motivating force of solidarity include conservative societies such as the Amish or Hasidic Jews. Both of those examples of identity maintenance are also closely linked to the religion of the communities and that can also serve as a source of motivation to maintain or acquire a language. In spite of often-justifiable criticisms of missionaries who imposed draconian language policies in the past, it is often the case that contemporary heritage language maintenance is strongest in churches where the language most closely associated with religious practice is the local language.

Ultimately, the motivation to maintain a language is economic, though perhaps it is not monetary. Communities will guard and treasure what they value and what is useful to them. If a language is associated with highly-valued functions its use will be sustainable. It may well be the case that language shift is precipitated by an ideological change, a value shift, where a heritage identity or heritage bodies of knowledge (i.e., heritage functions) are no longer perceived as providing enough benefit to make them worth maintaining.

7.2.4 Environment

The fourth condition for sustainable use is that the environment must be adequate to allow for the use of the language for its associated functions at the desired level of sustainable use. This condition focuses primarily on the language policy environment but the policies in view need not necessarily be those of a government. Organizations and institutions often have their own language policies. The influence of those policies can be felt well beyond the boundaries of the organization itself. There are many situations where policies are not codified in law or regulations but are still clearly enforced in practice and behavior.

A hostile environment such as the explicit prohibition of the use of a language obviously works against sustainable use. A more favorable or neutral environment may provide the political and legal space for a language to be maintained or even developed to higher levels of use in a wider range of functions.

Any discussion of policy inevitably requires the distinction between *de facto* policy (embodied in actual practice) and *de jure* policy (defined by law) which may or may not align with actual practice. Governments frequently establish language policies which are either not enforced (or are unenforceable) or are not effectively implemented. For the purposes of assessment of the status of a language, it is the de facto policy environment that matters most. No matter how positive de jure policy may appear to be, if it is not enforced or is inadequately implemented, the actual environment for language development may be much more hostile. As in any political process, the tendency of policy making bodies will be to conform to the pressures placed upon them in their current political context. Policy statements are often framed in terms that will "get votes," satisfy external pressure groups, or be most palatable to political forces in different ideological camps. This process of negotiation and compromise often leads to situations where the legal documents say what the policy makers need to say but none of the parties involved in that compromise strongly embrace the result. With no one championing the policy, implementation may be inadequate.

Cataloging and categorizing legal documents is certainly a very useful part of the analysis of the Environment condition, but a description of the actual practice and implementation of policy is a much more significant indicator of the state of the environment. An obvious observation is that in general, negative or hostile policies are more likely to hamper sustainable language use, while positive, but poorly implemented, policies may not do much to promote it. Frequently, a fully implemented neutral policy may provide more leeway for sustainable language use than a poorly implemented positive policy. For all of these reasons it is important for language development planners to carefully assess the actual state of the environment and not rely solely on a legislative review.

Policy micro-environments

The environment can be evaluated at various sociopolitical levels. Generally, national-level language policy is applied and practiced relatively uniformly throughout a nation-state or in a region within a nation-state. However, the existence of distinct micro-environments within any polity is always a definite possibility. Communities engaged in language development can benefit greatly from a careful consideration of these more local environment conditions.

Micro-environments might be created by social network associations that overlap with the speech community network. For example, a religious organization might span multiple speech communities and have its own policies (whether de facto or de jure) regarding language use in its activities. This network (with its language use policies) forms a micro-environment that is relevant for the local speech community. It may be impossible to introduce new functions for the local language in the activities of that organization if its policies and practices are hostile to local language use.

7.2.5 Differentiation

The final condition of sustainable language use is that the norms of language use that differentiate the separate functions for the local language and more dominant languages be widely shared within the community. Even when the preceding four conditions are adequate, without differentiation of the functions, sustainability is not assured since other languages are always present in the situation and are always competing for the "sociolinguistic space." If the local language and the dominant language are competing head-to-head in a given set of functions, without any concerted intervention, the more powerful and prestigious language will inevitably gain ground since it is generally perceived to provide more rewards and benefits.

The uphill battle for endangered languages is not only that they must develop and define their own legitimate domains of use (functions), but that they must also work to keep the dominant language from invading those spaces. A state of stable multilingualism can be established only by carving out (by assigning functions) and maintaining (through differentiation) a separate space for the local language.

In the case of local languages, this differentiation process requires not only the will and desire of the local community but also is aided, to a certain degree, by the assent and cooperation of the dominant language community through de jure language policy and, more importantly, through de facto acceptance and fostering of diversity within society. The Differentiation condition addresses the entire language ecology of the speech community. The focus of this condition is not so much on the fact that the local language has functions, but rather that the *norms* of use of the languages in the language ecology of the speech community are well-established and accepted in the speech community at large. The clear differentiation of language distribution (a complementary distribution of language use) renders the functional assignment of the local language considerably less vulnerable to the pressures of an encroaching dominant language.

The decision to assign particular functions to a language and the establishment of those functions as clearly defined and "watertight" compartments is what language planners have traditionally called status planning. Status planning has often been carried out from outside the language community with outsiders making decisions about what use will be given to a local language. Sustainable outcomes depend heavily on the primary agency of the local community itself in that status planning. Without that agency, the safety of the assigned functions will inevitably be in doubt. With that agency, there is a much better chance that status decisions will be implemented and sustained.

7.3 Some general observations

As mentioned at the beginning of this chapter, the EGIDS itself is a kind of shorthand categorization of a complex set of variables. Similarly, the FAMED conditions provide a way to summarize the complexities of the socioeconomic, sociopolitical, and sociolinguistic variables into a set of somewhat more manageable categories. Because situations are complex, we must continuously remind ourselves that the FAMED conditions are not completely separate from each other. They interact with each other. The choice of functions determines the nature and levels of strength of the other conditions. At the same time, however, the other conditions also influence the choice of functions. This interaction and interplay is what causes each language development context to be unique and to require a unique set of maintenance or development responses. The SUM as a whole, and the EGIDS and FAMED conditions in particular, provide us with a more widely applicable, principled framework for describing the complexity and diversity of such situations.

The advantage that comes from using the FAMED conditions as a framework for profiling the relative vitality of a language in a community is the diagnostic nature of the categorizations and the value of that kind of profile in identifying strategies and sets of activities which might address a particularly weak condition.

In addition, readers with sociolinguistic training will recognize that the FAMED conditions, in large measure, represent an alternative approach to describing the interrelated set of notions that revolve around the concepts of diglossia and domains of use. While we in no way wish to diminish the value of those concepts, the range of definitions that have been given to them (in particular, to the concept of diglossia) motivates us to find another way to talk about the dynamics of stable societal multilingualism. This was discussed at length in the Going Deeper section of chapter 4 and will be further dealt with in the Going Deeper section at the end of this chapter.

7.4 Assessing the FAMED conditions

Just as the EGIDS levels correlate with the sustainable levels of language use, so different states or levels of strength of each of the FAMED conditions correlate with particular EGIDS levels. As described above, the FAMED conditions constitute the components of sustainable vitality (as measured by the EGIDS). Thus, each of the five conditions in the FAMED acronym can be measured on its own scale. As the level of each condition rises on its associated scale, so also does its contribution to a higher level of sustainable use.

In the assessment scales that follow, each scale level is related to one or more corresponding EGIDS levels. This means that the situation described for the given level of the individual factor is typical for the indicated EGIDS levels. In using these scales to assess an actual situation, different factors may correlate with different EGIDS levels. This is to be expected. The final assessment must take all of the factors into consideration as is described following the description of the individual assessment scales.

The discussion which follows does not include correlations between FAMED conditions and EGIDS levels that are higher than EGIDS 4. Much of what needs to happen in order for a language to rise above EGIDS 4 is a political process at the national and even the international level that far exceeds the focus of this volume. Since we are focused on community-based language development, we have confined our analysis to the EGIDS levels that a local speech community is likely to be able to influence most directly. In the following subsections we describe

7.4 Assessing the FAMED conditions

briefly the different levels on the assessment scales for each of the five FAMED conditions.

7.4.1 Functions scale

The Functions scale is used to assess the degree to which the desired uses for the local language are available. It is summarized in table 7.1.

Table 7.1 Functions scale

Level	Description	Corresponding EGIDS Levels
F1	Adequate literature exists in this language for every function for which writing in this language is desired.	4 (Educational)
F2	Enough literature exists in this language for some functions to exemplify the value of literacy in this language.	5 (Developing)
F3	The language is being used face-to-face for the functions of day-to-day life, but there is no written use of the language.	6a (Vigorous)
F4	Some members of the community use the language face-to-face for the functions of day-to-day life, but an increasing number no longer do.	6b (Threatened) to 8a (Moribund)
F5	There is enough face-to-face use of this language to represent the identity of the group, but not enough for full communication.	8b (Nearly Extinct) and 9 (Dormant)
F6	The language is no longer used but there are enough archival materials that some functions could be restored in the future.	10 (Extinct)
F7	The language is no longer used and there is little or no documentation.	10 (Extinct)

Level F1: Adequate literature exists in this language for every function for which writing in this language is desired.

This level is the highest, strongest level of the Functions condition. If the Functions condition is at Level F1, there is written literature in existence for every body of knowledge for which the language is deemed to be appropriate and for which written materials might be needed. At this level, there is sufficient literature in existence for all of the life-crucial bodies of knowledge that the community wishes to transmit in written form from one generation to the next, or across the existing generations of language users. Level F1 corresponds to EGIDS 4 (Educational), the level of Sustainable Literacy.

Level F2: Enough literature exists in this language for some functions to exemplify the value of literacy in this language.

At this level, the existence of literature for the functions assigned to the language is only partial. This could mean that for every body of knowledge there is some exemplary literature being developed or it could mean that only some bodies of knowledge have adequate literature while others have none or only a few examples.

This level of the Functions condition occurs when literacy is being introduced and developed in a community. Only a few people may have sufficient proficiency in writing to be able to produce literature on their own and much of the existing literature may be translated works or products developed for a few specific bodies of knowledge (e.g., health information, agricultural development, etc.).

This level of the Functions condition could also apply when previously highly developed literacy in the language is in decline or being abandoned in favor of literacy in another language. As literary domains decrease, the extant literature will become sparser and less diverse in its content and coverage.

Level F2 corresponds to EGIDS 5 (Developing). It is important to note that EGIDS 5 is not a sustainable level of use. If a community that it is at level F2 wants to achieve Sustainable Literacy, it will need more investment in literacy promotion and expansion in order to raise the level on the Functions scale to F1.

Level F3: The language is being used orally for the functions of day-to-day life, but there is no written use of the language.

At this level, the language can be used to talk about every topic that the community wishes to discuss. That is, all of the life-crucial knowledge that a community desires to transmit in the local language can be transmitted face-to-face. There is no significant written use of the language though some individuals may engage in ad hoc attempts at writing for primarily personal use. Such ad hoc uses of writing, though not to be dismissed or overlooked, are novelties and anomalous. There may be historical examples of written use of the language, but if there are no living users of the language who make use of those materials then this is the correct level on the Functions scale. Level F3 corresponds to EGIDS 6a (Vigorous), the level of Sustainable Orality.

Level F4: Some members of the community use the language face-to-face for the functions of day-to-day life, but an increasing number no longer do.

At this level, face-to-face use of the language for everyday communication is restricted to a subset of the population. At first it is only some of the children who do not use the language for these functions, but as language shift progresses entire generations may no longer use it. Some may be passively bilingual, able to understand but hard-pressed to speak. In some cases one generation (often the parent generation) may be actively bilingual and act as the go-between for the older and younger generations who primarily use different languages. In addition, at this level, even those who are identified (or self-identify) as "speakers" may not be able to use the language for all of the functions that it was traditionally used for.

Level F4 corresponds to level EGIDS 6b (Threatened) when there are still members of the youngest generation who use the language for the functions of day-to-day life. It corresponds to EGIDS 7 (Shifting) when there are no children who use the languages, and to EGIDS 8a (Moribund) when no users remain in the child-bearing generation.

Level F5: There is enough face-to-face use of this language to represent the identity of the group, but not enough for full communication.

At this level, the life-crucial knowledge that is transmitted in the language is confined to heritage knowledge related to the ongoing preservation of the community's heritage identity. The function of the language is entirely identity-related. Language use is symbolic and ceremonial. It will largely be restricted to forms and structures which are closely associated with identity and heritage. This may include names, formalized "frozen" greetings, and poetic or other rhetorical forms. Genres and terminology related to music, dance, visual forms, and so on may be retained (or resurrected) but day-to-day communication is not possible because the language is no longer used for most activities. Those remnants of the language that are retained may be learned by rote and be little understood except by a few specialists.

Level F5 corresponds to EGIDS 9 (Dormant), the level of Sustainable Identity. It is also the level of the Functions scale for EGIDS 8b (Nearly Extinct) since at that stage in language decline there are so few L1 users left that those who remain do not have regular contact with others and are thus unable to use the language on a daily basis. If this is the case, the community needs to choose between investing in revitalization efforts that will move the language up the scale towards EGIDS 6a, (Vigorous), the level of Sustainable Orality, or working to ensure that their identity is retained at EGIDS 9 (Dormant), the level of Sustainable Identity.

Level F6: The language is no longer used but there are enough archival materials that some functions could be restored in the future.

At this level, all use of the language has ended but the language may still be associated with the heritage identity in the minds of the ethnic community. Fortunately, enough documentation of the language is available in archives that revitalization efforts could build on it to reclaim the identificational function of the language. Level F6 corresponds to EGIDS 10 (Extinct) at the level of Sustainable History. This means that language reclamation efforts could possibly achieve EGIDS 9 (Dormant) to restore Sustainable Identity.

Level F7: The language is no longer used and there is little or no documentation.

This level represents a situation where the language is extinct. The language is no longer used at all, not even for identity construction. The descendants of the former users of the language now associate their identity with some other language. The documentary materials on the language are not adequate for the ongoing historical preservation of even academic knowledge of the language. It would not be possible for future generations to reclaim this as a language of identity. Level F7 corresponds to EGIDS 10 (Extinct) where there is not even enough documentation for Sustainable History.

7.4.2 Acquisition scale

The Acquisition scale is used to assess the degree to which the skills needed for use of the local language are being acquired. It is summarized in table 7.2.

Table 7.2 Acquisition scale

Level	Description	Corresponding EGIDS Levels
A1	Literacy in this language is being taught by trained teachers under the auspices of a sustainable institution.	4 (Educational)
A2	There are adequate materials in this language to support literacy instruction in the language and some members of the community are successfully learning to read and write about some bodies of knowledge in the language.	5 (Developing)
A3	There is full face-to-face transmission of this language to all children in the home and community; literacy acquisition, if any, is in another language.	6a (Vigorous)
A4	Only some of the child-bearing generation are transmitting the language by normal means to their children.	6b (Threatened)
A5	The only transmission of the language is for identificational use (often in institutional settings rather than the home).	7 (Shifting) to 9 (Dormant)
A6	There is no transmission of the language.	10 (Extinct)

Level A1: Literacy in this language is being taught by trained teachers under the auspices of a sustainable institution.

This level is the strongest level on the Acquisition scale. At this level, literacy has "taken root" and there is an infrastructure in place that makes the acquisition of literacy skills accessible and available to those who wish to learn to read in the language. Level A1 corresponds to EGIDS 4 (Educational), the level of Sustainable Literacy.

Two key indicators of the attainment of this level of Acquisition are the existence of a sufficient number of trained teachers (who are, in fact, teaching) and the

7.4 Assessing the FAMED conditions

existence of sustainable institutions for the teaching and learning of literacy skills where those teachers can and do teach.

It is important to keep in mind that this evaluation (as for all of the FAMED conditions) is to be made in terms of a particular language. The ability to read and write consists of a set of skills that are generally learned first in one language and then transferred and applied in the other languages within a person's linguistic repertoire. The focus here, though expressed in terms of the acquisition of literacy (at this level on the Acquisition scale), is the acquisition of "local language literacy."

What constitutes a sufficient number of trained teachers and what makes an institution "sustainable" are evaluations that we leave somewhat vaguely defined at this point since every situation will be different. No precise numbers or even percentages can be given. Primarily what an evaluator should be concerned about is the level of accessibility and availability of the means of acquisition. In a very small group, living in a concentrated population center, a single institution (perhaps even a single literacy class) with a single teacher may provide sufficient access and make literacy acquisition adequately available to the majority of the population (to "most of those who wish to learn"). In larger, more dispersed groups, a larger and more complex infrastructure will be required to reach the same general level of adequacy. In some cases, formal institutions may be required or desirable. In others, a less formal infrastructure may be more effective. Whatever form the acquisition infrastructure takes, at this level it should be inclusive, not exclusive, and economically, socially, and politically accessible.

Sustainability also needs to be contextually defined here. As we indicated in our discussion of institutional support for literacy at EGIDS 4, sustainable institutions need not necessarily be self-funded or government supported. There are many contexts where a community lacks the resources needed to be able to sustain even a very small formal institution or where such a formal organization is not really necessary. The important factor to consider is whether literacy has become a community-wide value. In many cases external subsidies, whether financial, technical, or in-kind, may always be needed. Sustainability in such a setting, however, will focus on the will and the capacity of the community to identify, recruit, and retain that outside resourcing and to build and maintain the needed infrastructure over the longer term.

Level A2: There are adequate materials in this language to support literacy instruction in the language and some members of the community are successfully learning to read and write about some bodies of knowledge in the language.

This level on the Acquisition scale represents the situation where some members of the community have learned to read and write using the local language, but the means of acquisition are not widely available throughout the community or are not taken advantage of by large numbers of people. The materials to support literacy acquisition (i.e., primers, early reading materials, teacher's guides) exist, but the infrastructure for mass deployment may not be in place. This may mean that there is not yet an adequate cadre of trained literacy instructors, or that there are not yet enough venues where literacy instruction can be provided.

Instruction may be carried out by outsiders or by peers as in "each one teach one" approaches. More fundamentally, the community-wide positive evaluation of the acquisition of literacy may not yet be fully realized, that is, it has not yet achieved sustainability as we have defined it in chapter 6.

In some cases, the introduction, promotion, and dissemination of literacy instruction, the development of pedagogical materials, and the production of vernacular language literature may be largely in the hands of outsiders. A community-based literacy acquisition infrastructure may not yet exist or may be only in its early stages of formation. Level A2 corresponds to EGIDS 5 (Developing).

Level A3: There is full face-to-face transmission of this language to all children in the home and community; literacy acquisition, if any, is in another language.

This level describes the situation where the means of face-to-face acquisition of the local language are firmly in place. Most often, this acquisition takes place in the home with parents passing the language to their children. Level A3 corresponds to EGIDS 6a (Vigorous), the level of Sustainable Orality.

There are some cases where the normal means of acquisition of a language may be through other societal institutions. Deaf Sign Languages, for example, are more often acquired outside of the home setting in Deaf schools. In such cases, deaf children are often learning the language as their first language while their hearing parents may be acquiring it as a second language. There may also be some settings where local language acquisition takes place in adolescence rather than in childhood with the local language being acquired initially as a second language but eventually becoming the primary (albeit not the chronological "first") and nearly exclusive language of the individual. Thus, while the description speaks of the language being acquired by children in the home, what is in view is the normal acquisition path for each community. What is specifically excluded in this description is what is typically understood to be "second language acquisition" where language acquisition takes place in an explicitly pedagogical, more formal, and somewhat artificial setting.

In addition, "all children" should be understood not in absolute terms but in terms of the general pattern in the population. If there are anomalous cases of language transmission, the evaluator need not necessarily exclude level A3 as a description of the situation. Some discretion and judgment is required in determining when the number of exceptional cases is a leading indicator, foreshadowing a growing trend toward language shift, as opposed to being a trailing indicator that represents a remnant of a past trend. Similarly, a somewhat subjective evaluation is required to determine if the "exceptions" have reached the point where it can no longer be said that essentially all children are acquiring the local language through the normal means of transmission.

Level A4: Only some of the child-bearing generation are transmitting the language by normal means to their children.

When the "normal" means of acquisition are only partially present in a community, it can be judged to be at level A4. If a noticeable number of parents are not passing the local language on to their children but are instead using another language in the home, then this level of acquisition is indicated. All of the considerations described above regarding exceptions and what is meant by the terms "all" and "some" apply here as well.

The primary focus of level A4 is the disruption (beginning or more advanced) of the process of intergenerational transmission of the local language. Level A4 corresponds most directly to EGIDS 6b (Threatened) but may also reflect the more advanced stages of disruption described by EGIDS 7, 8a, and 8b.

Level A5: The only transmission of the language is for identificational use (often in institutional settings rather than the home).

This level describes the situation where intergenerational transmission of the language for day-to-day communication has ceased. As with other aspects of the FAMED analysis, this state of affairs should not be understood in quantitatively absolute terms. There may be a few anomalous cases where parents or grandparents make occasional use of the local language with children or where some language acquisition is taking place, but for the purposes of community-wide language maintenance and sustainable use, those instances, as admirable as they may be, are inadequate for the ongoing preservation of language use among the general population. In many cases, these remnant local language users are, in fact, champions of the identity, and the ongoing use of the language is largely symbolic of their pride in their heritage identity. That enthusiasm for the language and identity is noteworthy and can be encouraged but it does not alter the general categorization of the state of the Acquisition condition, which is what needs to be described by this analysis.

In most cases, language acquisition at this level centers around memorization and performance of traditional stories, poems, songs and dances which reinforce the heritage identity. Like the preservation of traditional ways of dress, crafts, arts, and technologies, language is another tool in the identity construction and maintenance repertoire of the community.

Level A5 corresponds to the EGIDS levels in which normal intergenerational transmission of the language has been completely broken. This begins with EGIDS 7 (Shifting) and culminates with EGIDS 9 (Dormant), the level of Sustainable Identity.

Level A6: There is no transmission of the language.

This level on the Acquisition scale describes the situation where no language transmission for any purpose is taking place. Generally, this indicates that there are no means of acquisition available to the community. However, where language documentation exists (Level F6) it might be possible for a community to develop a means of acquisition and many local speech communities are doing just that. Level A6 corresponds to EGIDS 10 (Extinct).

7.4.3 Motivation scale

The Motivation scale is used to assess the degree to which members of the speech community perceive use of the local language to be beneficial. It is summarized in table 7.3.

Table 7.3 Motivation scale

Level	Description	Highest EGIDS Potential
M1	Members of the speech community perceive the benefits of reading and writing in this language.	4 (Educational)
M2	Some members of the speech community perceive the benefits of reading and writing in this language, but the majority of them still do not.	5 (Developing)
M3	Members of the speech community perceive the benefits of using this language for face-to-face communication, but they perceive no benefits in reading and writing it.	6a (Vigorous)
M4	Some members of the child-bearing generation perceive the benefits of using this language for face-to-face communication, but others find more benefit in shifting to another language.	6b (Threatened)
M5	The child-bearing generation perceives no practical benefit in using this language, though they still perceive symbolic benefit.	7 (Shifting) to 9 (Dormant)
M6	Descendants of the language community associate neither practical nor symbolic benefits with the language.	10 (Extinct)

Level M1: Members of the speech community perceive the benefits of reading and writing in this language

This level identifies a high level of motivation for the use of the local language in written form. The community believes that communicating life-crucial knowledge in the language in writing (and being able to read it) will produce a great deal of benefit for them. The rewards and benefits that the community expects from the written use of the language should go well beyond merely the preservation of the language. Almost always, the rewards should be seen as being both practical and symbolic of the group identity. This means that there are a significant number of functions (see level F1) with which the local language is associated and those functions are also associated with a written modality. Level M1 corresponds to EGIDS 4 (Educational), the level of Sustainable Literacy.

7.4 Assessing the FAMED conditions

Level M2: Some members of the speech community perceive the benefits of reading and writing in this language, but the majority of them still do not.

At this level, some members of the community perceive that the transmission of life-crucial knowledge in this language through written means will be beneficial, but that value is not widely held. These champions or early adopters of local-language literacy represent a segment of the community that is larger and more significant than a few innovators and experimenters. They may be motivated to become literate for a variety of reasons but often their enthusiasm parallels and is spurred on by other social and economic factors in the community context. Level M2 corresponds to EGIDS 5 (Developing).

Level M3: Members of the speech community perceive the benefits of using this language for face-to-face communication, but they perceive no benefits in reading and writing it.

This level describes communities where face-to-face use of the local language is strongly valued and perceived as providing both practical and identity-reinforcing rewards and benefits to the community. While there may be a few who aspire to having the language written, they are exceptional cases. The prevailing sentiment within the community is that little or no benefit is derived from reading or writing the language. Level M3 corresponds to EGIDS 6a, the level of Sustainable Orality.

Level M4: Some members of the child-bearing generation perceive the benefit of using this language for face-to-face communication, but others find more benefit in shifting to another language.

At this level, many in the child-bearing generation (parents) do not believe that there are sufficient rewards and benefits to be gained for themselves, or more often, for their children, from using their local language in face-to-face communication. Among those who are able to use the more dominant language, this can be observed in the fact that they have begun using that language with their children. However, observable language shift is not a requirement for identifying a community at this level. Parents might place little value on the local language, but not have enough proficiency in the dominant language to be able to use it with their children. Level M4 corresponds to EGIDS 6b (Threatened).

Level M5: The child-bearing generation perceives no practical benefit in using this language, though they still perceive symbolic benefit.

At this level the parent generation believes that the best tool for economic, social, and political mobility is a more dominant language. As parents look to the future prospects for their children, the most fruitful path they can see is one which is primarily through the acquisition and use of another language. However, they may still have strong emotional ties to the heritage language and their identity is still strongly tied to that language. Use of the language is valued as a marker of identity and is common in formulaic and ceremonial performances of the language. The perceived benefit of this kind of language use is that it identifies the user as a member of the community and strengthens community solidarity.

Despite this strong sentimental attachment to the language, parents feel that it is a higher priority for their children to learn the dominant language. As a result, that is the language they choose to use with their children.

Level M5 corresponds to the EGIDS levels in which normal intergenerational transmission of the language has been completely broken. This begins with EGIDS 7 (Shifting) and culminates with EGIDS 9 (Dormant), the level of Sustainable Identity.

Level M6: Descendants of the language community associate neither practical nor symbolic benefits with the language.

At this level, no one in the community retains any sense that the language provides any benefit, and no one is willing to invest in acquiring it and using it for any purpose. With no extant community associating itself with the language, primary interest and motivations related to the language come exclusively from linguists, anthropologists, and other scholars who make use of the archival records of the language. Level M6 corresponds to EGIDS 10 (Extinct).

7.4.4 Environment scale

The Environment scale is used to assess the degree to which the external policy environment supports the use of the local language. Generally, this refers to official language policies, most often those of a governmental agency. However, environment should be understood more broadly than that. It may be that there is a major non-governmental institution such as a regional church body which has a language policy that is highly influential and significantly affects language use. Where there is a stated government policy, it is probably more significant than that of any other body since the risks of ignoring or disobeying legal requirements are generally of greater significance than the risks associated with failure to align with an organizational policy. For this reason, the levels on the Environment scale are expressed generally with reference to official government policies. Where government polices are favorable or neutral, the policies of significant institutions then become more salient in shaping the environment as described in our earlier discussion of micro-environments. The Environment scale is summarized in table 7.4.

Table 7.4 Environment scale

Level	Description	Corresponding EGIDS Levels
E1	The external policy environment calls for the cultivation of this language and cultural identity and the policy-making bodies are putting this into practice by endorsing an official orthography and using their institutions to transmit literacy in this language.	4 (Educational)

7.4 Assessing the FAMED conditions

Level	Description	Corresponding EGIDS Levels
E2	The external policy environment encourages the development of this language, but the policy-making bodies are making no investment in the implementation of such policy.	5 (Developing)
E3	The external policy environment has nothing to say about ethnolinguistic diversity or language development and thus raises no impediment.	5 (Developing), 6a (Vigorous)
E4	The external policy environment affirms the oral use of this language, but calls for the language to be left in its current state and not developed.	6a (Vigorous), 6b (Threatened)
E5	The external policy environment is hostile toward ethnolinguistic diversity and calls for the elimination or suppression of this language.	7 (Shifting) to 10 (Extinct)

Level E1: The external policy environment calls for the cultivation of this language and cultural identity and the policy-making bodies are putting this into practice by endorsing an official orthography and using their institutions to transmit literacy in this language.

The strongest level on the Environment scale describes the situation where there is full support, both de jure and de facto, for the cultivation of languages and the identities associated with them. This level only applies if there is both a codification of this policy in law or administrative regulations and the policy is "given feet" through vigorous efforts to implement it, including the provision of funds and the creation of agencies, additional legislation, implementing regulations, and training and resourcing of implementers. Most often, the implementation of this level of language policy is carried out through the national education system but other means may be employed as well. In some cases, evaluators may select this level on the Environment scale when government policy is favorable, as described, but implementation has been delegated to or otherwise taken on by non-governmental agencies rather than the government-run education system, and that implementation is widespread, effective, and sustainable as we have defined that term in chapter 6. Level E1 corresponds to EGIDS 4 (Educational), the level of Sustainable Literacy.

Level E2: The external policy environment encourages the development of this language, but the policy-making bodies are making no investment in the implementation of such policy.

At Level E2, government policy is positive but lacks the same level of commitment to implementation. Funds and technical resources may not always be forthcoming to implement the development of local languages. In some cases, this state of affairs is a reflection of the actual scarcity of resources (financial or technical or both) which limits how broadly and extensively the generally positive policy can be promoted. In other cases, it may reflect a more cynical effort on the part of those in power to conform rhetorically and legislatively to requests for language development, while withholding personnel, or technical support, so that no real development can take place. Level E2 differs from level E1 in that there is neither direct implementation of policy through government schools nor officially delegated and resourced implementation through other agencies. Implementation, while permitted, is simply not on the horizon for policy makers. Any implementation efforts will be carried out by non-governmental institutions. These private sector initiatives can be every bit as effective and far-reaching as a government program but the dynamics of working within such a system of language development will be considerably different for the local communities. Level E2 corresponds to EGIDS 5 (Developing).

Level E3: The external policy environment has nothing to say about ethnolinguistic diversity or language development and thus raises no impediment.

This level represents the "neutral" environment state where either there is no government language policy at all or that policy does not address the issue of local language development. This may be because the government policy only focuses on recognition of national or regional languages at EGIDS levels 1 or 2. In addition, at level E3 no non-governmental agency has a stated positive policy in regards to local language development. Local languages are simply not explicitly acknowledged or singled out for specific mention by any significant policy making body.

For level E3 to apply, this lack of an explicit policy must, at least, carry with it the implication that there is no prohibition of local language development. Where high levels of institutional support are available the situation would more properly be characterized as at level E2. At level E3 however, language development efforts would necessarily be carried out by more local, less-well-resourced agents of change. Their efforts may not be well-known or widespread throughout the speech community and may not be sustainable for the longer term. At level E3, the corresponding EGIDS level can be as high as EGIDS 5 (Developing) since there is no external impediment to development, but EGIDS 6a (Vigorous) is also typical.

Level E4: The external policy environment affirms the oral use of this language, but calls for the language to be left in its current state and not developed.

At this level on the Environment scale, efforts aimed at the development of a local language for written purposes would either be actively opposed and penalized by government authorities, at worst, or be ignored and officially unsupported, at best. Efforts by any non-governmental agency would not be looked upon with favor, though those efforts might not be actively opposed.

While it might be possible to engage in some very informal and low-profile literacy development work, it is unlikely that those efforts would be able to spread and flourish enough to even achieve EGIDS 5 (Developing). Level E4 typically corresponds with EGIDS 6a (Vigorous) or EGIDS 6b (Threatened).

7.4 Assessing the FAMED conditions

Level E5: The external policy environment is hostile toward ethnolinguistic diversity and calls for the elimination or suppression of this language.

Level E5 on the Environment scale represents a policy environment in which government authority (and resources) are marshalled against not only the development of local languages but against their continued use.

Such overtly hostile policy environments are quite rarely openly stated (de jure) though they may exist much more commonly in terms of practice and implementation (de facto). If such policies achieve their ends, languages that are at the weaker EGIDS levels are likely to lose strength more quickly than might otherwise be the case. The demise of these languages, however, is not a certainty. Many speech communities have found ways to maintain the oral use of their languages covertly or in very restricted domains. Obviously, a minoritized speech community that wishes to develop its language beyond those restricted domains in such a hostile policy environment will face a great deal of opposition and achieve its goals only at great cost.

For these reasons, the long-term prognosis at level E5 is EGIDS 10 (Extinct), though if a community can maintain its identity (even covertly) in defiance of government opposition, EGIDS 9 (Dormant) may be achievable. As a prohibition against transmitting the language goes into effect, the corresponding EGIDS level is EGIDS 7 (Shifting) and it will drop from there.

7.4.5 Differentiation Scale

As we mentioned earlier, the FAMED conditions provide an alternative way to talk about what is required in order to achieve stable multilingualism at each of the levels of sustainable use. For that reason the FAMED conditions often overlap and interact with each other and all of them make reference to the decisions the community has made regarding functions and the resulting association of each of the bodies of knowledge that have been identified as "life-crucial" with a specific language. The Differentiation scale looks at the degree to which there is a complementary distribution of those functional assignments to languages in the repertoire, and the degree to which those norms of use are disseminated and re-enforced within the speech community. What is in view is the degree to which the actual behavior of the community reflects the assignment of the different languages in the community's linguistic repertoire to distinct functional niches. The Differentiation scale is summarized in table 7.5.

Table 7.5 Differentiation scale

Level	Description	Corresponding EGIDS Levels
D1	Members of the language community have a set of shared norms as to when to use this language orally and in writing versus when to use other languages.	4 (Educational)

Level	Description	Corresponding EGIDS Levels
D2	Members of the speech community have a set of shared norms as to when to use this language orally versus when to use other languages, but for writing some use this language while others use another language for many of the same functions.	5 (Developing)
D3	Members of the speech community have a set of shared norms as to when to use this language orally versus when to use other languages, and they never use this language in written form.	6a (Vigorous)
D4	Some members of the child-bearing generation use this language orally for functions of day-to-day life, while others use a different language for many of the same functions.	6b (Threatened)
D5	The only functions for this language that remain for all in the speech community are identificational and there is a set of shared norms as to when and how they use the language as a marker of their ethnic identity.	7 (Shifting) to 9 (Dormant)
D6	For some members of the speech community the only remaining functions for this language are identificational, while others use a different language for many of the same functions.	9 (Dormant)
D7	Descendants of the language community do not use this language for any functions (oral or written).	10 (Extinct)

Level D1: Members of the language community have a set of shared norms as to when to use this language orally and in writing versus when to use other languages.

At this level on the Differentiation scale, the norms of use are focused primarily on the written use of the languages. Which bodies of life-crucial knowledge will be transmitted in written form in which of the languages in the community's linguistic repertoire is clearly defined and widely known. This clear differentiation results in a level of sociolinguistic confidence (i.e., predictability), the knowledge of which language and modality to use in which context. That clarity results in a certain amount of comfortableness in those uses and greater ease of use of the

7.4 Assessing the FAMED conditions

local language for those functions. Level D1 corresponds to EGIDS 4 (Educational), the level of Sustainable Literacy.

Level D2: Members of the speech community have a set of shared norms as to when to use this language orally versus when to use other languages, but for writing some use this language while others use another language for many of the same functions.

At this level, while community members may clearly know which language to use for which body of knowledge, the differentiation between written and oral use of the local language is only beginning to emerge (or is disintegrating from an earlier, clearer state) and the functions with which the written local language is associated are limited or are not widely known.

Depending on the trajectory of the language on the EGIDS, the limited number of functions could represent the development and emergence of bodies of life-crucial knowledge associated with the written modality as the language gains strength and develops. Alternatively, it could represent a stage in which a once flourishing literary heritage is waning and being retained for fewer and fewer functions. Level D2 corresponds to EGIDS 5 (Developing); the level must be raised to D1 to achieve Sustainable Literacy at EGIDS 4.

Level D3: Members of the speech community have a set of shared norms as to when to use this language orally versus when to use other languages, and they never use this language in written form.

At level D3, shared norms of behavior regarding language use exist but the complementary distribution of the functions associated with the languages in the community's repertoire limits the use of the local language to the oral modality only. Functions associated with the written modality are associated with the dominant language in the speech community.

In many cases, the goal of the speech community may be to achieve Sustainable Literacy and the lack of written use may reflect a lack of development efforts needed to introduce writing and reading in the local language. Efforts to achieve Sustainable Literacy, which is the tacit goal of most language development projects, will result in success or failure to the degree to which the necessary FAMED conditions are addressed. If a clearly differentiated niche for written local language cannot be created in the common practice of the speech community, those efforts are not likely to succeed. Level D3 corresponds to EGIDS 6a (Vigorous), the level of Sustainable Orality.

Level D4: Some members of the child-bearing generation use this language orally for functions of day-to-day life, while others use a different language for many of the same functions.

This level on the Differentiation scale characterizes situations where language shift is beginning or in progress. The dominant language present in the speech community has begun to occupy domains traditionally associated with the local language for everyday face-to-face communication. The number and nature of the functions that have been given over to the dominant language will correlate to the status of the local language on the EGIDS based on the generation of the youngest remaining users of the language (see the "Y" scale description below). Level D4 corresponds to EGIDS 6b (Threatened); the level must be raised to D3 to achieve Sustainable Orality at EGIDS 6a.

Level D5: The only functions for this language that remain for all in the speech community are identificational and there is a set of shared norms as to when and how they use the language as a marker of their ethnic identity.

At this level, all of the functions of day-to-day communication for up-coming generations have become associated with the dominant language. The only remaining functions for those generations are those related to identity construction and maintenance. This level reflects the community's level of acceptance and participation (conscious or not) in that distribution of language functions. While there are still times when the community needs to identify the local language as "the language to use," those are infrequent and fleeting, largely confined to holidays and ceremonial occasions. All other functions, the major portions of a community's day-to-day existence, are assigned to the dominant language.

Level D5 corresponds to those EGIDS levels in which the transmission of the language as the means for day-to-day communication has been completely broken. This begins with EGIDS 7 (Shifting) and culminates with EGIDS 9 (Dormant), the level of Sustainable Identity.

Level D6: For some members of the speech community, the only remaining functions for this language are identificational, while others use a different language for many of the same functions.

At this level, the only functions for the language that remain are identificational, but this functional assignment is not clearly differentiated since some community members have abandoned the language as a marker of their ethnic identity or have abandoned that identity altogether. Level D6 corresponds to EGIDS 9 (Dormant), but at a weak and unstable state. The level must be raised to D5 to maintain Sustainable Identity at EGIDS 9.

Level D7: Descendants of the language community do not use this language for any functions (oral or written).

At this level, differentiation of functional assignments is not an issue since there are no functions assigned to the local language. All of life, including identity construction, is carried out using another language. Level D6 corresponds to EGIDS 10 (Extinct).

7.5 Using the FAMED conditions to assess language vitality

The FAMED conditions provide a more detailed way to analyze the situation of a speech community in order to determine its EGIDS level than was presented in chapter 5. The five conditions that form the acronym FAMED are components of ethnolinguistic vitality. At the same time, they represent multiple ways of

7.5 Using the FAMED conditions to assess language vitality

examining the state of stable multilingualism in the speech community, which is the key to sustaining local language use in the context of an ecology involving other languages. We describe stable as primarily the assignment of functions (bodies of life-crucial knowledge) and the differentiation of those functions (i.e., compartmentalization, in which those domains are "watertight" as opposed to "leaking"). Acquisition, Motivation, and Environment represent the contextual and programmatic factors that affect the ability of a community to maintain (or alter) the association of those functions with a language.

The five conditions are sufficient to assess the vitality of a living local language when it is in the range of EGIDS 4 to EGIDS 6b. However, when full intergenerational transmission has been broken, an additional factor is needed to assign the situation to an EGIDS level, namely, the generation of the youngest first-language (L1) users. For this purpose, the Y scale with the following values is used:

- Y1—The youngest L1 users are children.
- Y2—The youngest L1 users are parents.
- Y3—The youngest L1 users are grandparents.
- Y4—The youngest L1 users are great-grandparents.
- Y5—There are no L1 users.

Table 7.6 summarizes the correspondence between levels on EGIDS and levels on the five FAMED Conditions scales and the youngest L1 users scale.

Table 7.6 FAMED conditions summary table

EGIDS Level	Functions	Acquisition	Motivation	Environment	Differentiation	Youngest L1 Users
4 (Educational)	F1	A1	M1	E1	D1	Y1
5 (Developing)	F2	A2	M2	E2, E3	D2	Y1
6a (Vigorous)	F3	A3	M3	E3, E4	D3	Y1
6b (Threatened)	F4	A4	M4	E4	D4	Y1
7 (Shifting)	F4	A5	M5	E5	D5	Y2
8a (Moribund)	F4	A5	M5	E5	D5	Y3

EGIDS Level	Functions	Acquisition	Motivation	Environment	Differentiation	Youngest L1 Users
8b (Nearly extinct)	F5	A5	M5	E5	D5	Y4
9 (Dormant)	F5	A5	M5	E5	D5, D6	Y5
10 (Extinct)	F6, F7	A6	M6	E5	D7	Y5

In assessing the status of a language in any given speech community, the evaluator looks at each of the scales individually and selects the level that best describes the situation of the local language. (The selected level can be circled in a copy of table 7.6.) When the value of the Youngest generation scale is from Y2 to Y4, the value on that scale determines the current EGIDS level. Otherwise, the current EGIDS level is typically the row in which the levels of the individual scales predominate. If one scale has a lower value than that which corresponds to the predominant EGIDS level, then assigning that EGIDS level is an optimistic assessment since the condition really needs to be raised to comfortably fit that EGIDS level. Assigning the EGIDS level corresponding to the lower factor might give a more realistic assessment. If two scales indicate a lower EGIDS level than the predominant one, then the lower EGIDS assessment is certainly called for.

The value of using this assessment table is not only for estimating the current EGIDS level, but also for projecting the future trajectory of the language on the EGIDS. The model predicts that any condition with a lower value than the predominant current level is pulling the situation downward and must be addressed by specific language development activities if the EGIDS level is to stay where it is. When the current EGIDs level is not one of the sustainable levels (4, 6a, 9, or 10), the model further predicts that the situation will naturally slide down to the nearest sustainable level in the absence of language development activities that are aimed at moving the situation up to the next higher sustainable level. Each of the assessment scales for the FAMED conditions can be used to identify the gap between the current state and the state that would be needed to achieve sustainability. This helps a community-based language development program plan activities that are aimed at addressing the situation. This is the subject of the remaining chapters in this book.

7.5.1 The SUM assessment grid revisited

We have already briefly mentioned the SUM Assessment Grid in chapter 5 as one of the tools that can be employed to evaluate the EGIDS status of a local language. However, as described there, this tool begins not with an overall evaluation of the EGIDS but with the finer-grained analysis of the FAMED conditions.

Designed to be used by someone with an in-depth knowledge of the local language situation, the grid asks the user to score the situation on each of the five conditions with respect both to sustainable oral use and to sustainable written use, the two most commonly identified goals of language development. The evaluator must select the descriptor that best fits the language community's current status or practice. The scales used in this tool align with but are not the same as the scales that we have described above. The user of the tool reads all of the descriptions in a row of the grid and selects the description that best fits the situation for the speech community in focus. Each column in the grid is assigned a number from 0 to 3, and the number of the column for the chosen descriptor is recorded. When a description for all five of the conditions on the page has been selected, the numbers are summed and the sum is looked up in a table to convert that score to an EGIDS value. The SUM Assessment Grid can be accessed and downloaded here: http://www.sil.org/resources/publications/entry/57632.

In addition to serving a descriptive purpose as a more detailed and refined EGIDS evaluation, the FAMED conditions serve an even more valuable purpose as a diagnostic tool that provides community-based language developers with an agenda to guide their planning and implementation. By identifying which factors are weak (i.e., not at a level sufficient to support a desired level of sustainable use), the FAMED conditions help language development planners establish better plans of action that focus effort on activities that specifically address the conditions that must be improved in order to achieve the desired level of sustainable use.

7.6 Going deeper

7.6.1 Functions

Our notion of Functions largely coincides with the concept of domain of use, whether understood traditionally (Fishman 1965) or as a "body of life-crucial knowledge" as we've already described in chapter 4.

7.6.2 Acquisition

There is a vast literature on language acquisition both from the perspective of child language acquisition and as a second or foreign language which we will not even attempt to mention here. In terms of language development, especially at the stronger levels of the Acquisition scale, it is the acquisition of literacy that is in focus. That literature is also large, though the work on literacy as "community development" is somewhat more manageable. We would especially point out some very practical references for community-based literacy development from UNESCO: UNESCO (1996, 2005a, 2007); Kosonen, Young, and Malone (2006); and Malone (2004).

Where oral re-acquisition of a language is in focus, we suggest Hinton 2001 as a useful model to be considered. Other case studies of oral language acquisition can be found in chapter 9.

7.6.3 Motivation

Karan (2000) developed the Perceived Benefit Model which specifically focuses on the motivations behind language maintenance or shift. "Its foundational element is that individuals with certain *language use motivations* modify and exploit their linguistic repertoires in such a way as to bring about what they perceive to be their personal good" (emphasis in the original, Karan 2000:65).

The Perceived Benefit Model identifies four types of motivations: communicative motivations, economic motivations, social motivations (which can be further distinguished in terms of power-oriented or solidarity-oriented intentions), and religious motivations. The model views community-wide change in language use in terms of the aggregate of individual choices affected by these different types of motivations. The model provides a helpful way to analyze motivational factors in a way that goes much more deeply into the topic than we cover in the Motivations scale of the FAMED conditions.For a direct application of the Perceived Benefit Model within the SUM, see Karan 2015.

Language empowerment

The language empowerment model is an alternative approach that addresses three major components: linguistic empowerment (previously referred to in this volume largely under the notion of corpus planning and in chapter 10 as "building the capacity of the language"), sociopolitical empowerment (addressed in the FAMED conditions largely as advocacy under the Environment condition and in chapter 10 as "building the capacity of the community"), and economic empowerment (which generally aligns with the FAMED condition of Motivation). This model is described in one of the examples in chapter 9. We mention it here because of its more direct relationship to the FAMED conditions.

- Linguistic empowerment involves a collaboration with the community to develop the language.

- Sociopolitical empowerment involves assisting the community to facilitate its own literacy programs, build self-confidence, and assert itself and its ethnolinguistic rights within the wider political context.

- Economic empowerment involves helping the community develop an economic base to increase its income while teaching community members better utilization of the income.

When these three areas are satisfied, the people find previously nonexistent benefits in choosing their language over a lingua franca (Batibo 2008:4).

The empowerment model is also an alternative approach to describing what we discuss in chapter 10 under the general label of capacity building. There are some significant points of overlap and agreement between this approach and the approach we are taking in the SUM. Linguistic empowerment can be thought of as building the capacity of the language itself to serve the needs of the community, that is, language development as we have defined it. Sociopolitical empowerment and economic empowerment parallel, in complementary ways, our notion of building the capacity of the local community to meet its own needs through training and infrastructure development.

7.6.4 Environment

As described above, we see the policy environment as being more than just the set of laws, statutes, and regulations which overtly address official language recognitions. Though the legal framework is important it is not the only tool by which policy is created and implemented. As we point out, there is often a significant amount of discrepancy between the legal and rhetorical policy and its actual implementation. In this volume we have combined without commenting on it what was identified first by Neustupny (1974) as policy planning and cultivation planning approaches to language planning. Much of what we have focused on falls, using that scheme of things, under cultivation planning since we place a heavy emphasis on the identification of functions and on language maintenance, revival, re-acquisition, and revitalization. Policy planning focuses more on the formal role of languages in society with issues of recognition and uses for governmental and official functions being at the forefront. When we attempt to categorize the state of the environment, our focus therefore must shift from the more cultivation-oriented issue of the assignment of functions to include a policy-oriented perspective. Hornberger (2006) provides a very helpful overview and summary of how the Cooper (1989) model of language planning integrates with the perspectives of Neustupny and others. See also the *Ethnologue* (Lewis, Simons, and Fennig 2016; especially https://www.ethnologue.com/methodology/#Status) for a systematic elaboration of possible categories of Official Recognition.

Most treatments of policy planning focus on the role of governments in establishing policy. As a largely political process, that kind of policy development almost always begins by establishing the status of the dominant language(s) at the national or provincial level. Beyond that, policy planning often makes only brief mention of the less powerful and politically inconsequential local languages and their place in national society. In contrast, the development of language policy can also be viewed as a component of a broader diversity policy (Lewis and Trudell 2008). That diversity policy, whether formally stated or tacitly practiced, often informs and shapes the policy planning of non-governmental institutions and agencies as we have discussed above.

Another perspective on the Environment condition can be gained by examining and categorizing the education policies of a country. A useful set of descriptive categories are those developed by Churchill (1986) and very fruitfully applied by May (2001). Churchill's stages parallel but are not exactly the same as the levels we have identified on the Environment scale.

7.6.5 Differentiation

We use the term differentiation to describe what is, in our view, one of the key components of diglossia. (See discussion in the Going Deeper section of chapter 4). As described there, we focus primarily on the compartmentalization of functions, the close association of a linguistic variety with a particular topic or body of knowledge (and its associated participants and locations), as an essential component of what we call stable multilingualism.

In developing the FAMED conditions we have essentially taken two major components of diglossia and identified them explicitly as essential conditions for stable multilingualism. Understanding the term as we do—as a set of functions which are clearly differentiated—we see diglossia as a highly desirable, indeed, an essential state of affairs if sustainable language use is to be attained.

Where the Functions condition aligns well with the notion of domains of use, the Differentiation condition corresponds closely to the notion of compartmentalization. In order for stable multilingualism to exist, there must not only be a clear association of a language with a function but that association must be seen as a norm of use by the community as a whole. By making Differentiation an explicit condition for achieving sustainable use we also emphasize that for the purposes of language development there must be overt, directed, intentional activities aimed at establishing those norms. This focus also aligns with our assertion that it is the speech community, characterized by shared norms of language use, that is the primary focus of community-based language development.

In their application of the FAMED conditions in the Democratic Republic of Congo, Bagamba and Boone (2015) observed that in order to accurately describe the state of endangerment or vitality of languages a more nuanced study of language dynamics was needed that, among other things, concentrated more on differentiation of functional niches, than on the presence of diglossia *per se*.

Activities aimed at differentiating the functional assignment of the languages in a speech community's linguistic repertoire may sometimes be seen as quite prescriptive. Differentiation activities can range from being nothing more than a gentle correction of a grammatical error or the suggestion of a word or term in the local language when a borrowed term from the dominant language is used, to public calls for purism and criticism of those who fail to use the local language when they could. Often, activities aimed at motivation can be understood to be addressing differentiation as well. Public promotional campaigns that encourage local language use, broadcasts and publications that model and demonstrate appropriate use, and any method of achieving community-wide consensus regarding the norms of language use can be helpfully employed as means of differentiation. Some specific examples are presented in chapter 9 and in the Appendix.

7.6.6 An alternative framework: The COD(P) model

An alternative descriptive framework is that developed by the language economists Grin and Vaillancourt (1997) which uses three situational factors, Capacity, Opportunity, and Desire (COD), to evaluate the potential for language maintenance. This model looks at language retention and use through the lens of economics using the concept of "constrained utility maximization" in particular. That perspective starts with the premise that "there are many ways in which language can be fitted into an individual's utility function" (Grin 1990:161). That assertion aligns with the Functions condition in the SUM. In the COD model, Capacity, we would argue, aligns in large part with the FAMED Acquisition condition; Opportunity with Environment; and Desire with Motivation.

7.6 Going deeper

More recently, an additional factor was added to the model by the European Language Diversity for All research project (Laakso et al. 2013) where it was noted that an additional essential factor for ongoing language use was the existence of Products in the local language. In the FAMED conditions scheme, the existence of such products most closely corresponds to the Functions condition as evidence of the association of a particular body of knowledge with the local language.

8

Language Development: Addressing the FAMED Conditions

As communities make choices regarding which bodies of life-crucial knowledge they will transmit in their local language, they must also make decisions about how the capacity of the language to perform those functions will be developed.

8.1 Introduction

The preceding chapters have identified the major components of the Sustainable Use Model (SUM): the notion of life-crucial knowledge transmission, the EGIDS, sustainable levels of use, and the FAMED conditions. There remains one more significant conceptual piece to be considered before we turn to the processes and activities of language development. We have proposed that communities need to be able to transmit life-crucial knowledge from one generation to the next. We have described those bodies of knowledge as *Functions* and we have made reference to that concept throughout the discussion so far. Recall the idea we introduced earlier that information (including language proficiency and norms of use) is transmitted across geographic and social space, as well as chronologically. The members of a speech community can consciously make decisions (or those decisions will be made without their conscious awareness in response to a changing environment) about which bodies of knowledge they will transmit within those dimensions. That set of decisions we have described as the assignment or association of a language (or languages) to particular functions. In this chapter we will discuss in general terms the process of developing the capacity of the languages themselves to carry out the functions the community wishes to associate with them.

The identification of life-crucial bodies of knowledge (both internal and external) is the starting point of the process by which a language is associated with Functions. In addition, a body of knowledge may also be closely associated with a particular modality of the associated language—oral, written, digital, or some combination of these.

This interplay of knowledge, language, and modality forms the sociolinguistic ecology of a speech community—the shared norms of linguistic behavior. In addition, it constitutes the primary focus of a community's efforts as that community engages in its own language development: Which language(s) will be used for the transmission of which bodies of life-crucial knowledge in which modalities? The answers to those interrelated questions constitute an agenda for community-based language development that takes into account current levels of use (as measured by the EGIDS); the community consensus about a desired level of sustainable use; a diagnosis of what needs to be addressed (via the FAMED conditions) to achieve that sustainable level of use; and a set of concrete identified Functions that provide focus for the more general strategic aims of the language development program. These are the major building blocks of the SUM.

8.2 Building the capacity of the language

With those concepts laid out and described, we can now turn to the steps needed to actually engage in the development of each Function. As mentioned above, the overall nature and scope of the development program will be affected by the community consensus regarding a desired level of sustainable use. That desired future provides the overall vision for all language development efforts in the community. The language development program will also be constrained by the community's current level of language use and vitality (its current level on the EGIDS). A language that is at a very weak level of vitality will require a great deal more effort and investment to achieve Sustainable Literacy (in even one or two identified bodies of knowledge) than a language that is at a much higher level. Additionally, if the factors to support intervening sustainable levels of use are not in place (as measured by the FAMED conditions), the desired level of sustainable use cannot be achieved until the relevant FAMED conditions are adequate. A more detailed description of specific activities required to achieve these goals is given in chapter 9 and some example scenarios will be provided there. For now, we will confine our discussion to the more general features of the process of developing the capacity of the language to serve its assigned function using the general conceptual framework of language planning as described earlier in chapter 3.

8.2.1 Status planning

The association of a function with a language and a modality is equivalent in many respects to the language planning process called status planning. Once that association is made for each identified function, a set of development activities must be carried out in order to enhance the capacity of the language to fulfill the functions assigned to it. Within the language planning framework, these activities are called corpus planning.

Identifying and defining functions

The first step in this knowledge management process is to identify each of the bodies of knowledge that is to be maintained or developed. This process relates to the Functions condition in the FAMED acronym. As we have framed it, a body of knowledge corresponds to a Function. A language functions as the means of transmission of a specific body of knowledge. The body of knowledge or the topic is what the language is used to talk about. As we saw in chapter 4, this association of a language with a function or a set of functions is essential for the achievement of stable multilingualism at one of the levels of sustainable use.

Some typical bodies of internal knowledge

A short list of different bodies of *internal* knowledge might include the following:

- Folklore and origin stories
- History of the community
- Life histories of community members
- Folk taxonomy and uses of flora and fauna
- Traditional religion and cosmology
- Traditional art forms
- Health and healing
- Local technology
- Food and clothing
- Subsistence practices and technologies

In many cases it is a relatively straightforward process for a community to identify the internal bodies of knowledge that are important for the maintenance of the community's distinctive identity. The same methods can be used to identify external bodies of knowledge that are seen to be life-crucial.

Some typical bodies of external knowledge

A short list of different bodies of *external* knowledge might include the following:

- World history
- World religions
- Scientific taxonomies of flora and fauna
- Science and technology
- Mathematics
- Nutrition and hygiene
- Medicine and pharmacology
- Agriculture and food production

For each body of knowledge, however, there is more to do than simply applying a label such as Foods, Clothing, Agricultural Methods, Health and Healing, Religion and Cosmology, etc. The task of formally defining each body of knowledge requires some thought and careful consideration. The question to be answered is: What facts, behaviors, skills, and artifacts make up this body of knowledge? The inverse of that question is also important. What facts, behaviors, skills and artifacts do *not* make up this body of knowledge?

This process of definition can be difficult since, as with many things in the real world, boundaries are often not clear and well-marked. In addition, communities in either recent or longstanding contact with others are often characterized by mixed, synthesized, and syncretized bodies of knowledge that draw a little from the "inside" and at the same time (and at various periods in history), are, or have been, significantly influenced by the "outside" as well. There are a variety of techniques that might be used within the community setting to explore the content and the range of each of the identified bodies of knowledge. One of these, Rapid Word Collection (SIL International 2014), has proven to be both productive and relatively straightforward to implement by systematically exploring semantic domains. While identifying and documenting semantic domains is not all there is to identifying and delimiting a body of knowledge, it does provide a helpful and practical starting point for that process.

The point of this identification process is not to develop fixed, immoveable boundaries between categories of knowledge that can never be altered. Rather, the process is intended to provide the community with a clearer perspective regarding the kinds of knowledge that they deal with and to help them recognize the value they place on the knowledge they already possess and use as well as the new knowledge they would like to know and use. An exploration of the range of linguistic resources that comprise each identified body of knowledge not only provides a linguistic corpus for the language development effort itself, but also has the potential to enhance the prestige of the local language by demonstrating its usefulness. Once this broad categorization has been done, the community will have a clearer picture of what their language development task will look like.

It is important to note that it serves little useful purpose to assign either positive or negative evaluations to inside and outside knowledge. Inside knowledge is not inherently better or more authentic than outside knowledge. Neither is outside knowledge necessarily more advantageous. The point of this distinction is to provide a community with a way to identify the knowledge resources they have at their disposal and to engage in an informed consideration of which of those bodies of knowledge meet their needs. In whatever context a community finds itself, it needs to evaluate how best to manage knowledge transmission so as to serve its needs in all areas of life both now and into the future. This decision is closely related to the identity choices that community members are making. Few communities are able to maintain themselves in complete isolation and eliminate any contact with the outside world. Some community members are very likely going to value some bodies of external knowledge more highly than others, and other community members will value and wish to retain the internal knowledge that is a distinctive part of the heritage identity. Many will be actively constructing hybridized identities that participate in and make use of multiple bodies of knowledge from both the inside and the outside. Each community will want to find its own path and needs to be able to make these important decisions with the best information and most helpful perspectives available.

> **A point to ponder**
>
> "Being able to talk about the complexities of modern life emphatically does not mean having to give up the native language. Unfortunately the issue is too often framed in this way as a choice, putting the language in a museum mode as being of value only for expressing traditional cultural matters but otherwise of no use. Community psychology must change to embrace the use of the language for all aspects of life, adopting terms and adapting usage as needed to maintain relevance."
> (Rudolph Troike, c. 2010, personal communication)

Communities that find themselves near the lower end of the EGIDS scale may find it difficult to identify what is truly their internal knowledge and what is not. They may find that many of their heritage bodies of knowledge have become reduced and limited or so overlaid with external knowledge that they are indistinguishable as separate at all. Efforts to reclaim cultural heritage knowledge and to revitalize the language associated with that knowledge often tend to focus on purifying and restoring some replica of the past. A truly vital culture and language, however, reflects that past but engages dynamically with the present and with the future.

This definition process gives the community concrete areas of focus for language development efforts. Where the distinction between internal knowledge and external knowledge is unhelpful or is simply too difficult to distinguish, it can be abandoned. The important point is that a set of valued (i.e., life-crucial) bodies of knowledge be identified and defined so that the community has an inventory of potential language development projects.

8.2.2 Corpus planning

Some corpus planning activities can serve broadly for all of the different Functions. In most cases, a single writing system, called an orthography, should serve all bodies of knowledge associated with the same language, but there may be cases where a particular body of knowledge is deemed to be better communicated using a different writing system or script. In such cases, separate orthography development activities may be required for some of the Functions. Similarly, general standards may be developed for grammar or vocabulary that might apply to all the Functions.

Standardization

Standardization is the process of establishing norms of language use. Particularly when a new function for a language is being introduced, establishing such norms is a foundational aspect of bringing use for that function into existence. The intent of standardization is to reduce variation and to reduce the undesirable obstacles to communication created by such variation. For each identified Function, a set of norms can be established that will facilitate the use of the language for the communication of that body of knowledge. These norms will differ in accordance with the desired level of sustainable use. If the desired level, for example, is Sustainable Literacy, standardization may focus more on the written norms of use and pay less attention to norms of oral use. If Sustainable Literacy is not in focus, standardization will very likely focus more on issues of pronunciation and accent, acceptable lexical choices, grammatical correctness, and other features of the spoken language. Where Sustainable Identity is the desired level of sustainable use, a canon of "traditional oral literature" may be defined and stylistics and rhetorical conformity to a "classical" standard form of the language may be the primary concern.

As described above, establishing an orthography is a standardization activity. Orthography development includes not only the choice of a script but the norms of use for that script including conventions for spelling, word division, and punctuation. If the desired level of sustainable use is not Sustainable Literacy, there may be no need to develop fully an official practical orthography designed for widespread use. Often it is enough in such cases to have a "working" orthography for those relatively limited occasions when having a written version of an oral text is useful. For the purposes of achieving Sustainable Orality and Sustainable Identity, the elaboration of orthographic norms may, in fact, be counter-productive since orthographies unavoidably enshrine in a very visible way specific phonological and grammatical features of one variety of the language that has been chosen as "the standard." That choice may alienate users of other varieties and make written materials unacceptable or a source of division. An alternative is to use one or more working orthographies. These less elaborate, often ad hoc, and unstandardized, or only partially standardized working orthographies may be used for the purposes of language development work, such as for the elaboration of written scripts for radio or video productions. They serve an immediate practical purpose but are not intended for widespread public dissemination and so need to be less rigorously designed. They may not be standardized to any great degree. In contrast, "public" or "practical" standardized orthographies must be much more rigorous in regards to their linguistic fit, their pedagogical aptness, and their sociolinguistic acceptability. A weakness in any one of these areas can make the orthography more difficult to be accepted, to be learned, and used. In the end, along with the issue of acceptance, orthography problems may work against the goals of the language development program rather than promoting it by adding to the perception that the local language is defective or inferior. Another factor to be taken into account is that, often, "official" standardized orthographies require review and approval by a government agency before they can be used in government educational institutions. In situations where the policy environment is negative, gaining such approval may be difficult or impossible, severely limiting the possibility of widespread dissemination and working against the establishment of a consensus of acceptance of the standard.

Standardization involves more than accurately representing the sounds of a language. There are extremely important sociopolitical and pedagogical concerns that must also be considered and which may, in fact, be more significant than the accurate representation of the sound system.

Orthography development: More than sounds and symbols

Orthography development involves much more than the development of a set of symbols which represent the sounds of a language. There are many other factors which need to be considered. These include:

1. Government policies and restrictions
2. Internal linguistic (dialect) variation
3. Attitudes towards the languages in the language ecology
4. Script choices
5. Pedagogical considerations
6. Ease of transfer to literacy in other languages
7. Typographic and computer localization issues

It is often the case that these factors outweigh the linguistic considerations in orthography design. (Cahill 2014)

In addition to orthography development, the community may also wish to define other language-related, but often non-linguistic, features that are to be associated with a Function. A particular function may, for example, be most authentically communicated through certain speech styles or genres. These styles may be falling into disuse and will need to be recalled from the memories of elders or specialists and formally described so that they can be taught and learned. Some Functions may be accompanied by music or dance and these and other artistic forms will need to be revitalized if they have been waning, or promoted if they are not adequately known and mastered.

Oral standards

Implementing a standard is difficult, and an oral standard even more so, but it is not uncommon. In English, for instance, school teachers, parents, and peers regularly correct others' failure to use the standard pronouns in the objective or subjective cases in non-standard English sentences like these:

- "Me and him went to the store."
- "They gave the books to her and I."

The relentless but largely unsuccessful suppression of non-standard oral forms such as "ain't" exemplify the promotion of a standardized form of the language that is considered appropriate for specific functions. The instruction in and enforcement of norms of usage deemed to be socially desirable is also a type of standardization (e.g., grammar correction, non-sexist language).

In these efforts, societies generally call upon their institutions of education (formal or informal) to provide the means of learning the standard (Acquisition) and to enforce the standard (Differentiation). The tools employed for this in schools and other places of learning include everything from modeling of correct behavior, punishments and rewards for incorrect and correct usage respectively, pedagogical materials such as grammar texts, spelling books, reading primers, and dictionaries, to name just a sampling. In many well-developed languages where specific functions are both identified and well elaborated (see the next section), style manuals lay out in clear detail how the language is to be used (either orally or in writing) for the communication of the specified kinds of knowledge. Beyond these more formal means, however, the reinforcement of norms of use within the social networks that constitute a speech community (i.e., peer pressure) is often the most effective and powerful means of promoting and enforcing an oral standard.

Elaboration

If it doesn't already exist, the terminology needed to use a language for the transmission of a particular body of knowledge must be developed, and agreed upon. This process is often referred to as *elaboration*. Particularly when a new body of knowledge is being introduced within a language, establishing the terminology that is needed to talk about it is a foundational aspect of bringing the new function into existence. For every body of knowledge there is likely to be a set of "key terms," frequently used and highly nuanced terms, which express not only the scope of the knowledge but also the conceptual framework of the body of knowledge itself. For most bodies of internal knowledge, this terminology may already exist and be rich and expressive. However, if the language is at a weak level of vitality and language shift is in progress, much of the specialized terminology may have been lost or may be remembered only by the oldest members of the society. In such cases, the terminology needs to be recovered and disseminated. Where a body of external knowledge is being introduced into a community and is becoming increasingly associated with the local language (rather than being transmitted in the dominant language), it may be necessary for the community to come to a consensus on what terms will be used to communicate the key concepts of that external body of knowledge.

If elaboration is not proactively addressed by a community, users of the language will inevitably find a way to talk about whatever they feel they need to talk (or write) about. However, as local languages are pressured by dominant languages and as bodies of internal knowledge are increasingly encroached on and taken over by those dominant languages, the tendency will be for both external knowledge and an increasing number of bodies of internal knowledge to become associated with the dominant language. Important concepts, and the key terms that express them, may be lost as dominant language terms are borrowed and increase in frequency.

The challenge to community-based language developers is to achieve the proper balance between directed and managed language change on the one hand and spontaneous dynamic language change resulting from a community's responses to its ever-changing environment on the other. Too heavy a hand in managing change can be stifling or lack authenticity and may well be ignored by users of the language. Too little direction or a lack of conscious effort in language development may result in too little too late in terms of language maintenance and revitalization. Unsystematic, ad hoc elaboration, where each speaker invents their own terminological system and puts that out in the linguistic marketplace to see if there are any "buyers," assumes that the language has the luxury of time in which the forces of the linguistic market can play themselves out and a clear consensus can develop around one of the options. The risk associated with this approach is that it ignores the presence of the more powerful, better resourced, and encroaching dominant language competing in that same marketplace. Unless there is a concerted effort on behalf of one of the alternatives proposed in the local language, none of the local-language options is likely to be able to compete adequately against its stronger competitor(s). If the local-language options in that marketplace are further divided among competing proposals, their position in the "market" is weakened even more. The chances are that few or none of the local language terminological proposals will find acceptance and use. Where language development is being undertaken consciously, overtly, and proactively, with a community-based consensus already in place, it is likely to be far more viable. If that effort fails, it is likely that the identified body of knowledge will be more closely associated with the dominant language and the local language will be associated with one less function. This loss of functions or uses, as we described earlier, leads inevitably to a loss of users and ultimately to the demise of the language at worst or to a reduced level of use at best.

By reducing ambiguities and minimizing the need for circumlocutions, the elaboration of such terminology enables people to use the language more easily, more precisely, and more comfortably for the transmission of the body of knowledge. For the purposes of fostering language maintenance and sustainable use, utility and ease of use are highly desirable.

As with standardization, much has been written about how to go about the process of elaboration. There are decisions to be made regarding the preferred approach to elaboration (purism vs. borrowing vs. the creation of wholly new words, for example) and many of the same sociopolitical and pedagogical concerns apply in this process as in the elaboration of an orthography.

8.2.3 Acquisition planning

Once the decisions are made regarding which bodies of knowledge will be communicated in the language and in which modalities, and the corpus decisions (standardization, elaboration) are made and implemented, the means of acquiring the forms of the language associated with each of those functions must be developed and made accessible to the community. The standards have to be taught, usually in schools, and are subject to their being accepted and adopted by the wider community. These aspects of language planning have been called acquisition planning.

If the goal of language development is to preserve or restore Sustainable Identity, then the functions most closely associated with identity maintenance must be specified, standardized (if no standardized forms already exist), elaborated (where terms and linguistic structures may have gone out of use), and then made accessible and available to all those in the community who wish or need to use them. This may take the form of cultural heritage training in stories, songs, poems, dances, and crafts. Opportunities for exposure to the genres and styles associated with the heritage identity must be created and promoted.

In cases where language transmission is significantly disrupted and the goal is to achieve Sustainable Orality, this may take the form of language learning classes for adults or language nests for children. Not only must basic oral proficiency in the language be achieved, but also proficiency in the vocabulary and genres of each of the bodies of life-crucial knowledge must be considered and made accessible.

If the goal is to achieve Sustainable Literacy, then beginning reading and writing must be taught, literacy teachers must be trained, and literacy materials must be developed, produced, and distributed. The results of the standardization and elaboration processes for each identified body of knowledge must be made known and taught so that people have the ability to use the language for the desired functions.

Motivation: Internal advocacy

If a significant majority of the community has not achieved a consensus as to the desired future, or if prevailing language attitudes in the community are not supportive of the language development goals, an action plan must be developed aimed at developing an awareness of the potential benefits of sustainable language use (at whatever level) generally and for specific functions in particular. This process has been referred to at times as prestige planning and requires advocacy on behalf of the language and the functions with which it is associated. The goal of these efforts is to make as many community members as possible aware of the rewards and benefits that can be derived from using the language for the identified functions.

This advocacy requires significant effort. In most cases, a language community has to combat the prevailing perceptions that external knowledge and the dominant language associated with it are more useful and more valuable. There may be an equally strong perception that the heritage identity and its associated language are out-of-date, old-fashioned, and not very useful. That perception is strengthened when there are few (if any) functions closely associated with the local language.

An important component of this internal advocacy is the overt association of the local language with valued functions that reflect and re-enforce the heritage identity as well as demonstrating that valuable external knowledge can also be helpfully communicated via the local language. By associating language and identity with valued functions, the value, usefulness, and worth of the language associated with those functions is enhanced.

Environment: External advocacy

If the external policy environment is hostile to the sustainable use of the language, actions must be planned that will address policies that work against sustainable use. Policies that are tolerant or favorable towards the community's language development goals must be proposed and promoted. This may require that a community organize itself to address policy issues through the political processes that are available to it. If a community is too small or too isolated to be able to mount such an advocacy campaign on its own (or to draw attention to its pleas), the community may wish to join with other local communities to seek policy changes at higher and broader levels, perhaps regionally or nationally.

Methods and principles of external policy advocacy are not within the scope of this volume. However, advocacy need not be understood as being essentially adversarial. Just as internal advocacy (Motivation) may require a good deal of orientation, education, and perspective building in order to give community members the information they need to make well-informed decisions about language development, so too external advocacy may include a large investment in informing and educating policy makers regarding the dynamics of identity and language, the importance of achieving a sustainable level of use, and many of the topics that have been covered in this volume. A carefully constructed introduction to some of the concepts of the Sustainable Use Model may go a long way towards influencing policy makers to think about the situation of local languages more holistically and more equitably.

Differentiation

Deliberate focused attention on achieving functional compartmentalization is arguably the least attended to, least appreciated, and most difficult factor to address in most language development efforts. As described in chapter 7, we are calling this process Differentiation.

There are various reasons why there are difficulties in achieving an adequate level of differentiation. For one, many communities are simply unaware of the sociolinguistic situation that they find themselves in. They are either unaware of the language shift that is taking place or feel no sense of urgency about the declining use of the local language. Even in cases where there may be some awareness of what is happening, many users of local languages simply do not know what to do about it. Being below the level of conscious awareness for most speakers, it is often the case that language choice is neither thought about nor actively addressed. Making people aware of their unconscious behavior can be difficult.

Another reason why differentiation may not come into focus for language developers (especially community-level language workers) is that it may seem to be beyond their reach. The idea that community-wide linguistic behavior can or should be overtly modified is one that most self-deprecating language workers don't see as being within their sphere of influence.

A third reason why differentiation is not directly attended to in some cases is that the activities required to bring about a stable complementary distribution of functions are seen as being too prescriptive, too purist, or too ideological or unrealistic. Differentiation, especially in cases where language use is particularly weak, requires a level of militance and activism that many do not feel comfortable with. This is why we argue for as much participation as possible by community members in community-based language development. A local movement focused on sustainable use provides a much more supportive context for activism. While lone champions for language and culture may arise and have significant influence, their efforts require greater risk and sacrifice when they stand alone. The safety and greater effectiveness of greater numbers is an important consideration in achieving sustainable language use.

In spite of these obstacles, those who are promoting sustainable language use must become champions of the language and proactively insist on the use of the associated language(s) for the desired Functions if the sought-after sustainable level of language use is to be achieved. This prescriptive behavior may not always be comfortable for those who engage in it. However, as with the process of elaboration described above, a highly endangered language may not have the luxury of time to allow less direct and slower methods to influence community norms of use. The promotion of the idea that "for this Function we use this language" need not always be confrontational nor adversarial. Positive motivational campaigns (associated with enhancing the Motivation condition) can also serve to clarify when use of the local language is to be preferred. Differentiation can also be promoted by means of Acquisition activities in which not only the linguistic forms and structures of the language are taught and learned but also the norms of use of the language. By whatever means, the functional distribution of the languages within the language ecology of a speech community must be made as clear and as unambiguous as possible if sustainable use is to be achieved.

8.3 Going deeper

Much of the theoretical content of this chapter has already been dealt with in earlier chapters. See especially chapter 2 for a discussion of the distinction between internal knowledge and external knowledge. In chapter 3 we discussed language planning at some length. The concept of functional distribution of languages and the identification of domains of use by topic was introduced in chapter 4 and the idea of compartmentalization of those domains, dealt with in chapter 7 and here as Differentiation, was also discussed in the Going Deeper section of chapter 4.

8.3.1 Bodies of knowledge, functions, literacies

Many practitioners in education and community development have come to refer to bodies of knowledge that a community or individual possesses as Literacies. Literacies, so defined, are more than literacy skills, the ability to read and write. Paradoxically they may not even include the use of the technologies of reading and writing at all. This more technical usage is not as unusual as it might at first appear. In common parlance we have become accustomed to talking about "computer literacy" or "financial literacy" when referring to specific bodies of knowledge and the behaviors (and skills) associated with them. Thus, another way of talking about the transmission of life-crucial knowledge might be to talk about what Literacies a community wishes to develop and pass on to the next generation.

There can be oral Literacies, bodies of knowledge that are entirely transmitted through oral means. And increasingly, there are Literacies that involve the so-called "new media" which rely much less on the traditional coding and decoding of written text that has generally been associated with being literate. These

Literacies are transmitted digitally and involve both alphabetic and graphic representations of text that are subject to ad hoc and developing standards.

Using this terminology, an initial step in the language development process, then, is to identify the life-crucial Literacies that the community deems to be necessary, valuable, and useful for the maintenance of its identity and to meet its needs in day-to-day communication. Because of the potential for confusion between the traditional understanding of the term literacy and the expanded denotation of the term Literacies, we have chosen to continue to refer to bodies of knowledge and to associate those with the FAMED conditions by using the term *functions*. More extensive discussions of the notion of Literacies can be found in references such as: Street 2008; Hornberger 2002, 2003; Hornberger and Skilton-Sylvester 2000; and others.

8.3.2 Standardization, elaboration, prestige planning, and advocacy

We've already given a fairly extensive overview of the traditional approach to language planning in chapter 3. In this chapter we described some of the practical outworkings of status planning decisions. Our three components of language planning—status planning, corpus planning, and acquisition planning—follow Cooper 1989. Other introductory volumes to language planning in particular, each of which takes a somewhat different approach to the topic, include: Eastman 1983, Haarman 1990, and the previously cited Ricento 2006 introductory volume. Another overview of both language planning and language policy is Wright 2004.

Standardization and elaboration are but two labels that have been applied to corpus planning activities. The same or similar actions are described under various labels in earlier work on language planning and language development such as Haugen 1966, Ferguson 1968 Fishman 1973, and many others. The term prestige planning is used by Ager (2005), Chríost (2005) and Hult (2005) though the notion of prestige itself has a very extensive literature indeed: Dorian 1994, Kahane 1986, Ryan 1979, Sallabank 2005, and many others. It should not be forgotten that one of the defining features of a High language in Ferguson's (1959) seminal article on diglossia is prestige. Trudgill (1972) identified that while often speakers are most aware of overt prestige, covert prestige also can work powerfully to affect language use patterns.

A very helpful collection of papers and case studies on orthography development is Cahill and Rice 2014.

Advocacy both on behalf of and by local speech communities has not generally been considered part of the core set of activities of linguists and anthropologists until fairly recently. Even applied linguists have struggled to a certain degree with the tension between their scientific role as "disinterested observers" and analysts on the one hand and their desire to work positively to assist local communities and individuals on the other. Much of the literature on advocacy in the language policy arena has been produced by community developers and educators who, generally, focus on the educational benefits to be had through the use of local languages, particularly in early education. See especially Malone 2007 for a very useful "toolkit" for advocates of multilingual local–language–based education. Lewis and Trudell (2008) identify an adequate diversity policy as an essential element in fostering the cultivation of local languages in multilingual settings.

Alisjahbana (1974), Coulmas (1984), Davis (1994), Heath (1978), Litteral (1999), Paulston and Heidemann (2006) and many others have pointed out the significant role of language policy in achieving higher levels of literacy or improving general education levels in developing nations.

More recently, the importance of advocacy has been overtly recognized as part of the implementation of multilingual education programs in many local communities. A helpful reference in this regard is Kosonen, Young, and Malone 2006.

In addition to advocacy in support of education there is also a growing body of literature on the relationship of policy to human and language rights. Indeed, in many ways, advocacy for linguistic rights has become an area of major focus for language policy scholarship. Since much of language policy focuses primarily on official recognition of dominant languages within a nation-state, a growing number of scholars have turned their attention to the "negative space" in the policy environment, taking note of the failure of much language policy legislation to provide and protect a favorable environment for local languages.

The volume by Ricento (2006) provides a good overview of the issues and especially provides an orientation to the role of critical theory in shifting the perspective of language planning to take into account the inequalities that result from the top-down formation and implementation of policy. Of particular interest in that volume, and as a starting point in exploring the earlier and broader literature on the topic, see especially Tollefson 2006, May 2006, and Skutnabb-Kangas 2006. In addition there are numerous international and regional documents, such as the Universal Declaration of Linguistic Rights, that make assertions regarding linguistic rights intended to affect the formation of policy. A summary overview and evaluation of some of these can be found in Skutnabb-Kangas 2006.

8.3.3 Differentiation

Beyond the description of stable multilingualism as a situation where there is clear compartmentalization of functions, we have proposed that differentiation includes a prescriptive component, sometimes referred to as linguistic hygiene. This is often the activity of language academies, committees, and individual language champions to promote and enforce. Much of the published literature on this topic deals with issues of purism, (e.g., Hill and Hill 1980) or cases where champions of the language attempt to purge the local language of all borrowed terms and to wean users of the language away from code-switching. Cooper 1989, in his discussion of corpus planning and especially codification and modernization, is a good place to start for a general orientation to this topic.

9

Language Development: Achieving Sustainable Use

> Using the EGIDS and the FAMED conditions, the SUM provides guidelines for how local communities can implement focused sets of activities that will most effectively result in a sustainable level of language use.

9.1 Introduction

The basic concepts that we have covered to this point provide an outline of a process for formulating a language development strategy that a reflective practitioner of community-based language development can work through with a local speech community:

1. Identify the speech community that will be the focus of the language development work (chapter 3).
2. Identify, with the community, the bodies of life-crucial knowledge that they wish to maintain and develop (chapter 4).
3. Evaluate the current vitality status of all of the languages within the speech community using the EGIDS (chapter 5).
4. Establish what sustainable level of language use the community desires to achieve (chapter 6).
5. Assess with the community the FAMED conditions and identify those that need to be addressed in order to achieve the desired level of sustainable use (chapter 7).
6. Identify and plan general language development activities that will span all of the identified bodies of life-crucial knowledge (chapter 8).

7. Determine specific language development activities to be carried out to address the FAMED conditions that are inadequate for the desired sustainable level of language use for each identified body of knowledge (this chapter).

This process represents a logical sequence within the Sustainable Use Model and it is assumed that all of the components of the SUM, or as many as possible, will be carried out with the full participation and agency of the local speech community. In practice, all of these steps in the process are happening to one degree or another at the same time and are affecting each other as they progress. That dynamic interaction of local contexts, which are naturally changing over time, and the effects of language development interventions can take many forms.

- Initial decisions regarding the local communities that might profitably participate in a language development program together may change over time as the results of language-development activities indicate that either inclusion or exclusion of certain segments of the population is appropriate. The determination of the boundaries of the speech community in focus has a significant impact on the number of languages that are included in the community's linguistic repertoire. The vitality status of the languages within that language ecology also affects what kinds of decisions the community might make or wish to revise.

- As language development work progresses the speech community may recognize that their original decision regarding the desired sustainable level of local language use was either too ambitious or not ambitious enough.

- The sociolinguistic situation is changing even as it is being analyzed and described and language development interventions themselves are part of that changing context. The decisions made about which bodies of knowledge will be developed is affected by and in turn affects the choice of a desired level of sustainable use.

- The choice of the desired level, in turn, affects decisions regarding modality (oral, written, digital).

- Those decisions then significantly shape the number and nature of the activities that will be engaged in to bring about the desired alterations in the FAMED conditions.

The categories and the overall conceptual framework of the SUM provide a useful way to think about the complexities of community-based language development, but practitioners would do well to recognize that the model is not a straitjacket meant to confine and constrain responses. The model provides a way to conceptualize the sociolinguistic situation without necessarily prescribing specific solutions. The development of a plan and its implementation very much depend on the community's resolve, the resources available, and the contexts in which community planning is taking place.

We turn now to an overview of some of the principles that can help community members identify and select activities aimed at altering the status of a language on the EGIDS. The discussion that follows is organized in terms of "moving" a language from one level of the EGIDS to another. The goal, of course, is to achieve a sustainable level of language use but the SUM operates on the premise that movement on the scale must be incremental. It is not advisable to attempt to skip a level while moving up the scale. In general, we advise that language development efforts are most effective if small gains are achieved successfully rather than aiming for drastic change and failing to achieve it. Additionally, we are suggesting that the process of language development needs to be managed by the community itself and the aim of the SUM is to give local speech communities the conceptual tools they need in order to be able to manage their own language development. For each step, we describe the major components that language developers should focus on (described in terms of the FAMED conditions). Examples of activities that have been used are given in the Appendix.

Mainly due to space constraints, we primarily discuss how to achieve an upward movement on the EGIDS rather than the cases where downward movement might be desired. There aren't many documented instances where a local speech community has consciously decided to achieve a "soft landing" at a lower EGIDS level (e.g., aiming to land at EGIDS 9). In most cases, the downward slide happens, as we have described, unconsciously and as the result of external pressures and the loss of internal motivation. Much more experience is needed in the application of the model, in order to be able to describe how to assist a community in moving intentionally to a lower level of sustainable use.

The principles elaborated in the next sections are intended to help the community invest resources more efficiently, focusing on the priority areas of need for language development work and not expending resources on efforts that may not provide as much benefit. There are, of course, many variables to be considered. Not only must the language development practitioner be concerned about doing the "right" thing, but there must also be enough of that right thing applied over a long enough period of time, with the right recipients, and the right practitioners. That statement puts it far too simply but gives a hint of the complexities to be dealt with in implementing effective community-based language development.

As mentioned earlier, language development efforts which have regional or national recognition as their goal, that is, those aimed at moving a language to EGIDS levels stronger than EGIDS 4 as their primary objectives, are more often exercises in applied political science (lobbying, advocacy, legislation, policy formation) though those efforts can very profitably be informed and guided by the concepts embodied in the SUM. More importantly, efforts to establish a language as an officially recognized national or regional language go well beyond the scope of local community-based language development which is the primary focus of this volume. For those reasons, we will not directly address those higher, broader, and more ambitious levels of language development. We will instead start with the level of Sustainable Literacy (EGIDS 4) and consider each of the sustainable levels of use in turn.

9.2 Achieving Sustainable Literacy

As described in earlier chapters, Sustainable Literacy corresponds with EGIDS 4. If a community sets Sustainable Literacy as its goal, it must evaluate its current vitality status on the EGIDS and move incrementally up the scale. The discussion that follows describes what must happen for a community to move from Sustainable Orality (EGIDS 6a) to Sustainable Literacy (EGIDS 4).

9.2.1 Introducing written functions (from EGIDS 6a to EGIDS 5)

At EGIDS 6a adequate face-to-face use exists in every function for which such use is desired, but there is no written use. The primary goal of activities at this level is to move from purely face-to-face use of the local language to incipient literacy. The fundamental work needed to introduce literacy skills in a local language is well-documented and the general process of standardization and orthography development was described in chapter 8. This requires analysis of the language's sound system, the development of a practical orthography suitable for widespread use in the community (not only for linguists or other specialists) which involves consideration of sociolinguistic and pedagogical factors, the development of literacy acquisition materials (primers, beginning reading materials, and the like), the training of literacy teachers, the teaching of a significant number of readers, and ultimately (generally when moving to EGIDS 4) the development of a corps of authors and translators who will produce additional literature as desired and needed. In addition, in order to achieve Sustainable Literacy (at EGIDS 4), even at these early stages, the development of the community's capacity to maintain and enhance the production of those resources over the longer term must be addressed. This can be done either through efforts to gain government recognition and inclusion of the local language literacy in its approved curriculum or through the establishment of local community-based institutions that will sustain the transmission of literacy.

> **Introducing literacy: Getting to EGIDS 5**
>
> "Before a minority language community can start their education program, they need a writing system that:
>
> - is acceptable to the majority of the Mother Tongue (MT) speakers of the language;
> - is acceptable to the government;
> - represents the sounds of the language accurately;
> - is as easy as possible to learn
> - enables MT speakers to transfer between minority and majority languages; and
> - can be reproduced and printed easily." (Malone 2004:38)

Functions

When bringing a language community to EGIDS 5, the objective in terms of the Functions condition is to bring enough local language literature into existence for enough Functions to exemplify the value of literacy in the local language. As we've already described, the SUM proposes that local communities make conscious, well-informed decisions regarding which bodies of life-crucial knowledge they

9.2 Achieving Sustainable Literacy

wish to transmit to future generations in this way. In addition to determining in which language that knowledge will be transmitted, the community must also decide which of those bodies of knowledge will be transmitted only through face-to-face language use and which might be better transmitted in written form as well. Obviously, if the chosen language of knowledge transmission has never been written, and the community wishes to preserve their knowledge in a written form, a greater investment in development of the needed literacy technologies and in community capacity to institute and sustain literacy will be required. We have suggested that the general development of written usage of a local language is better served if all segments of the community reach a consensus about the nature of the written standard. Reaching that consensus is a significant part of that investment.

Local language literature can be very effective in teaching traditional cultural values and social norms, thus enhancing the prestige of the local identity and creating greater motivation for language use. Community members and outsiders can work together to develop materials that can be used in the local education system or in the home and community to disseminate this cultural knowledge. Community members can be enlisted in remembering and recording old proverbs, for example, which can then be consolidated into a booklet. Traditional stories can be recorded and transcribed and new stories can be authored and published.

The importance of this activity lies in the development of literature that can be used to re-assert traditional values that have been lost through assimilation to the dominant culture. In many cases, literacy is perceived to be a tool of the dominant culture but it can be just as powerfully used by a local community as a tool to maintain the community's distinct cultural identity.

Where a speech community has left its physical homeland or where the majority of the community lives outside of that area, internet websites can become a virtual homeland for the community. In these situations, the internet can be used to create a virtual global speech community. It can unite the people through forums devoted to issues affecting the community, or through online language classes, internet radio, and social networking sites, to name just a few possibilities.

An important aspect of creating such a virtual global community is communication through the medium of the common heritage language. This overtly includes the language used and displayed on the websites, and represents a specific example of how the community can participate in the explicit assignment of new functions to a heritage language.

Specific issues related to the expansion of functions for a language into this kind of new media have to do with how the language will be represented digitally. If the script is non-traditional or has never been implemented electronically, the speech community will need to develop an appropriate font or contact font designers and encoding specialists who can provide assistance in that regard.

Beyond encoding and font development, the provision of a computer operating system and software that is localized specifically for the local language may also contribute to the strengthening of the language. In order to do this, the language community needs to have advocates or leaders adept at effectively communicating their needs to technology providers. Once the provider agrees to make the operating systems in the minority language available, new terms may need to be coined for basic computing commands and related terminology so that a truly localized user interface can be developed.

Acquisition

In order to achieve EGIDS 5 (Developing) it is necessary that, in addition to full face-to-face language acquisition, literacy acquisition be made accessible through the development of adequate materials to support local language literacy instruction and some members of the community must be successfully using those materials to learn to read and write the language.

In general, the means of Acquisition are many and should be carefully selected to fit the context of the community. Some Acquisition activities require more resources and greater levels of expertise while others are simpler and easier to implement. Literacy acquisition requires a different set of resources than oral language acquisition. Factors such as the size of the community, its geographic distribution, and how concentrated or dispersed the population centers may be are very practical but significant factors to be considered. A set of Acquisition activities that work well and are easily implemented in a very small community may be exceedingly difficult and costly to implement when attempted in a large, widely scattered population.

Conversely, an Acquisition activity that is highly effective on a large scale may have more overhead in terms of costs, personnel, and expertise than a small community can muster. It is often better to start with smaller, easier, and simpler approaches and then augment those that show themselves to be effective and abandon those that do not produce the desired results. At the same time, when a local language is critically endangered, the community may not be able to take the time to start small, go slow, and see what works. A major intervention may seem more appropriate in such cases, but planners and implementers should monitor such interventions carefully and be prepared to make needed adjustments and reallocations of resources as they evaluate results.

Another important factor to consider is how learning and teaching is done within the community. We make reference to "the normal means of language acquisition" in our discussion of Acquisition in recognition that spoken languages are most often acquired primarily in the home and occasionally through community institutions, whereas signed languages are much more often acquired in Deaf schools or Deaf associations rather than in the home. Similarly, literacy skills are not so often learned first at home, but more often are acquired in a formal school setting. In some communities, learning of many skills and behaviors takes place much more through observation and emulation than through formal instruction. Traditional methods of knowledge transmission may be more effective or receive more acceptance than external, imported approaches to education. In some cases, these traditional methods of instruction may themselves be a part of the content of the identity restoration and preservation effort. When that is the case, "learning how to learn" may be one of the Acquisition objectives. On the other hand, outsider approaches to teaching and learning may be prestigious and so widely accepted that attempts to use alternative modes of education may not be credible or readily accepted.

Finally, acquisition planners may not only need to plan the content and means of acquisition but also may need to develop plans for the promotion and distribution of that content and those means. Developing awareness that the means of acquisition exist and are accessible may be as important as the creation of the acquisition resources themselves.

Many communities will need training and technical support in the skills needed for local language literature production and publication. This support allows for language development by people from within the speech community itself and can lead to an increase in the use of reading and writing for a wider range of bodies of knowledge. Initially this training may be offered to adults who, as they become increasingly confident and competent, become the authors and developers of other materials, including pedagogical materials for use by children. SIL's BLOOM software (http://bloomlibrary.org/landing) may also be of assistance in facilitating the production of a significant body of literature relatively quickly. Over the longer term, writing and authoring skills, in particular, can be built into early education curricula, laying a foundation for ongoing sustainable literacy.

Motivation

In order to achieve EGIDS 5 in terms of the Motivation condition, the community must achieve a state in which at least some members of the language community perceive the benefits of reading and writing their local language for the Functions that they have identified as being life-crucial.

One strategy by which this objective can be achieved has been called language empowerment. The goal of language empowerment is to foster and develop positive attitudes in local-language users towards their language. The strategy is twofold, attempting to increase the capacity of the language and the capabilities of its users. The aim is to engage in activities that will raise the status of the language while developing it in preparation for use in public domains, which generally accompanies the introduction of written use of the language.

Language empowerment activities might include explicit references to linguistic human rights, which will raise public awareness of them. Further, advocacy for appropriate legislation (addressing the Environment condition) may be needed. Language development itself has the potential to raise the status of the language. Adoption of second-language norms (addressing Differentiation), use in education (Acquisition), provision of incentives to users (Motivation), and expansion of domains of use (Functions) comprise the comprehensive scope of language empowerment.

One significant issue to be confronted is that, in most cases, literacy in the dominant language is already well-established (though not always easily accessible in many local communities) and has the potential to meet all of the FAMED conditions for Sustainable Literacy. In these situations, the dominant language has an already identified set of Functions and a means of Acquisition. There is clearly identifiable motivation with ample perceived benefits and there is a supportive policy environment. As a result, there are few reasons to engage in Differentiation activities on behalf of the local language. Efforts to increase the motivation for local language use in these settings becomes a significant concern for local language champions. Why should a community member invest in acquiring local language literacy skills—no matter how little effort that may require—when nearly all of a community's needs for knowledge transmission are perceived to be met through the dominant language?

In such situations, the goal is to identify written functions that community members perceive as being beneficial and to spread awareness and acceptance of those benefits through all possible means. We have described these functions as bodies of life-crucial knowledge and we emphasize again that the status decision to identify those functions and the corpus development activities that follow are a fundamental cornerstone of the process we are describing. Often, it is the Function itself that is so obviously useful and attractive that nothing more than awareness raising is needed. This by no means dismisses awareness raising as a trivial activity. Making any innovation widely known can be daunting, particularly in large or very fragmented or dispersed groups. The entire process requires great effort and strong resolve as the community attempts to push back against an encroaching dominant language.

Environment

In order for a language community to achieve EGIDS 5, official policy should either encourage the development of the language or have nothing to say about ethnolinguistic diversity or language development and thus raise no impediment to the written use of this language. On the other hand, if official policies are hostile toward the development of writing in the language, then the long-term prospects for establishing sustainable local language literacy within the community are not good.

In order to effectively advocate for an adequate language policy environment, the community needs to exist in a political environment that is amenable to change. When a group tries to foster new uses for a language that are contrary to current policies, it is imperative that there be an advocacy group that can take the case before the proper authorities to change the current state of policy or practice. This group can help focus the needs of the community, mobilize people, and hire appropriate legal counsel when necessary. Modifying the environment creates a "space" for local-language use. The other conditions in the FAMED framework provide the means by which the community can fill that space.

It is often necessary for communities to advocate for policies that are advantageous for their survival. The community often has specific goals in mind for new policies in contexts where domains of use have shifted to the dominant language and the group wishes to reclaim those domains. Direct advocacy of officials and policy makers by community members may be the most effective way to bring about the desired policy changes.

Merely changing legislation does not always result in changes in practice. An adequate environment for language development requires not only statutory improvements but adequate implementation of those changes as well. While changing legislation is important and creates the possibility of changed practice, the two must go hand in hand.

We have already mentioned that the external environment is not only determined by government or its agencies. Often there are other institutions, employers, religious groups, schools or universities, which apply their own language polices

Differentiation

In order to achieve EGIDS 5 (Developing) Differentiation activities must aim to help some members of the speech community use the local language in written form for particular functions routinely as part of their day-to-day life.

As described above, activities aimed at enhancing Differentiation should build on the motivation strategies aimed at increasing awareness within the speech community of the possibility of using the local language both orally and in writing for the selected functions. As awareness of the possibility of using the local language for written functions increases, additional differentiation activities may focus on increasing the use of the written materials in the local language as a "normal" practice and to decrease exclusive reliance on written materials in the dominant language. Ultimately, as local-language literacy begins to take root, clear norms of use should emerge and become more widely adopted within the speech community.

9.2.2 Establishing mass literacy (from EGIDS 5 to EGIDS 4)

In order to achieve Sustainable Literacy it is necessary that adequate local language literature exists in every domain for which local-language writing is desired and that awareness, proficiency, and motivation to make use of those resources be widespread. Thus, the focus of activities at this level is not only to expand the functional distribution of the language but, importantly at this stage, to build the capacity of the community to sustain the written use of the language. Many of the areas of activity that we have already described remain in focus, but now with the focus on strengthening, sustaining, and expanding the literate behaviors that are only incipient at EGIDS 5. This work focuses not so much on the language and its capacity to communicate life-crucial knowledge as on the infrastructures within the community that will support that knowledge transmission. This infrastructure development includes human resources such as authors and editors as well as material resources such as computer systems, printing and distribution systems, and an economic model that supports the needed literary production.

> **Getting to EGIDS 4: Building the capacity of the community**
>
> "If community members are to develop and expand a body of literature in their own language, they will need to develop infrastructures (people, methods, materials and other resources) for writing, illustrating, editing, testing, revising, producing, storing and distributing graded reading materials as their program expands. Equipping program leaders and the community in general to develop their own literature requires helping them build the vision and the capacity for each part of the process." (Malone 2004:87)

Functions

In order to achieve EGIDS 4 (Educational) in terms of Functions the community must move to the state where adequate local language literature exists in every domain for which local-language writing is desired (EGIDS 4). In order to achieve this level on the Functions scale, the capacity of the community to produce literature relevant to the bodies of life-crucial knowledge must be developed. This involves the elaboration of the terminology needed in order to be able to produce that literature as described in the previous chapter. It also may require that additional bodies of life-crucial knowledge be identified and that the appropriate written materials be developed. Beyond that, however, the capacity of the community to produce literature that transmits these bodies of life-crucial knowledge must be enhanced. In terms of Functions this might include the identification and training of "experts" who could become both the producers and the standard-setters for the relevant literature.

Acquisition

If EGIDS 4 (Educational) is to be achieved, the focus in regard to Acquisition is to bring the community to the state where local-language literacy is being taught by trained teachers under the auspices of at least one sustainable institution.

Multilingual Education (MLE) is one way in which relatively stable resourcing for the development of the needed literature for each identified body of life-crucial knowledge can be made accessible to the community. Formal MLE enables production and distribution of literary products, and it facilitates acquisition of literacy skills as well.

In addition to the direct benefits of MLE in terms of the acquisition of literacy skills, MLE programs have been clearly demonstrated to result in better educational outcomes for all students (both users of dominant and non-dominant languages) and to make education more accessible to communities which otherwise would be underserved educationally.

Because it is most often part of a government initiative, MLE frequently is better resourced and more scalable to larger, dispersed populations. As with many bureaucratized programs, however, MLE can be susceptible to poor implementation (failure to adequately include the community in the planning and implementation, for example), lapses in allocation of materials and personnel, and failure to adequately monitor and evaluate the results of the program.

Language and culture

"A language learned outside of its traditional cultural context will lack the ability to reflect traditional culture." (Hinton and Hale 2001:9)

Where members of the language community are already literate in a dominant language and have good access to technology, another strategy that can be employed to extend local-language literacy acquisition in the community is to use technology-mediated methods. Transferring reading skills from the dominant language to the local language could be facilitated by a self-paced application on a computer or cell phone. Learning to write in the language could be made possible by adding spelling and grammar checking modules to a word processing program that is already familiar. This requires not only specific software programs designed for these applications but, as described above, an overall computing environment that makes possible digital use of the language.

Motivation

The focus of Motivation activities when the goal is to establish mass literacy at EGIDS 4 (Educational) is partially the same as when literacy is being introduced at EGIDS 5 (Developing). Whereas initially a smaller segment of the population is made aware of the benefits of local-language literacy, at this stage the aim is to expand that awareness to the general population. In many cases this is a matter of "scaling up" the program activities to encompass the broader audience. In smaller, more concentrated communities this process may be relatively straightforward. Where there are large populations and where the population is dispersed or fragmented, expanding motivational activities will require a greater investment and more innovative approaches.

> **New genres**
>
> "Developing languages add more than just new vocabulary: they also add whole new genres of speech. A language that had previously not been written will, if used in schools, develop such genres as readers, essays, poems, or short stories. Oral book reports, plays, and formal debates may enter the language. Outside of school contexts, the language may be used for court proceedings or the writing of tribal or even national constitutions." (Hinton and Hale 2001:16)
>
> This expansion of the language for these new genres can motivate speakers of the language to become readers and writers of it as well.

A significant additional component of Motivation at this level may be the development of a "market" for the literary production of the community. A strong incentive for the ongoing production of written materials may be that it is economically beneficial to those who write, edit, print, and distribute literature. We make the assumption that life-crucial knowledge that the community itself has identified will be sought after by potential consumers. That assumption may not always hold true and proactive marketing (internal advocacy) may be necessary, at the very least, to make a broader segment of the community aware of the literature and of its value. Often, even highly-valued literature fails to be used because it is not easily available or is too costly. In order to achieve Sustainable Literacy an economic model that motivates writers to produce and consumers to buy local language literature must be developed.

Environment

If EGIDS 4 (Educational) is to be achieved in regards to the Environment condition, policy must call for the cultivation of this language and cultural identity, and the policy-making agencies must be putting this policy into practice by adopting a standardized orthography and using educational and other institutions to transmit local language literacy. Where a neutral policy environment may be adequate for informal or incipient literacy development at EGIDS 5 (Developing), Sustainable Literacy can only be fully achieved where the environment is more positive and supportive. Most often, this includes the development of an educational infrastructure that enables community members to acquire high levels of proficiency in local language literacy.

As with the previously described levels on the EGIDS, communities can engage in the needed language policy advocacy in a number of different ways. At this level, the focus turns to gaining the institutional support needed to make local language literacy widespread and institutionally supported.

In many cases, advocacy, and often language planning in general, is carried out by a language academy. This can take many forms. Sometimes, it is a grass-roots, voluntary organization created by users of the language. The members of such an academy may be well-educated young people, though more formal academies often are made up of older, well-recognized poets, writers, and linguists. In every case, language academy members take upon themselves—or are assigned—responsibility to implement language development strategies. Such an institution, however it is constituted, can be useful where the government has a positive official policy towards local languages but poor implementation of those policies. By indicating their dedication to language development, the group can influence the government to act on its stated policies or look for alternative means of implementation. Language academies and other language planning agencies can also contribute significantly to community motivation to use the language.

Differentiation

If EGIDS 4 (Educational) is to be achieved, the focus of language development activities in regards to Differentiation condition is to promote widely the norms of use as to when to use the local language orally and in writing versus when to use a more dominant language.

In some cases, members of a minority speech community are able to understand and use their own language orally, but have difficulty communicating through the written word. Though this is partly an issue that needs to be addressed through Acquisition activities aimed at increasing proficiency in literacy skills, the Differentiation condition can also be addressed as that training is offered. By framing the acquisition of written functions in terms of Differentiation—"We should write about this kind of knowledge in our language, and here is how we can do it"—both FAMED conditions can be addressed simultaneously.

If both government and the local community desire the development of the local language, the education system can be used to keep the dominant language from overwhelming the local language by promoting the use of the local language in the school setting and, in particular, for the specific bodies of knowledge which are to be transmitted in written form. Differentiated use of the languages in the local community's repertoire can be both taught and modeled in the school and other public settings.

9.3 Achieving Sustainable Orality

When the life-crucial knowledge of a community is no longer being fully transmitted in the local language, it is important for the community to re-establish that transmission. Almost always the loss of uses (Functions) is paralleled by a loss of users so both aspects of language shift need to be addressed. The highest priority is to return to full face-to-face transmission at EGIDS 6a.

9.3.1 Cultivating the language (from EGIDS 6b and 7 to EGIDS 6a)

At EGIDS 6b, oral use exists within every generation for the Functions for which oral use is desired. The problem is that while some children are acquiring and using the language, many are not. Thus, the focus is on expanding the number of users who are acquiring the language through the "normal" means (i.e., in the home or community) and who can thus access the already-established bodies of life-crucial knowledge in the local language. Expanding the number of proficient language users may require a significant investment in a variety of strategies, some of which we have already described and for which examples can be found in the Appendix. These strategies may need to address multiple generations with some focused on children, others targeting their parents, and still others designed to work with elderly language users or language "rememberers," often involving them as tutors or instructors, especially in cases where additional Functions are being cultivated. Note that the title of this section does not mean to imply that a community can move directly from EGIDS 7 to EGIDS 6a. The progression of language development necessarily requires that the community move over time from no intergenerational transmission at EGIDS 7 to partial transmission at EGIDS 6b before achieving full intergenerational transmission at EGIDS 6a.

Functions

At EGIDS 6b, the Functions in which the local language is used orally are usually already clearly defined though there is no reason that additional Functions could not be added to the repertoire along with those currently in use. It should also be kept in mind, as we have already pointed out, that users and uses go hand in hand. It is often the case that fewer uses (Functions) assigned to a language results in there being fewer users. The weakening of the functional associations to a local language may be the root cause of the loss of users. In such cases, focused attention must be given to identifying and assigning Functions to the local language.

Where functional assignments are intact, the focus at this level should be on augmenting the number of users of the language for those Functions (essentially an Acquisition activity). If the important work of identifying the bodies of life-crucial knowledge has not yet been done or is inadequate, language development practitioners will need to lay that groundwork as described in chapter 8.

One strategy that has been used to re-establish community-wide language use is to divide up the language development work among several different working groups within the community. Each group focuses on a particular aspect of the task of augmenting the number of users. One or more of these groups might focus on the identification and specification of particular bodies of knowledge while others might focus on other FAMED conditions. Examples of how these working groups might be formed are given in the Appendix. There are also other ways to organize the community for language development work, which are discussed at greater length in chapter 10.

Acquisition

At EGIDS 6b the language is used for face-to-face communication within all generations but only some of the childbearing generation are transmitting it to their children in the home or community. The Acquisition objective is to help the community achieve EGIDS 6a where there is full face-to-face transmission of the local language to all children via normal means. One important feature of the acquisition process at this level is that those who are learning the language are acquiring it as their first or primary language (L1). In situations where intergenerational transmission is more disrupted (see below) that may not be the case.

Parents may need to be encouraged to use the local language for childcare in particular. Whether for childcare or for any other function, younger adults may benefit from being connected with elders of the language group that still have full command of the language if they lack confidence in their own proficiency. The elders may be able to teach the younger parents the vocabulary and traditions associated with parenting or with other functions that need to be further developed.

In language areas where immersion preschools and schools are already in place, the schools can serve as a helpful re-enforcement for language acquisition in the home. The children are exposed to additional language use during the earliest stages of their language development. A secondary benefit is the exposure their parents gain to additional bodies of knowledge that they may not be familiar with in the language.

Motivation

At EGIDS 6b some members of the childbearing generation perceive the benefit of using their language orally for some Functions, but for others they find more benefit in shifting to a more dominant language. The primary objective in terms of Motivation is to help the community achieve EGIDS 6a where members of the language community perceive the economic, social, religious, and identificational benefits of using their language in face-to-face interactions for all of the bodies of life-crucial knowledge. Activities aimed at augmenting motivation will be aimed at increasing the prestige, perceived usefulness, and general acceptance of the language as we have already described. There are a number of ways in which this can be done including some of the activities we've already described above.

Local language media can supplement the dominant language media by focusing on local news from the minority language area. This creates a new form of the village square domain which is still dominated by the local language, even if the people use the dominant language in most other domains. It also allows for a sense of identity within the new world of media which may lead to an increased desire to be identified publicly with that language and ethnic group. The differentiation of local news from national or international news through this association with local language forms can work powerfully to enhance local-community prestige.

Environment

The goal of activities in reference to the Environment condition at this level is to make language policy more positive and affirming of local language use. Where achieving a clearly positive policy environment is not possible, the minimal goal is to arrive at a neutral policy that will allow for ongoing face-to-face use of the language.

As described earlier, advocacy with policy makers in this situation might consist of ongoing educational and informational exchanges to make policy makers aware of the desires of the community and their plans and activities in regards to their own language cultivation. In these interactions policy makers could be informed regarding the benefits of maintaining strong face-to-face use of local languages. A more favorable environment may be achieved through the collection and dissemination of culture and language information. This information can be used both to remind the speech community members of their identity (addressing the "internal environment," i.e., the Motivation condition), giving them a renewed sense of worth in that identity, and more specifically focused on the Environment condition, to raise broader awareness of the existence and aspirations of the local community among outsiders.

In addition to language policy changes themselves and the use of media campaigns to establish use of the local language as a normal fact of life, providing multiple opportunities for use can be an important strategy in rectifying the policy environment. The creation and administration of internet websites can be used in this way as well as for other aspects of language cultivation.

Alongside other major media outlets, websites can be used as a method of defining the identity of a speech community, while uniting geographically separated members of that community. The web is also an accessible location to store language data for use in cultivation as repositories for standard terminology for the various bodies of knowledge. Websites may also serve the needs of the speech community in areas where policy is either actively hostile or simply absent. Websites are often created by community outsiders or dispersed members who no longer live within the core language area. This has the potential to become a side project or hobby taken up by outsiders instead of an effective revitalization tool. However, websites can be used to bring attention to governments that are not actively promoting the cultivation of local languages. Often this is easier to accomplish from the outside. Websites that are visually stimulating and new media products of other types that are well-designed are more likely to attract young people and increase the prestige and validity of the language among members of that important age group.

In areas where the minority language group is experiencing extreme political suppression, it may not be possible for those who are located in the homeland itself to promote the maintenance or development of the local speech community's culture and language. Community insiders that have left their homeland to avoid government pressure may initiate advocacy efforts on behalf of their language from abroad.

In less extreme situations, organized advocacy groups can work through public consciousness-raising campaigns to influence politicians and policy makers. Often a starting point is to simply make the general public aware that local languages exist and that these languages have their own histories and cultural traditions. Frequently, members of the dominant society have no awareness that some of the lore around which their national identity has been constructed is actually drawn from earlier societies and cultures which are still represented by the local languages and cultures which remain. By making those connections apparent, the prestige of the local languages can be enhanced and an environment in which association with that heritage identity is not only acceptable but desirable can be fostered.

Where governmental controls on freedom of expression permit it, the speech community can be mobilized to bring the needs of the minority community to the attention of the government. These efforts can focus on language rights issues and often advocate for government policies that are favorable towards language maintenance and development. This approach can also be used to promote activism within the community itself towards language and culture preservation and local-language education.

Where local advocacy can be freely engaged in, of course, the community is in a much better position to engage with policy makers to present their case for a more favorable policy environment.

Differentiation

At EGIDS 6b some members of the childbearing generation use the local language for face-to-face Functions that were traditionally reserved for the local language, while others use a more dominant language for many of the same Functions. In these situations, there is no clear differentiation regarding which language should be used for which Function. Activities at this level would be directed towards helping the community achieve EGIDS 6a where members of the language community have a set of shared norms as to when to use the local language versus when to use a more dominant language for face-to-face interaction.

Within the SUM, the Functions and Differentiation conditions are closely related. If Functions are thought of as the "spaces" where the local language is to be used, then Differentiation can be thought of as the identification of the boundaries that separate those spaces. In multilingual communities where one language is more dominant, the tendency will be for that language to take over more and more of the available space. Differentiation focuses on maintaining the boundaries so that encroachment doesn't go too far. We believe it is important, given the differences in power and prestige, for a local language community to engage in this boundary maintenance wisely. There is nothing wrong with a dominant language being used for some bodies of knowledge. And attempts to exclude all use of the dominant language are almost certainly futile. If a local community has adequate cultural boundaries (and a sufficient number of community members are motivated to maintain them), the people can intentionally use the dominant language in domains that are more contact-intensive while simultaneously strengthening use of the minority language in more intimate domains. This strategy of promoting dominant language use for some Functions may seem counterintuitive if language revitalization is in focus, but can be very strategic where the local language and the dominant language are competing for the same functional space. When a local language is losing ground, it is important for cultivation efforts to be seen as successful in order to foster Motivation. Failed efforts to fend off the use of the dominant language are demotivating and work against the goals of language development generally.

One location that characteristically fosters contact with the dominant culture is the school. It is important for the purposes of language maintenance that the local community retain as much control of local schooling as possible. By conducting some classes in the dominant language accompanied by appropriate use of the local language for other Functions, the overall language development program can take into account the entire linguistic repertoire of the community in such a way as to foster sustainable language use by modeling face-to-face (and written) use of the languages for their respective functions. In this way, the local speech community protects the more intimate domains of home and community by creating a clear distinction between internal and external bodies of knowledge through how they handle the differentiation of these functions in the school domain. In some cases, the differentiation in language use may parallel the distinction between internal knowledge and external knowledge as described in chapter 2. In other cases, the community may prefer that some external knowledge be transmitted orally through the local language. The introduction of this knowledge through the local language will require translation and with that the kinds of corpus planning we described in chapter 8. This face-to-face use of the local language does not preclude the possibility of its being used for written functions as well, but here, with Sustainable Orality in view as the desired outcome, we focus primarily on the differentiation between the face-to-face uses of the languages in the school setting.

Having local input into education policy and its implementation in the schools is essential if this approach is taken. That input, which is relatively rare in most countries, gives the speech community the ability to become the gatekeeper for their children in how much exposure to the dominant culture and language they receive. In most cases, local communities have relatively little influence on the level of contact their children will have with the dominant society in the school setting, but to the extent possible, community involvement in overt knowledge management is precisely what the SUM encourages. Frequently, local communities deal with this by supplementing the formal schools with heritage schooling programs that take place on weekends or in the evening or at home. However it is done, it is important for the speech community to identify the domains that bring the most contact with the dominant culture and those domains which they wish to maintain closely linked to their heritage culture. In this way they can promote the use of the dominant language in those domains where it is appropriate while simultaneously re-enforcing local language use. This allows the adults to develop in their children an appreciation and awareness of what is part of their ethnic identity while at the same time enabling them to participate more globally.

9.3.2 Revitalizing the language (From EGIDS 8a, 8b to EGIDS 7)

While EGIDS 7 is an unsustainable level where the language is threatened, there is still at least one generation that retains proficiency in the language even if they are not passing it on to their children. As the EGIDS level weakens, the age of the youngest speaker grows progressively older. At EGIDS 7, re-acquisition of the language as a child's first or primary language via normal means (the home, the community) is still possible. However, the levels between EGIDS 8a and EGIDS 9 (i.e., EGIDS 8a, 8b) are levels where the local language will generally be acquired as a second language through some formal channel that is outside of the home and family setting. Endangered languages that are still in day-to-day use by some segment of the population generally fall within one of these levels where intergenerational transmission is disrupted but, at least potentially, not totally absent. Where all generations may be using the language but the bodies of knowledge or functions which they associate with the language are being reduced, the language is very likely at EGIDS 7 (Shifting) or EGIDS 6b (Threatened) and the activities described above are more appropriate. For dying languages, the process of moving upwards on the EGIDS is seen as being primarily one focused on the Acquisition condition with efforts directed at increasing the level of intergenerational transmission. However, there may also be a need to direct significant attention to the Functions condition in order to increase the opportunities for use of the language. The focus in that case would be on identifying bodies of knowledge that go beyond the internal knowledge most closely associated with sustaining the local identity (as at EGIDS 9) and which provide a useful niche for sustainable daily face-to-face use of the language for a broader range of topics.

Functions

At the EGIDS levels below EGIDS 6b (Threatened) there are entire generations that no longer have full oral use of the language. Though full Sustainable Orality (EGIDS 6a) should be the ultimate goal in most cases, the objective of the following activities is to enable the community to progressively move up the EGIDS scale until they are able to re-establish at least partial intergenerational transmission (EGIDS 6b) where adequate oral use exists for at least some bodies of life-crucial knowledge.

The goal is to identify the full range of bodies of life-crucial knowledge, engage in their development through the needed corpus planning activities as described in chapter 8, and then promote the oral use of the local language for those functions by addressing the other FAMED conditions (e.g., Acquisition or Motivation) as necessary. This goal will be achieved when at least some members of the childbearing generation are once again successfully transmitting the language to their children for the desired Functions.

As we have stated previously, when a language loses users and declines on the EGIDS scale, it also loses uses (functions). This may eventually result in the complete loss of functions, but along the way it involves partial loss as individual vocabulary items or semantic sets fall out of use and as particular traditional stories are forgotten and entire bodies of knowledge are either lost or shift to another language. If this has happened, one activity related to restoring functions of the language is to locate archived documentation and then study it to find forgotten words, phrases, and stories that can be reintroduced.

In many cases, this level of language development involves a local community and an outside agency such as a university or development organization working together. The agency provides expertise in language documentation, corpus development, and teacher training. The local community gives the agency the chance to diversify and to serve their community. Where the outside agency is a university, students are provided with opportunities for experiential learning in the field.

The agency can be involved by sending students and instructors on short and long term research assignments into the language area, creating a long term presence within the language community, developing relationships with the local group leaders, training teachers from the language area, promoting language maintenance activities, or all of the above. The involvement of an outside agency may also serve to enhance the prestige of the language, thus addressing the Motivation condition. Sometimes the outside agency can also serve the community by advocating for an improved policy environment.

Acquisition

At EGIDS levels below 6b, transmission of the language may be for identificational use (often in institutional as well as non-formal settings other than the home) or highly segmented by generation. The objective of acquisition activities should be to help the community achieve EGIDS 6b where the language is used orally by a significant number of members of all generations especially in the home setting.

In many communities, revitalization programs start by employing the older generations, who still maintain knowledge of the language, as teachers of the younger generations. These efforts are sometimes frustrated due to the assumption that those who know the language can also teach the language. Training users of the language to become effective educators with state-approved qualifications may be one way to avoid the frustration. Because of scarce resources, members of various local communities may wish to cooperate to create a partnership with universities or teacher training institutions in order to address the specific educational needs of their community members. Along with the facilitation of higher levels of education generally, such a cooperative program offers specific classes to train mother tongue teachers and offers those classes on a schedule that is helpful to those communities.

A less formal, but well-designed approach to involving elders in the process of revitalization is what has been called the master-apprentice approach. As the name indicates, an elder is identified and trained to be a mentor (master) in the language to a younger learner (apprentice). This apprenticeship provides a social context consistent, in many cases, with existing cultural structures whereby experts can transfer their skills and knowledge to other members of their community. This approach has been extensively developed and put into practice in Native American communities in the United States.

Other acquisition strategies might include formal classroom instruction augmented with day-to-day practice in the community, online language learning, informal learning groups, and the provision of ample safe and encouraging venues for use of the language at any level of proficiency. There are no limits to what a community might attempt. Each situation will require a unique response. The ultimate goal is to have speakers make the conscious decision to transmit the language to their children in the home. As an interim step in that direction, other means of language acquisition may be employed. Language developers can encourage this process of re-acquisition by promoting language use in the home as a supplement to the other venues where language instruction and learning are taking place.

Language immersion camps can be organized by the language community and advertised as a summer camp. The camps generally accommodate children, from kindergarten to high school, but could also be organized as family camps where multiple generations could be exposed to and given opportunity to use the language.

The focus of these acquisition activities is on creating a safe environment for participants to learn the language, while teaching it in a manner that encourages use outside of a classroom setting. Much of the formal learning time is spent learning cultural lore such as how to play traditional games, make traditional clothes, and how to create traditional crafts. Use of the dominant language is intentionally avoided so the students are fully immersed in the local language during class time as well as during recreational time.

When students attend a school that promotes local language use, that school can encourage and train parents, in addition to the students, to start using the language in their homes. Teachers can share with parents the benefits of using the language at home and offer helpful advice. If the parents need to learn the language themselves, it can be effective to offer night classes that the parents can attend with their children.

Language acquisition can also be facilitated using technology and, to the degree that it enhances the prestige of the language, technological innovation may also serve to re-enforce motivation.

Motivation

At EGIDS 7 the childbearing generation finds no practical benefit in speaking the language, though they may still find sentimental benefit in associating the language with their identity. In terms of addressing the Motivation condition, the major intermediate objective is to help the community achieve EGIDS 6b where at least some members of the childbearing generation perceive the benefit of using their language orally for some purposes, even though for other purposes they may find more benefit in using the dominant language. Since the primary motivation for language shift away from the local language is often economic, the most effective way to reverse that trend may be to link ongoing or renewed local language use with tangible economic benefits. This doesn't mean that non-economic motivations may not also be important. Community language developers need to examine the entire range of motivational factors and determine which might be the most effective ones to prioritize.

Motivating language use

"A person who knows a language will use it if he or she is spoken to in that language. It is the learners who must bring the native speakers back into language use. In a language revitalization program, perhaps the most important first step of second-language learning is to teach the learners things they can say to speakers. Simple greetings and conversational openers are important. This creates a tiny place where the language can be spoken again. This is just a first step, though; a native speaker cannot continue the conversation beyond the greeting if that is all the learner knows. It is very important for learners to practice everything they learn on speakers, both for the sake of learning and for the sake of encouraging the speakers to use the language." (Hinton 2001a:14)

Environment

In many cases users of languages that are at EGIDS 7 (or below) find themselves in a hostile policy environment. External policy may not favor ethnolinguistic diversity and may actively work to eliminate or suppress ethnic and linguistic diversity. Even when the policy is not so overtly hostile to local language use, it may simply ignore or fail to recognize the existence of diverse ethnic identities, making them invisible in terms of any appeal to the government or external agencies for assistance. When this is the case, advocacy is called for. A focus of these advocacy efforts may be on the human and linguistic rights recognized under international conventions and agreements of various types.

Human and linguistic rights

Numerous international agreements and instruments focus on the basic human rights of individuals. Awareness of these accords and their contents can be useful in developing a case for the recognition of a local language. Important fundamental topics considered by these instruments include the following:

- The International Bill of Human Rights
- The Rights of Indigenous Peoples
- The Rights of the Child
- Minority Rights
- The Rights of Migrant Workers
  (Adapted from Skutnabb-Kangas 2000:483)

Differentiation

At EGIDS 6b and below, intergenerational language transmission has been disrupted and bodies of knowledge are either coming to be associated with the dominant language or are being lost altogether. The primary objective in terms of Differentiation is to help the community achieve EGIDS 6b where at least some members of the childbearing generation are clearly aware of the Functions that have been reserved or are being reclaimed for the local language. As described above, Differentiation involves a certain amount of prescriptive "policing" of language use. In order for intergenerational language transmission to be effectively reinstituted in a community, parents must exercise a considerable amount of discipline within their homes in order to defend and promote the functional assignment of the languages that the community has agreed upon. Similarly, those adults who choose to reinstitute use of the language will need to make public demonstrations of that resolve.

9.3.3 Awakening the language (from EGIDS 9 to EGIDS 8b)

The primary focus for a community that wishes to move up the scale from EGIDS 9 is to identify the life-crucial bodies of knowledge that are important not only for the maintenance of a heritage identity but which also serve useful functions in daily life. In many cases, this will involve not only the identification and elaboration of Functions but also the revival of linguistic competence with phonological and syntactic proficiency being rediscovered and put back into use. Re-associating the local language with those bodies of knowledge and promoting the re-acquisition of the language for those functions constitute the priorities for action at this stage. In many cases, unlike the downward progression where children are the first to stop using the language and only elderly speakers remain, for revitalization and reintroduction of language use, it may be young adults or those of the childbearing generation, who are the first to reacquire some elements of the language. Though some revitalization projects begin with programs aimed at school age children or younger, generally some adults need to (re)learn the language sufficiently first so as to serve as the children's teachers and models.

Functions

The assignment of Functions and the corpus development that accompanies that has been described in general terms in chapter 8. Each community will want to identify and prioritize specific bodies of knowledge for this development work. Documentary sources, elders' memories, and any other available resources, including comparisons with still-living related languages can be called upon. In many situations, the language revitalization movement might benefit from a centralized and coordinated plan of action which recognizes that there are multiple components of the language development effort, as described by the "Working Group" strategy mentioned above. Each of these components requires somewhat different kinds of activities but the strategies guiding them should be coordinated and not be at odds with each other. In general, the desired level of Sustainable Use sets the general direction with specific strategies for development work being set for each of the identified bodies of life-crucial knowledge.

It is becoming increasingly common for the members of a speech community who have lost the use of their heritage language to ask linguists to help them understand the documentation that is in archives so that they can learn how to speak their language once again. Nevertheless, the descriptive materials that have traditionally been produced by linguists and archived (e.g., grammars, dictionaries, analyzed texts) fall far short of what is needed. Such documentation makes it possible to construct grammatically correct (though sometimes archaic) sentences, but gives little clue about how to use the language in actual situations. These more pragmatic aspects of language use have not generally been described in traditional descriptive materials. It is particularly important that authentic patterns of language use, that cannot be predicted by a grammar and dictionary alone, be identified and documented.

For instance, how would one express affection to a friend or to one's child or a spouse? How would one praise good behavior or scold bad behavior? How would one express gratitude or ask for a favor in different settings? Within this arena of functions of a language, it is particularly important to uncover the idiomatic speech formulas that cannot be learned from descriptions of grammatical structure or lists of lexical items.

The traditional focus of linguistic data gathering has often been on folklore, amassing a collection of text material that does not provide a well-rounded corpus for fostering present-day use of a language. For the purposes of language revitalization and in order to achieve adequate documentation of the language, it is best for language documentors to work with a range of local experts in specific bodies of knowledge (such as health, law, botany, etc.). This will uncover not only traditional knowledge and terminology, but also the neologisms and borrowings that demonstrate how the community is dealing with innovation from the outside.

Acquisition

As the Functions are recovered and assigned to a language, planning for how the language will be learned must also be done. Where terminology that was previously lost has been recovered or re-created, those terms need to be disseminated, taught, and learned. And, as described above, conventional ways of speaking must be recovered or developed for different, and often new, contexts in which the language is being used.

Adequate learning opportunities must be devised for specific audiences. Adults will learn differently and in different settings than children. In some communities women may learn in separate settings from men and the means of instruction may differ as well. Initially, this reintroduction of the language may be structured as an academic, highly formal learning program such as a college course where the local language is taught as a subject. As students in those courses gain proficiency they may begin to use the language in "real life" and in turn become instructors in the language for others. As the language is reintroduced and gains users, the development process would then consider how to expand uses (Functions) until all of the bodies of life-crucial knowledge identified by the community are restored to use in the language.

Motivation

At EGIDS 9, members of the language community have a strong sentimental attachment to their language, but are no longer able or motivated to speak it regularly. The objective in terms of the Motivation condition is to help the community achieve EGIDS 8b, 8a, and 7 in succession, where at least some members of each of the generations find a benefit in using the language for face-to-face communication.

As described above, activities aimed at developing motivation will focus on enhancing the prestige of the identity and the language associated with it. Initially these activities may not be focused directly on the language itself but would create an awareness of the benefits and positive attributes of the heritage identity that goes beyond being purely symbolic as at EGIDS 9 (Dormant). From there the focus would develop to demonstrate the usefulness of the local language for the Functions with which the community wishes to associate it.

Environment

In moving from EGIDS 9 to the next higher levels, the focus of activities for the Environment condition is to affect language policy so that it is at least neutral in regards to oral language use. Government policies should not prohibit full face-to-face use of the language. Where policies are inadequate, advocacy efforts are called for and local communities may find it advantageous to join with other local communities who are in the same position or to call upon international bodies to help them represent themselves before government authorities. Though in such situations interactions between the community and the relevant government authorities may be adversarial, it is often the case that a reasoned, evidence-based presentation of the value of linguistic diversity within a nation can help to raise awareness among policy makers and implementers. Interactions with these authorities can be bolstered significantly by also focusing on public awareness and prestige-building campaigns aimed at the wider population.

Differentiation

As the inventory of Functions for a language expands, so too must the efforts of language developers expand to emphasize the clear identification of the local language with those Functions. As described above, this may be achieved through public promotional campaigns which stress the importance of using the local language. These efforts often address Motivation most directly as they stress the value of using the local language and make community members aware of the benefits that can be had through language maintenance and daily use. Such publicity is helpful, but probably is not sufficient for the purposes of Differentiation without a more targeted effort in the moment of language use to point out to community members that "we can talk about this topic in our language." Continuous modeling of the desired communicative behavior by those who are able to do so is required. These opportunities for Differentiation can occur in the home and the community, where the language needs to be used appropriately and consistently.

Where the identified Functions are more public or formal, failure to use the language when it could be used must be remarked on and, again, those who are able to do so should model the desired behavior for others. As with the introduction of any linguistic innovation, repeated, consistent use over a long period of time will enhance the likelihood of adoption and spread of the new behavior. If well-known and respected persons can be recruited to participate in the effort, all the better.

9.4 Achieving Sustainable Identity

Sustainable Identity at EGIDS 9 (Dormant) is most frequently arrived at through the natural processes of language shift as the repertoire of Functions associated with the local languages is reduced to those that are largely ceremonial and traditional. More and more bodies of knowledge gradually become associated with the dominant language until the point is reached where the only functions remaining for the local language are symbolic and ceremonial. In some cases, Sustainable Identity can also be arrived at by design if the community feels that it is important to halt the language shift process before the language becomes totally extinct. In these cases, the community may set Sustainable Identity as their goal. This means that a very limited number of specifically identified Functions will be associated with the heritage language and the focus of language development for that community will be the preservation of those Functions. In contrast to these preventative efforts in response to the continuing process of language loss, achieving Sustainable Identity may be the goal of a concerted language revitalization effort where an "extinct" language is being brought back into at least limited use. Where achieving stronger levels of use may be viewed as too ambitious or too costly, a community may opt to aim for Sustainable Identity as a first (or perhaps only) waypoint in the proactive recovery of a language that has gone completely out of use. This section discusses both of these situations.

9.4.1 Landing at Sustainable Identity (from EGIDS 8b to EGIDS 9)

The primary objective of language development activities for a language that is losing its last speakers is to halt the decline at a level where at least the community identity can be preserved. In some cases, a community arrives at EGIDS 9 and maintains its identity for many years without significant intentional efforts. In other cases, the slide down the EGIDS scale will continue unabated if nothing is done to bring language and identity loss to a halt.

Before a language has fallen completely silent, documentation activities should be part of a planned effort to preserve a historical record of bodies of knowledge which are going out of use. Such documentation, though urgently needed, may not actually serve to maintain ongoing use of all of that knowledge nor the on-going use of the language, but certain bodies of knowledge may be preserved as markers of the heritage identity and the vocabulary and linguistic structures associated with those markers may remain in use solely for the purpose of identity maintenance. In addition, thorough language documentation may provide a sustainable record for possible future use by scholars and by the community itself.

Such efforts contribute to a "soft landing" of the language at Sustainable Identity (EGIDS 9) and build a foundation for any future efforts to reawaken the language.

Functions

When the community intentionally opts to move *down* the EGIDS scale and achieve a "soft landing" at EGIDS 9, they will work to preserve their identity while giving up the language as a means of day-to-day communication. The only use they will make of their language is symbolic and ceremonial, using it as a marker of identity with only very limited communicative functionality. The focus of their efforts in regards to Functions will be to identify those bodies of knowledge that best serve them as markers of their identity. As described earlier, this will often consist of traditional knowledge, lore, stories, songs, poems, and a limited set of vocabulary items, phrases, and "frozen" utterances such as greetings.

Acquisition

While the Functions assigned to a language at this stage are relatively few, because intergenerational transmission has been disrupted, it is important that the community develop the means by which enough of the language can be learned for use in transmitting the retained bodies of knowledge. In most cases, these Acquisition activities take place outside of the home in formal language learning settings. Nevertheless, parents may have a significant role in passing on the knowledge of the language for those limited Functions and should be encouraged to do so.

Motivation

Most of the efforts at increasing Motivation at this stage will be focused on increasing positive attitudes towards the identity and only secondarily on the language associated with that identity. The focus will largely be on making the perceived benefits of maintaining one's local identity widely known and accepted. Even limited use of the local language as a marker of that positively-evaluated identity becomes one way in which community members can demonstrate their pride in their heritage.

Environment

It may be the case that official policies are or have been hostile toward ethnolinguistic diversity resulting in the elimination or suppression of the local language. Even if policy has not been overtly hostile to language maintenance, non-committal policies or policies of neglect, especially where other FAMED conditions are weak, may also have negative results. The objective at this level is to bring about a change in official policy so that it, at least, affirms the maintenance of the local identity and even minimal oral use of the language.

A fundamental first step in affecting policy may involve nothing more than getting the language "on the radar" by requesting that it be assigned an ISO 639-3 code if one does not already exist (http://www.sil.org/iso639-3). The assignment of a code under this standard may provide a scientific basis for arguing for the

9.4 Achieving Sustainable Identity

rights of the speakers to use their language in a variety of functions. A speech community may need to solicit the assistance of a linguist in order to make a well-founded argument for this recognition.

Where speakers of the language have been conditioned, through oppressive government policies, not to use their language in public domains, the fear of such public use must be overcome and use of the language, at least for identity maintenance, must come to be seen as normal and acceptable. There is a strong motivational component to these activities since along with de jure policy there may also exist a de facto set of language practices that will be very difficult to alter. The focus here is on addressing official (de jure) policy. However, a public relations campaign using the power of media and marketing techniques may also be employed to address Motivation as described above.

Differentiation

For identity maintenance, an important aspect of Differentiation is to define clear cases where public use of the language, albeit only for ceremonial or symbolic purposes, is to be expected. In some locations, the village square was where at one time local news and events were communicated person-to-person. Modern technologies have rapidly functionally replaced the village square, but the new media, such as mobile telephones, text messaging, and the worldwide web, can also be identified as venues for local-language use and sharing of identity-re-enforcing knowledge. Even though mass media is increasingly an avenue for the dominant culture to facilitate the assimilation of local communities, it can also be used to maintain links between the core speech community and those that have moved away as well as to build solidarity within the local community itself. Because television, radio, newspapers, and new media allow for anonymity, they can also provide a way for the language and identity to be promoted without requiring any individual to place his or her social standing at risk by using a non-prestigious language publicly.

Whether a community has a functional equivalent of the village square or not, the point of Differentiation is to mark and re-enforce the boundaries between local and dominant language use. Without sufficient differentiation efforts, the tendency will be for the dominant language to expand its range of use and gradually replace the local language in all Functions.

9.4.2 Reclaiming the language of identity (from EGIDS 10 to EGIDS 9)

There are some cases where a community decides to re-identify with a now-extinct language. These situations are distinguished from those we've just described by the fact that not even the symbolic and ceremonial language use associated with identity maintenance is intact. Such a reclamation project depends crucially on a credible champion (an individual, group of individuals, or an agency) to promote the revitalization of the language, and the existence of enough documentation to preserve knowledge of the language and to constitute what we have termed Sustainable History.

The role of language revitalization activists is significant in restoring the association of the language with the identity as these champions of the language make the community aware of the language and of the possibility of its return to use. They provide the energy and direction for the revitalization effort and can be most effective if their influence is respected and has broad acceptance. Much of the activity of the language revitalization activists will very likely be focused on motivation primarily, but the other FAMED conditions will also need to be addressed appropriately.

At the beginning of this kind of endeavor, a major amount of the effort may be invested in locating and gaining access to the existing documentation. Older documentation may need to be retranscribed or updated from an obsolete technology. Sometimes the language of description used in the documentation may be antiquated or require the services of a translator. If an older script is used, a paleographer may be needed to render the documentation in a more readable form.

It is valuable for as many community members as possible to be involved in the work of finding and connecting once again with the historical documents that have records of their heritage language. By being so engaged, the people may be reminded of the value of their heritage identity and perhaps also become aware of the unique features and nuances of their forgotten language. This may serve to ignite an even greater desire to revive the language by restoring forgotten forms and functions. To restore the language to its former role as a language of everyday communication is an extremely ambitious goal and is probably not a realistic one in most cases. However, a more practical first step in the revitalization process is to reclaim the heritage language as a language of identity for the ethnic community. Once that is achieved additional planning can focus on re-establishing the means of production (Acquisition) and the means of reproduction (intergenerational transmission).

Functions

If adequate documentation is not immediately accessible, language development efforts focused on the Functions scale would be primarily invested in searching archives and other repositories to see what kinds of documentation can be found. Sometimes there are descriptions of the language embedded in diaries of travelers or explorers. The records kept by early missionaries or others who had sustained contact with the community in the past often are helpful documentary resources. Though these ad hoc records may not contain the systematic thorough sampling of the language that current documentary linguists would prefer, they can be used as a start to at least improve the documentary status of the language (and thereby achieve Sustainable History).

With considerable additional effort, sometimes involving wholesale reconstitution of language forms and structures, it may also be possible to re-establish Sustainable Identity (EGIDS 9). Using the available documentary resources, the primary objective of language development at this stage should be to help the community reconstruct, at least partially, some bodies of knowledge in order to achieve enough oral use of the language to be able to symbolize their identity at EGIDS 9 (Sustainable Identity). The functions assigned to the language would largely be related to the transmission of cultural heritage knowledge. The life-crucial knowledge that would be in focus at this level of language development would consist of highly symbolic heritage knowledge such as greetings, names, and formulaic utterances that could be learned easily. Once Sustainable Identity is achieved, further revitalization might then be possible.

In most cases this will involve bringing back into use local language greetings, vocabulary for common items in the community, and restoring the use of animal names, color terms, numbers and counting systems, and any other identity-linked language content such as stories, poems, songs, and the like. In language groups that use geographical place names to represent significant cultural, sociological, and subsistence information, language developers can work to preserve those names to help maintain the community's identity and association with its history. At EGIDS 10, such local place names may no longer be in wide use, may have been significantly modified from their original forms, or may not be understood to have any significance. An effective way to elicit place names is through storying with elders of the speech community that have maintained the cultural and linguistic knowledge necessary to interpret the place names. In many cases the older geographic place names may only be discoverable from written documentation.

There are many different ways in which this re-establishment of functions related to identity can be achieved. Sometimes only a small group, often only one person, may champion the discovery process at the start. If the SUM process is followed, however, the decision to initiate rediscovery and reclamation of a language should be the result of a community consensus and should elicit the involvement of as many community members as possible. Each community will organize itself for this work in their own way. Sometimes it may be by forming a language committee or by organizing into working groups. In other cases, the community may have the resources to hire or collaborate with external agencies, with a professional linguist or anthropologist, or with other sources of assistance. For the longer term, it is advantageous to develop from within their own community the needed capacity to carry on the language development work.

Acquisition

At EGIDS 10 there is no ongoing transmission of the language. The objective of the language development work in terms of the Acquisition scale at this level is to help the community achieve EGIDS 9 where the transmission of the language is restored for identificational use (most often in public or institutional ceremonial settings rather than the home). Most often, this is done through a focus on identity maintenance or preservation and through the rediscovery and celebration of heritage values and lore. Much of this activity is necessarily backward looking, reminding community members of their past and preserving what the community perceives as being life-crucial knowledge which preserves and fosters community cohesiveness.

For the purposes of achieving EGIDS 9, the knowledge content of the acquisition planning is likely going to be relatively restricted. The goal is not to achieve high proficiency in day-to-day use of the language but rather, to achieve only enough proficiency in the language so as to be able to transmit the limited content of the identity-related bodies of knowledge. If the language is at EGIDS 10 there will be no remaining fluent speakers. The content to be learned will need to be recovered from documentary sources or perhaps will be partially remembered by a few, usually older, community members. Language proficiency goals will largely center around the acquisition of the needed vocabulary and linguistic structures for the life-crucial bodies of knowledge. Generally, grammar skills will be limited to those needed for those Functions and most learners of the language will not be able to use the language at a level where they can produce very much, if any, original speech. Much of the teaching and learning methodology may concentrate on memorization of "frozen" text material along with any associated performance skills (song, dance, gestures, etc.).

Sustainable Identity need not be entirely rooted in the past, however. Members of the community can opt to construct a contemporary identity built on their heritage internal knowledge but incorporating and assimilating external knowledge by clothing it in their language and imbuing it with their own cultural features. Sustainable Identity should not be conceived of as static or frozen in a revered past. A truly sustainable community identity needs to be dynamic and alive, able to interact with and to cope with the changing world in which it finds itself. This means that in some cases members of a community might opt to transmit some internal bodies of knowledge by means of a language other than their heritage language. Identity construction of this type should not be seen as inauthentic or fabricated. As long as there is a general consensus within the community and the community itself is the agent behind the identity construction, any efforts to transmit life-crucial knowledge can only be seen as useful. Even when the language of knowledge transmission is a widely used and well-developed one, some work will be needed to find the best translation equivalents for the heritage knowledge content. When this "other language transmission" of life-crucial knowledge is opted for, Acquisition activities may include facilitating proficiency in the dominant language for those functions.

Motivation

At EGIDS 10 descendants of the language community have abandoned all use of their heritage language and do not regret it. The objective of the activities at this level is to help the community perceive the benefits of achieving EGIDS 9 (Sustainable Identity) where members of the language community once again have a strong sentimental attachment to their heritage language, even though they are no longer able to speak it. Building motivation for even minimal restoration of language use will require efforts to re-establish the prestige of the language in the local speech community. Many of the activities aimed at Acquisition may simultaneously contribute to the fostering of Motivation and the perception of the usefulness and value of the language may also be closely linked to the "uses" (i.e., Functions) assigned to the language. In any situation where Motivation isn't adequate for the desired level of sustainable use, specific activities aimed at increasing awareness of the benefits of using the language for the desired Functions will be called for.

Motivational activities may be most needed in situations where the local language and its speakers have been belittled to the point of eradicating any desire to use or learn the language. Where there is a history of abuse (physical, emotional, verbal) aimed at a language community, the people may no longer feel safe speaking their language. An attempt to revitalize the language will not succeed if the people continue to equate shame and embarrassment with the language and culture.

Initially, the focus may need to be on cultural features other than the language (i.e., rebuilding an appreciation for the heritage identity through costume, food, song, dance, or ceremony). A program that requires minimal commitment and promotes positive feedback in a safe environment enables participants to regain a sense of sentimental attachment to their identity and, eventually, to its associated language. Learning dances and songs is much easier than going through the rigors of language learning and the people are able to see tangible manifestations of their heritage culture.

Environment

Once a language is extinct, the policy environment may not be a significant issue. It may have been a hostile environment that caused the extinction, but now that the aim of the hostile policy has been achieved, the hostility may have been forgotten. In fact, there might even be remorse. If this is so, the external environment could become an ally for funding to support reclamation of the heritage language and in some small measure right some of the wrongs of the past. The focus of activities to address the Environment condition if it is now neutral or positive, might be on identifying and gathering the resources needed to fund the revitalization effort.

Where the Environment remains inadequate for any kind of language development work, any and all of the activities described above aimed at advocating for a more favorable Environment may be called for.

Differentiation

At EGIDS 10, descendants of the language community use the dominant language for all Functions (oral and written). The Differentiation objective at this level is to help these community members to achieve EGIDS 9 where the local language use is being reintroduced for identificational purposes. At that level on the EGIDS there will be clearly identifiable occasions when use of the local language is appropriate and the goal will be to see the majority of community members approving of and practicing those norms of use.

As described earlier on, the Functions condition deals with the association of a language with a body of knowledge. The Differentiation condition focuses on the dissemination, implementation, and promotion of that functional assignment. Differentiation can be carried out in a variety of ways. It is the conscious maintenance of the language through overt actions aimed at setting the boundaries between local-language Functions and dominant-language Functions.

9.5 Going deeper

This chapter summarizes the strategies and activities that constitute the focused efforts needed to move a language from one level on the EGIDS to another. Brief descriptions of specific activities categorized using EGIDS and FAMED scales are provided in the Appendix. That list is far from complete and only suggests some among a wide range of possible activities that could be engaged in. The organization of the Appendix parallels the outline of this chapter.

Since this chapter is primarily focused on the more practical aspects of activities aimed at addressing the FAMED conditions at different levels on the EGIDS, there is not a great deal of new theoretical information presented here. The paired notions of language production (Acquisition) and reproduction (intergenerational transmission) are borrowed from Riagáin 2001.

The general process of revitalization and language development proposed by the Sustainable Use Model and the stepwise description of movement up (or down) the EGIDS can be compared with the 9 steps of language revitalization proposed by Hinton (2001a:6), for example. Other practical approaches to language revitalization and language maintenance may propose somewhat different but generally parallel processes.

A reader who wishes to explore in greater depth any of the activities or strategies described is directed to the bibliographic citations associated with the examples in the Appendix. Those are drawn from journals, conference proceedings volumes, and personal communications, which collectively serve as a rich resource for those who are strategizing about what can be done in a particular setting. The Appendix is only a first step towards assembling a fuller catalog of what has been attempted and the outcomes of those attempts.

10

Organizing for Community-Based Language Development

> A language development program is a means to plan and carry out activities in a coordinated manner which will enable the community to attain the results they desire.

10.1 Introduction

The long-term goal for community-based language development in local speech communities is that the members of a speech community are better equipped to maintain their identity while at the same time participating fully in the changing world in which they live. Their heritage language plays an important role as a component of their overall linguistic repertoire and as one means of knowledge transmission. The Sustainable Use Model describes a framework for thinking about how to accomplish knowledge transmission and is particularly focused on the role of the local language as a tool for that transmission. Some strategies aimed at moving a local language from one EGIDS level to another were described in chapter 9 and examples of activities related to those strategies can be found in the Appendix. In addition, community-based language development programs need to be organized or structured in such a way as to bring about the changes which the community desires. There are, of course, many ways in which to organize language development efforts. No single organizational scheme will fit all situations. There are, however, some general principles that have been tried and which have been shown to be effective. In this chapter, we summarize those principles and offer some suggestions to organizers of community-based language development programs.

Language development programs begin with the speech community and include other stakeholders who have an interest or influence on the language development the community wants to undertake. The SUM provides both a theory and a methodology for members of a speech community and those stakeholders to become more aware of their language and knowledge transmission choices. The EGIDS helps them evaluate the current status of the languages in their linguistic repertoire and the FAMED conditions help them identify specific contextual issues that need to be addressed in order to reach a sustainable level on the EGIDS. Based on that analysis, the community can then make better informed, conscious decisions about the future of their local language and how they want to manage their life-crucial knowledge. With these decisions made, the task becomes one of identifying and engaging in activities which will bring about the desired results.

In the sections that follow, we discuss general planning and organizational issues related to the implementation of a community-based language development plan.

10.2 Planning a community-based language development program

A language development program is a means to plan and carry out activities in a coordinated manner which will enable the community to attain the results they desire. Unplanned, random activities, though carried out enthusiastically and energetically, are not in themselves sufficient to achieve sustainable language use. In some cases, such uncoordinated activity may actually work against the goals of the community, waste community resources needlessly, and further demotivate the community in regards to its language and identity.

10.2.1 Language users and speech community

Among the speakers of a local language there is generally more than one speech community. In chapter 3 a speech community is defined as a group of people who have a shared linguistic repertoire (whether varieties of a single language or multiple languages) and have shared norms that guide the use of that repertoire. In general, throughout this volume, we have discussed the application of the SUM to a single speech community, identifying the speech community as the most appropriate focus for setting the goals of a language development program. However, the general orientation of language development is on a specific language within a speech community's linguistic repertoire. That language may be part of the linguistic repertoire of multiple speech communities and in each of those settings it may have different functions and be at a different level on the EGIDS. Ideally, planning for language development should take into account the status of the language in all of the speech communities where it is present. This is particularly true for such language development aspects as codification (orthography development) and modernization (development of new terminology) which are usually most helpfully applied to the language as a whole, wherever it is in use, as described in chapter 8.

A language which is endangered in one speech community may be at a much stronger level on the EGIDS in another. The resources, prestige, and strength of the language in those stronger settings can be drawn upon in the settings where the language is not as strong. When development for a specific local language is done without reference to the other speech communities in which the language is used, there is a risk of separate orthographies being created and divergent terminology being developed which will limit or hinder the use of materials by all users of the local language. Sometimes there are good reasons why different development strategies might best be implemented in different locations, but in general, following divergent development paths unnecessarily duplicates efforts and wastes resources.

Most often, different development planning is motivated by significantly different FAMED conditions and sociolinguistic characteristics of speech communities that are located in different countries or that are widely separated by geographic or cultural barriers. For example, where the national language of one country is not the same as that of another country where the local language is also used, there may be good reason to use different scripts and to accommodate loan words from the different dominant languages. Increasingly, enclaves of members of language communities are dispersed globally and each of those local populations finds itself in a unique speech community configuration where language development goals and objectives need to be adjusted to account for the local dynamics.

Within a single country, there are two frequently occurring configurations that result in separate speech communities:

- Speakers who live in the traditional homeland, often a rural area, and speakers who live outside of their traditional area, particularly in urban centers.

- Speakers who have different religious, social, or occupational social network affiliations.

- Whether the distinct speech communities are within a single country, cross national borders, or are globally dispersed, the similarities and differences among them must be considered in attempting to coordinate language development for the local languages that they share.

10.2.2 Coordinating language development in multiple speech communities with the same local language

Planning a language development endeavor in speech communities that share the same local language must occur at two levels:

- Develop a proposed language development program plan for each identified speech community, and

- Coordinate and make adjustments if needed to the planned activities for each program to harmonize the language development as much as possible. This will increase efficiency and the probable sustainability of the minority language use for each community.

For example, a minority language at EGIDS 6a might be in use in two speech communities, one consisting of the rural population and the other made of an urban population. Using the SUM, both speech communities may decide they want to attain Sustainable Literacy (EGIDS 4) for the local language though perhaps the two communities may decide to assign different functions to the language in their respective contexts. To attain this level, a written form of the language will need to be developed. Since this activity can serve all of the speech communities where the same desired level of sustainable use is an identified goal, it would be best that the written form be developed jointly so as to serve all of the users of the language. Materials for the different functions might also be developed jointly where the functions are shared by both speech communities. Where the functions differ, separate materials may need to be created. In every case, the need for and the ease of facilitating the needed collaboration must also be taken into account. Great distances, difficulty in transportation or communication, hostility between the two communities, and other practical factors may all influence the ability of the language development programs to coordinate with each other.

In order for this kind of collaboration to take place, users of the local language from all of the speech communities must be connected by some means. While networking among local language users is increasing greatly as a result of globalization, at times it may be an appropriate role for an outsider to act as an intermediary between the different speech communities. Outside agencies may serve a valuable role in facilitating opportunities for local language users to interact with each other. These sorts of contacts contribute to the awareness and perspective of the local-language community as they see what others have done, learn about what can be done and at what cost, and come to understand better the nature of the task they are choosing to take on.

One language, multiple speech communities

The Nawda people, speakers of the Nawdm [nmz] language, belong to several different speech communities. Their traditional homeland is in northern Togo. During the past 100 years, many of them migrated to other regions of Togo and to the neighboring countries of Ghana, Benin, and others. As a consequence, today large populations of the Nawda live in several different geographical areas including: the rural traditional area, rural areas of Central Togo, rural areas of southern Togo, the Togolese capital city Lome, the city of Accra in Ghana, and so on. Patterns of language use are different in each of these different locations. Table 10.1 shows the languages used by the Nawda in different locations for various domains of use.

The Nawdm language is currently at EGIDS level 5 in the northern and central areas of Togo. It is at EGIDS level 6a in Lome and Accra.

The development goals for Nawdm may differ somewhat among the four identified speech communities. In Togo the dominant language contact for the Nawda people is with French while in Ghana the dominant language is English. In rural areas Nawdm is more generally the exclusive language in the home, while in the cities, both Nawdm and the dominant language are used. The policy environment may differ significantly between the two countries. In urban and rural settings, other languages represented in the speech repertoire appear in the work domain. Each of these speech communities might come to different decisions as to the role they want Nawdm to play in the transmission of life-crucial knowledge. They might also come to different decisions as to whether that knowledge transmission is better accomplished through oral, written, or digital modalities. What doesn't change, however, is the need, first of all, to preserve the shared identity of the Nawda through how their language is represented orthographically should it come to be written and how terminology is preserved for internal knowledge or introduced for external knowledge (Tom Marmor, 2013, personal communication).

Table 10.1 Language choice in Nawdm speech communities

Location	Home	School/Govt	Market	Work	Church
Traditional area	Nawdm	French	Nawdm	Nawdm	French, Nawdm
Central Togo	Nawdm	French	Tem	Nawdm, Kabiye	Tem, French
Lome, Togo	Nawdm, French	French	Mina	French, Mina	Ewe, French
Accra, Ghana	Nawdm, English	English	Ewe, English	English, Ewe	English, Ewe

10.3 Determining the program content

The activity components of a speech community's language development program are determined by the changes in the FAMED conditions that are required to attain the desired sustainable level of language use on the EGIDS. The SUM process contributes to this in a significant way by helping members of a speech community frame their understanding of the role of the local language in their overall linguistic ecology. Planning a community-based language development program requires an assessment by the community of its current language situation and the identification of its desired future situation.

10.3.1 Building capacity

Besides the factors identified by the SUM, there are other, more pragmatic, factors that need to be considered when planning a community-based language development program. These include, for example, the community's capacity to carry out language development and the help they can expect from other stakeholders. This kind of capacity includes organizational capacity, technical skills, experience, and resources as well as the ability to secure help from others.

More broadly, there are three different, but interrelated kinds of capacity that language development program implementers need to think about: the capacity of the language, the capacity of the community, and the capacity of the language development organization itself.

The capacity of the language

Throughout this volume, much of what we have been discussing within the SUM framework has to do with the capacity of a language to serve the functions which have been assigned to it. Chapter 8, in particular, described efforts aimed at building the capacity of a local language. Corpus planning for the most part deals with the development tasks which will make the form of a language follow those functional assignments. Where a written function is assigned to the language, an orthography must be created if one doesn't already exist. Generally standardized spelling and punctuation norms are also seen as being helpful in facilitating communication. If a particular body of knowledge is to be transmitted in the language, the lexicon of the language may need to be enhanced and given the capacity to serve that function. While this kind of capacity building may be the most technical of the three categories we describe here, it is, in many ways, also the clearest and procedurally most defined (though not without its own inherent complexities). A local-language community may need to seek expert assistance to carry this out, but the capacity building process itself is relatively straightforward using well-developed and tested tools of documentary, descriptive, and applied linguistics.

The capacity of the community

The second category of capacity building is focused on the ability of the community itself to achieve its language development goals. Not all communities have a large enough population of interested participants to be able to sustain the kind of long-term commitment that an extensive language development program requires, especially if those goals are ambitious. Some communities have very low levels of education and even with a large population may have few community members who can carry out the needed language development tasks. Often there are no trained linguists among the population of language users and the corpus planning work needed to build the capacity of the language may need to be outsourced to external experts. There may be too few institutions or only very weak institutions that might give support to the language development effort.

Motivation among the general population may be low and too few people may have the skills to engage in prestige planning or to conduct motivational campaigns. The policy environment may be hostile and there may not be anyone who knows how to engage in effective advocacy to bring about changes. And crucially, the means of financing language development work within the community may be lacking. Though much can be done with volunteers, most often the magnitude of a language development effort, especially where a language is endangered, will require the full-time efforts of at least some staff (and even more-so where population numbers are large). Sometimes outside funding can be found but often that funding is encumbered with the particular agenda of the funders and almost

10.3 Determining the program content

without exception it is available only for a limited time period. Ongoing resourcing of language development requires that a community not only build its intellectual and technical capacity but that it also build its capacity to fund the work.

Where any of these constraints apply, efforts must be made to build the community's overall capacity to act on its own behalf. This kind of community organizing and community development work requires a set of skills that, again, may only be obtainable from outsiders. While dependence on outside expertise may be necessary at the outset, ideally the outside agency's contribution would be to train community members themselves in the needed skills. The prospects of sustainable language development are enhanced if a community's own capacity to carry out the work that needs to be done can be built. This process takes time, patience, and resolve.

The capacity of the language development organization

To the degree that local-language development becomes formally organized within a speech community, there will be a need for that organization to develop the capacity to carry out its mission. This parallels the need to develop community capacity in that, to the greatest degree possible, the development of capacity within and among community members themselves is highly desirable. Similarly, the ability of a local language development committee, language academy, or whatever organizational structure is created, to carry out its mandate, will require that there be an adequate number of sufficiently trained personnel working as part of that unit. As with community capacity generally, initially a local working unit may require considerable assistance and participation from outsiders. However, a goal of the language development program should be to achieve the greatest level of internal organizational capacity possible. This places control, direction, and implementation of the language development program more firmly in the hands of the community itself.

For community and organizational capacity in particular, the identification of and engagement with additional stakeholders is of crucial importance as these stakeholders can be important sources of assistance or can stand in the way of the language development effort.

10.3.2 Capacity assessment

The SUM provides a set of tools that can be used to assess the capacity of a local language to serve the functions assigned to it at a sustainable level. The assessment of the current state of a local language and the identification of the desired results of language development efforts provide a basis for determining the capacity of the community generally and of the organizations that it develops specifically to achieve those results. Based on the language capacity assessments using the EGIDS and FAMED tools, general estimates can be made as to what needs to be done and what human, technical, and financial resources will be needed. Then, an assessment of community or organizational capacity should focus on the three areas we have just described:

- Capacity for Language Development – Are there people within the community with expertise and technical skills in language development? How many? At what levels of proficiency and training?

- Organizational Capacity – Is there one or more organizations able to initiate, direct, and manage language development endeavors? Are those organizations able to support needed training? Are they able to carry out promotion and distribution activities? Are they able and willing to work together?

- Resourcing Capacity – Is the community able to provide financial resources to support the language development effort? Does the community have adequate infrastructure (buildings, equipment, etc.) for the language development effort? Is the community able to engage other stakeholders? Are there stakeholders who have enough capacity of their own to be able to assist?

This sort of comprehensive assessment of the language, community, and organizational capacity clarifies for the community the scope of the goals that they have set for themselves. They may initially feel overwhelmed by what they find, but the assessment also gives them a clearer picture of what needs to be done and gives a more concrete sense of where to begin as well as how to prioritize activities.

In summary, planning a language development program requires attention to these two major components:
- The current and future desired level of sustainable language use and the activities which will bring about the desired future, as framed by the SUM.
- The current and future capacity needed (language, community, organization) to achieve the desired level of sustainable use.

10.4 Planning language development endeavors

Language development is a long-term effort (minimally 10, but frequently 20 or more years depending on the overall goals) and takes place in an environment that is subject to change. At the same time, it seeks to initiate change in the behavior of people and institutions. Programs and projects are a means to identify and organize activities that are expected to produce a desired result. They serve as a guide for implementing the program (doing the activities) and tracking progress. The SUM places the capacity of a language to meet the community's needs and desires within a coherent framework. There are also planning frameworks which assist language development workers in addressing the other aspects of community-based development.

Results-Based Management (RBM) is one well-developed model for planning programs designed to bring about change in communities and people. It also provides a methodology for implementing the program which focuses on achieving the desired results by monitoring progress and making adjustments to the plan when expected progress is not being achieved. For more background and explanation of the Results-Based Management methodology see the literature references in the Going Deeper section of this chapter. RBM is particularly well suited for community-based language development programs for these reasons:

10.4 Planning language development endeavors

- The focus is on changed behaviors (results).
- The community's participation and that of other stakeholders is essential in all phases of the program.
- The plan is expected to change during implementation as results are monitored and evaluated. As the desired results fail to materialize (or exceed expectations), as conditions change, or as new approaches are developed, there is room within the RBM approach for any part of the plan to be adjusted accordingly.

Detailed descriptions and instructions on the creation of a well-formed results plan are beyond the scope of this volume. A companion volume lays out the major features of such a results-based planning and program management system with specific application to community-based language development. In brief, it should be noted that results plans can be developed at different levels and durations. That is, long-term and program results can include a lot of change and a large number of people or be much more limited in their scope. Also, different components of a larger results plan can themselves be specified with their own results plans and those sub-plans combined into a master plan. Organizationally, different parts of the master plan might be implemented by different agencies or combinations of agencies working collaboratively. This flexibility allows a community to involve diverse segments of its population in different aspects of the overall language development effort.

10.4.1 Developing an overall language development program

Following the SUM analysis and capacity assessment, the next step in planning a community-based language development program is to elaborate the desired long-term Impact and the intermediate results of the endeavor (Outcomes). This long-term plan will generally encompass a years-long effort requiring several different shorter-term projects to complete.

Community-based language development takes a global view. It is larger than just about languages. It is about the people who use those languages and their need to transmit life-crucial knowledge. It is about helping people have and use the linguistic tools that enhance their overall quality of life. In the Results-Based Management model, desired results are expressed in terms of changes in behavior rather than in terms of static products or states. A generic long-term goal, the Impact, of a language development effort aimed at achieving Sustainable Literacy, might be expressed in the form:

> The members of the _____ speech community, in this and the next generations, are accessing and passing on life-crucial knowledge and information through the use of their local language in written form.

Such a general statement does not specify what needs to be done for this change of behavior to be realized. It does describe the changes in behavior that the language development effort hopes to achieve.

In terms of the SUM, the Impact statement will very likely reference one of the Sustainable levels of use as the desired long-term result. The example statement above indicates that the overall goal is to achieve Sustainable Literacy. As the planning process moves along, planners identify the changes in community behavior that are needed to bring about that result. These are the intermediate results (Outcomes) that are believed by the planners to be necessary in order to achieve the desired Impact. In many cases, the Outcome statements will involve reference to specific FAMED conditions that need to be brought to the desired levels as well as other changes needed for sustainability such as the community's capacity to carry on with its own language development or the organizational capacity of local community agents. This cycle of more and more detailed planning continues with the identification of other needed results (Outputs) that will contribute to bringing about the desired Outcomes until a list of specific activities are identified and planned for.

Near the completion of each set of activities in the plan, an evaluation should be conducted and adjustments made to the plan based on lessons learned from previous efforts, the progress made toward desired results, and a review of the context. This cycle continues for the life of the language development effort until the desired Impact is achieved.

10.5 Implementing the overall language development plan in a single speech community

The implementation of a language development plan can be most clearly described by focusing on a single speech community rather than attempting to deal with the complexities that arise when there are multiple speech communities to be considered. The same principles described here apply in those more complex situations but it may be necessary to have supplemental plans that are tailored for each of the speech communities.

An overall, long-term, community-based language development plan is implemented by carrying out activities with the resources available. Where it is perceived that additional resources may be needed, the identification and development of those resources must be included as part of the planning. The overall plan is broken down into a series of projects so that the implementation is more manageable and able to be modified as there are changes in the environment and speech community. This division of the plan into projects also allows for a more efficient allocation of resources, with expertise, materials, and finances allocated to best meet the requirements of each project. The long-term result (Impact) for the overall plan and the intermediate results (Outcomes and Outputs) provide both direction (a clear vision of the goals) and constraints (clear boundaries that limit the potential for "mission creep") on the development of the individual projects.

10.5.1 Projects

For better management of its implementation, a large and complex language development program can be broken down into smaller units or projects. This provides a means to organize the work, assign responsibilities, and monitor progress. Projects can be identified in several ways. One approach defines the project as all of the short term results (Outputs) and associated activities designed to facilitate the same Outcome in the overall plan. Each project focuses relatively narrowly on achieving that single Outcome but may include a number of quite different sets of outputs and activities aimed at realizing the desired Outcome. When the Outcome is achieved the project ends. These sorts of projects involve a greater level of internal complexity as they may require the participation of personnel with quite different sets of skills and expertise. The manager of a such a project may not have expertise in any of those skills but will be required to have sufficient understanding to be able to evaluate when a particular skill is needed or could be better used. Since Outcomes generally represent intermediate-term results, projects structured around Outcomes are frequently of somewhat longer duration and therefore might require long-term pledges of financial support if they are to reach completion. If the Working Group strategy is used as described in chapter 9, different groups might be formed around these kinds of projects or the projects themselves might be structured using internal working groups.

Another organizational approach defines a project as a single short term result (Output) and all of its associated Activities. Such a project will be much more narrowly focused and often of much shorter duration. Often a project of this type will be constrained not only by the particular results that it is focused on, but by a period of time in which it is to be carried out. A one- or two-year project with clearly defined objectives provides a working environment that is not only more easily managed and directed, but also more easily resourced. A project of this type, for example, might focus on the production of initial literacy acquisition materials and the training of teachers to use them. Once those materials are developed and a corps of teachers is trained, the project may be considered completed. An evaluation of the results may indicate that additional work is needed but that work can be structured within a new project that reflects what has been learned and that builds on previous results. At that point, project personnel may be reassigned to the new project or to another project and funds redirected as appropriate.

Within a language development program there can be a combination of these types of projects. A project leader is given responsibility for achieving the results of the project, no matter which type. The project leaders might report to or at least coordinate with the manager of the overall program. An advantage of organizing around projects in this way is that different segments of the community may be more interested in one set of Outcomes than others and so will be more willing to participate in a project that aligns more closely with their interests. Where there are religious or social differences in the community it may be impossible to effectively involve a cross-section of the community in all of the development activities together, but they may be willing to work on specific projects separately.

10.5.2 Organization and management

No matter how many projects are at work, overall coordination of the language development program as a whole still must be provided. That is greatly enhanced if there is a community-wide consensus on the higher level goals and desired results. This program-level management function is responsible for supporting the projects, monitoring their progress, and evaluating their contribution to the desired

Impact. This management role will take different forms in different communities. It may be carried out by a single person acting as a "local language development czar". It may be handled by a committee or board. It may be distributed among a team of administrative personnel. In whatever way it is implemented, the program-level management agent is responsible to interact with the community and other stakeholders, maintaining communications and their involvement in program and project reviews and decisions.

10.6 Implementing programs in multiple speech communities

As we've already described above, there are good reasons for grouping multiple speech communities into a coordinated language development effort. In such cases, the overall language development program needs to take into account the differences in the role of the local language in each of the different speech communities and the sustainable level of use that each of those communities identifies as desirable. This may result in completely different programs being designed for each of the speech communities with different Impact statements and different intermediate and short-term results. In such cases, the coordination among the distinct programs may be purely technical with coordinated decisions regarding orthography and script, perhaps, but not much else.

In contrast, where there are large areas of agreement regarding higher level results among the various speech communities, much more can be done collaboratively and in coordination. As a result, many of the projects designed to achieve intermediate results may involve representatives from the different speech communities. At the very least distinct projects focusing on similar results should be communicating with each other and, to the greatest extent possible, sharing resources, learning from each other, and avoiding duplication of efforts.

10.7 Going deeper

The major new concepts introduced in this chapter are those related to Results Based Management. We raise again here, as we did in chapter 3, the notion of speech community as distinct from language community. That ground has already been covered in the Going Deeper section of that chapter, so will not be repeated here.

10.7.1 Results-based management

Results-Based Management (RBM) is a planning framework that has grown out of the experience of international development practitioners as they have learned from past experiences with traditional top-down, outsider initiated development attempts. We list here only some of the earliest and most introductory literature on the topic. Introductory summaries include Asian Development Bank 2006, Cox et al. 2004, and Cox 2009. These should serve as an adequate introduction to the method. Additional orientation and practical application of RBM specifically to community-based language development can also be found in the companion volume, *Managing Language Programs: Perspectives, Processes, and Practices* (Marmor and Bartels, forthcoming).

11

Conclusion

The Sustainable Use Model as we have described it provides a new lens through which to view the process of sustaining language use. Rather than focus first on language, the SUM focuses on local community identity and its preservation through the transmission of life-crucial knowledge. Language is clearly an essential element in that knowledge transmission, but is often so far below the level of conscious awareness that many local communities are unable to grapple with it. Community members are often much more able to identify knowledge that is being lost or knowledge that needs to be acquired without reference, at first, to the language issues related to those processes.

With a concrete body of knowledge in mind, however, the issue of the language of transmission can much more readily be dealt with. Further, the concept of sustainable levels of use provides a conceptual framework for envisioning a desired future. Using the EGIDS, community members can evaluate the current status of their language and thus better understand how much might need to be done in order to reach their desired sustainable level of use. The FAMED conditions provide a way to diagnose specific factors that need to be addressed in a language development program. All of these tools give a community a structured way to think through its current situation and to develop targeted responses that will more effectively move it towards its language development goals.

The idea of developing local languages Function by Function—that is, one body of knowledge at a time—also provides an organizing principle by which an overall language development program can be structured around more focused sets of related activities aimed at preserving and developing the features of a local language that are needed for the transmission of each specific body of knowledge. The goal of language development in the SUM is to carve out and preserve a "space" where the language is safe and can be used. As each of the desired functions is developed, that safe space for the language grows and strengthens. The maxim we propose is that as a language gains uses, it will also gain users.

While the SUM demystifies the language development process to a certain extent, there is no denying that achieving sustainable language use is neither easy nor simple. Local language communities need all of the tools and resources that they can muster to engage in the sorts of language development efforts that we have described. In particular, the SUM makes much clearer the importance of identifying and achieving a *sustainable* level of use. Language recovery, revitalization, and development activities, no matter how beneficial or how well resourced, which do not move a community towards the desired level of sustainable use, are not, in themselves, adequate. This perspective with its clearer identification of what it takes to achieve sustainability may be daunting. Nevertheless, it is essential that communities that undertake language development programs enter into those efforts with a clear understanding of the level of investment that will be required of them. Without that understanding they may lose resolve and grow weary as results are slow to be seen.

The aim of the SUM is to provide awareness and perspective for reflective practitioners of language development. It adds a significant set of tools that will make the task easier and maximize the investments of time, energy, and determination that local language communities must make. We are convinced of the great value of local heritage languages and encourage local language communities to make the needed investment in order to achieve sustainable language use.

Appendix

Examples of activities for promoting sustainable language use

A wide variety of activities can be used to help a speech community achieve the desired sustainable level of use.

A.1 Introduction

This appendix lists some activities that are representative of efforts to change the situation of a language within its linguistic ecology. It is not comprehensive but serves as the beginnings of a catalog of things that have been attempted by others in many different parts of the world. The SUM provides a way to identify which of the FAMED conditions need to be addressed. The following examples are categorized both by the change in EGIDS level that is desired in order to move towards a sustainable level of use and the specific FAMED condition(s) that need to be addressed. The sections that follow parallel the description of the principles involved in chapter 9. The examples presented here can serve as a point of departure for local practitioners. Not every example is necessarily applicable in every context. In every case, local language developers will want to make adjustments appropriate to their own circumstances. Even better, they should develop activities of their own that are more suited to the situation at hand.

It should also be clear that some of the activities given as examples may, in fact, address multiple FAMED conditions simultaneously or can be adjusted in ways that make them more appropriate for addressing one inadequate condition over another. Similarly, an example identified here as being applicable in achieving movement up or down between specific levels on the EGIDS, may also be useful, with or without modifications, in facilitating transitions between other EGIDS levels. Our categorization of an activity as addressing a particular condition does not preclude its use for other purposes or in other ways. We especially encourage practitioners to be reflective as they read and evaluate this catalog.

A.2 Achieving Sustainable Literacy

A.2.1 Introducing written functions (from EGIDS 6a to EGIDS 5)

Functions

Jicarilla Apache [apj]. Preschool teachers among the Jicarilla Apache in New Mexico organized and participated in a workshop aimed at developing written materials for language socialization. During the workshop, elders of the community and the teachers recalled sayings and anecdotes from their childhood that helped teach them the ways of the community. With the help of linguists from the local university, they put these proverbs together and created a series of illustrated booklets called "Jicarilla Teachings" that could be easily disseminated. Participants at another creative writing workshop elaborated on the booklets and wrote explanatory stories. The stories also included interactions between community members that demonstrated the appropriate manner of interacting on an informal level (i.e., teasing through proverbs).

The development of these booklets and stories increased the corpus of literature available in Apache, which had been limited. The participants fervently desired to use literacy as a means of both teaching the language and socializing their children (Gómez de Garcia, Axelrod, and Lachler 2002:51–58).

Acquisition

Heritage Language playschools in Malaysia. In 2007, UNESCO initiated a pilot project in multilingual education in cooperation with the Dayak Bidayuh National Association (DBNA) in Sarawak, Malaysia. As of 2012, DBNA was operating playschools in 8 villages and kindergarten classes in 3 others. The project included the development of ongoing pre-service and in-service teacher training, curriculum development, materials production, and monitoring and evaluation of the program.

The playschools provide opportunity and re-enforcement of language use for three- and four-year olds with community involvement. The focus of the curriculum is on pre-reading and pre-writing activities and reading readiness skills. The playschools are conducted entirely in the heritage language of the community. "Effective Multilingual Education allows the children to develop their thinking and reasoning skills first in their heritage language(s) and then add subsequent languages. In cases where the child has not been allowed to learn his/her heritage language, the parents' language(s), s/he is still able to learn the heritage language(s) as a second and/or third language. The teaching methods in a heritage language programme are designed to promote interactive and participative learning as it builds on what the child knows and moves from the known to the unknown" (Smith 2012:3).

Producing educational materials (Southeast Asia). Sometimes government and educational officials and even members of local communities themselves believe it is an insurmountable problem to produce culturally relevant curricula in many different languages. Language development workers in Southeast Asia have produced a manual that demonstrates how it is possible for any group to develop quality educational materials. Following Participatory Action Research methodology, the manual uses a three-stage process of Discovering, Deciding and Developing. Community members brainstorm together to Discover cultural resources, art forms, local wisdom, traditions and values by starting with the community's own cultural calendar. They then Decide together which topics they want to include in their curriculum. Finally, the community members work together to Develop, check, and improve their own teaching materials. Using this procedure it has been found that children learn more easily and quickly. They develop skills in listening, speaking, reading, writing, creativity, and crticial thinking. The school setting is more enjoyable and children become confident learners. Using a locally developed culturally relevant curriculum also raises cultural prestige and self-esteem while preserving heritage language, cultural art forms, and local knowledge (Foerster and Saurman 2013).

Naskapi [nsk]. Computer technical support and training was provided for members of the Naskapi community by a resident linguist allowing for desktop publishing using the unique Canadian syllabic script. This technical support made it possible to develop a Naskapi school curriculum on-site, which in turn made it possible to implement a mother-tongue-first multilingual education program, switching from English to Naskapi as a language of instruction in local schools for grades 1–3. Children not only learn to speak, but also to read and write in their language (Jancewicz and MacKenzie 2002).

Motivation

Naro [nhr]. Naro is one of 26 minority languages spoken in Botswana. There are 9,000 speakers along the border of Namibia and Botswana and despite shifting to the national language (Setswana [tsn]) and another dominant language of the area (Shekgalagarhi), the Naro speakers have begun the revitalization process through holistic empowerment.

There was minimal intergenerational transmission when the Naro speech community entered the 1990s. In 1991, a language project was begun that eventually led into a language empowerment project. As the language was developed and materials were produced (linguistic empowerment), literacy classes were started and control of those classes was placed in the hands of the elders (socio-political empowerment). Many people enrolled in the classes and what they learned spilled into their daily activities. They learned how to settle accounts and infused literacy into painting, crafting, sculpturing, and weaving. Eventually the people began to showcase their language and culture for tourists, thereby establishing an economic base (economic empowerment). Naro, once one of several endangered minority languages in the Ghanzi zone of Botswana, has become a lingua franca with a core speech community that is now aware of the economic and social benefits of their language (Batibo 2008, 2009:31–33).

Environment

Hawaiian [haw]. The 'Aha Pūnana Leo ('APL) was established in 1983 with the purpose of creating language nests similar to the successful language nest program in New Zealand. The 'APL was a nonprofit education organization that was made up of 8 board members from four different Hawaiian islands. Throughout its existence, the 'APL has maintained focus on its primary goal of facilitating educational opportunities for Hawaiian children in their own language. However, in the years directly following its inception, the group was forced to act as political activists for the rights of Hawaiian speakers instead of as educational facilitators.

In the mid-1980s, when the 'APL tried to start the first language nest, they ran into problems with the Department of Social Services and Housing of the State of Hawaii (DSSH). According to two different Supreme Court rulings, the state department had no jurisdiction over foreign language schools. Nevertheless, the DSSH argued that the language nests should be under state regulation because they were not like regular foreign language schools, the children were too young and the days too long, and the method of teaching by immersion was not a "true method of language teaching." The 'APL was forced to fight for their right to establish language nests. They hired the American Civil Liberties Union, motivated people in the speech community to testify at hearings, and, despite setbacks, kept the community behind the fight to change the legislation to more favorable terms. The outcome was a compromise that allowed them to begin opening language nests in earnest (Warner 2001:137).

Kazakh [kaz]. Throughout the 20th century, the Kazakh language steadily lost ground to Russian. In an effort to regain functions for the language, political and social leaders put pressure on the newly independent government to create a Kazakh-only policy in government offices. In 2002, Qyzylorda became the first province to create a policy encompassing this idea. Four more provinces followed their example and plans were implemented to shift all internal government communication to Kazakh. In reality, this has not panned out according to plan and even the offices in Qyzylorda still communicate in Russian when interacting with officials from the capital. However, this is an example of how governments can be pressured to create a statutory environment that at least makes allowance for the use of a non-dominant language (Fierman 2005:117–123).

Philippines: Advocacy for inclusive minority language policies in education. The language policy of the Philippine Department of Education required the use of two languages of instruction: Filipino [fil] and English [eng]. Other languages were permitted only as auxiliary languages in the classroom, not in textbooks or in written form. This policy, though intended to unify the country and promote fluency in the major languages, marginalized 70% of learners. A new language-in-education policy that prioritized access to quality education in the languages understood by the learners was needed.

A coalition of actors in the areas of language, culture, education, natural resource management, economic development and health, both governmental and non-governmental, was formed (the Philippines MLE Network) to advocate for a new policy. Research was done on the outcomes of mother tongue-based education providing the evidence needed to support a change in the language-in-education policy. The Philippines MLE Network worked with the highest placed officials in the Department of Education to obtain a Department-level order that established Mother Tongue-Based Multilingual Education (MTB-MLE) in the national curriculum. This established MTB-MLE as the foundational principle for basic education and permitted localization of teaching and learning materials. (Catherine Young, personal communication)

Differentiation

Identifying bodies of knowledge. Recent participatory research among the Akha people of Myanmar has attempted to identify the bodies of knowledge that are part of the Akha [akh] culture and to use those as a means of evaluating the status of the language on the Functions scale. Twenty-eight bodies of knowledge were specified and pictures found to represent these in a group activity that asked the participants to place the picture on a chart that had headings for the different levels on the Function scale. The pictures represented community life, community events, community development, art and music, family, farming, food, health, housing, crafts, religion, technology, self-advancement, law, business, and transportation. For some categories more than one picture was used. All of the pictures were assigned to a level on the chart, developing an overview of the way in which the bodies of knowledge were communicated. The Bodies of Knowledge were chosen such that some were expected to be internal and some external, providing a range of situations to be classified. The results of the study have been used to evaluate the status of the communities on the Functions scale and can serve as a basis for planning a language development initiative aimed at preserving and strengthening Akha culture (Ah Suhn 2015).

A.2.2 Establishing mass literacy (from EGIDS 5 to EGIDS 4)

Functions

Mayan mathematics. The ancient Mayan civilization is credited with being one of the first to develop the concept of zero and their well-developed mathematical knowledge was applied to the study of astronomy, the counting of time and calendrics, land measurement and to textile weaving and design. Mayan languages use a base 20 counting system and many aspects of daily life in Mayan communities still reflect that perspective. In several Mayan communities in both Mexico and Guatemala, primary and secondary school mathematics is being taught using these traditional bodies of knowledge as the basis for the curriculum. These curricula emphasize the usefulness of traditional Mayan mathematics in daily life in the community (Hirsch-Dubin 2010:7–8).

Acquisition

Me'en [mym] literacy in Ethiopia. The Me'en language community is located in the southwest of Ethiopia. Local language literacy in Me'en started in 1992 when the first new Christian converts (about 13 in number) wanted to study the Bible in their mother tongue. Literacy classes were initiated and the classes soon attracted many others. Those who were able to read and write in Me'en went out to the villages with their books and showed them to their extended families and fellow clan members. Within a year or two, almost all of the villages in the clan were requesting literacy classes. Following the "each one teach one" approach, the early literacy students became the literacy teachers. Children and adults who went through these literacy classes went on in the formal schools.

After a few years of this church-based literacy program, the government asked the church to help in training adult literacy teachers who would be paid and coordinated by the local government. The church trained 9 teachers who became part of the government-run non-formal education program in Me'en. In 2007 the Me'en Language Development Program (MLDP) was founded combining the government and church programs into a formal education program that now teaches thousands of children and adults.

In 2008, Me'en was introduced as a subject in 6 government schools and a year later expanded to 12 schools. As members of other language communities learned of this program they requested similar programs using their languages (Bench [bcn], Dizi [mdx], Sheko [she], and Suri [suq]) and a clustered approach to language development was begun with Me'en teachers and trainers sharing their experiences with the rest of the cluster team and with government officials. Currently, Me'en is used as a medium of instruction for the first primary cycle (grades 1–4) and is taught as a subject from grade 5 onwards. The other languages are on the same track and each has trained hundreds of native teachers with many attending teachers training colleges in preparation for employment in the local schools. (Tefera Endalew, personal communication)

Tharaka [thk] literacy in Kenya. Most indigenous African languages native to Kenya are not used in formal education though government policy allows for such use through grade 3. The Tharaka are agriculturalists living in a remote semi-arid region. They deal with drought, pollution, traditions that hinder health and education, and therefore have very limited access to educational opportunities. Where education is accessible, poverty and poor health cause low enrollment and high early dropout rates.

Local school district resources are extremely limited. Bible Translation and Literacy (BTL), a Kenyan NGO, began adult literacy classes in the area in 1996. In 1997 there were nine classes in operation using a pre-reading book and a primer. Completion of these classes was often delayed significantly for the reasons mentioned above and others. Teachers were volunteers and the turnover rate was high. The lack of roads and means of transportation made access to the communities difficult. Much of the effort of the project was invested in training replacement teachers rather than on expansion of the program to new locations. Upon evaluation it was determined that one of the major reasons for slow progress in the adult literacy program was the lack of a well-trained, salaried teaching corps.

That evaluation led BTL to change its focus to the development of curricula for a children's program in the schools and to use the development and teacher training processes as a means of strengthening the literacy proficiency of the adult educators. This shift answered the requests of the existing corps of school teachers, numbering in the hundreds, for assistance in teaching children to read in Tharaka. Local education officials were willing to experiment and support this initiative and contributed a core group of 12 administrators and teachers for a period of 4 years. They committed to an intense teacher training and supervision regime. In 2004, a pilot program at the preschool level was begun in a single test school in each of the Tharaka region's three divisions. The administrators and teachers who received the initial training produced new, imaginative stories, documented valuable historical and cultural information, and put many of their songs into print for the first time. They are now passing on the those skills and their love of their written language to the next generation. Hundreds of other teachers and administrators are receiving that training and practicing their skills daily in their work with children (Schroeder 2004).

Software localization. The localization of software is one way to move a language closer to being used widely in written form. Localization of software aims to literally "relocate" the software within a local language and culture. This means that not only are the appropriate script and fonts used but the entire "look and feel" of the localized product is adapted to make local users more comfortable and effective in using the software. For economic reasons, major software companies may not be willing to take on localization projects for every community, but some have made resources and tools available to those who might wish to do so. For a good overview of the process and the issues involved, consult online sources such as http://msdn.microsoft.com/en-us/goglobal/bb688139.

West Frisian [fry]: Software Support for Learning to Write. The Fryske Akademy in the Netherlands is a research center for Frisian culture and language. It was established in 1938 and has been collecting and developing a linguistic database for the Frisian language. They have been publishing writing support books for years, but had not developed a method of using the computer to disseminate the helps until they engaged with a local software company to develop a program that would help people learn to write Frisian.

Taalhelp ("Language help") is a module that operates within Microsoft Word to provide a dictionary, spell check, and thesaurus. Before this program became available, people were not using Frisian as much as Dutch when writing, simply because they lacked training. The software provides a means for the speech community to learn the rules of writing their language in a safe environment. There is no fear of ridicule when you are the only person to see the correction. Since the corrections are explained, learning can happen. As people learn how to write Frisian they are using it as a written language in more and more domains (Sijens 2008:136–137).

Motivation

Promoting the economic benefits of language use. In Comitancillo, Guatemala, language development was closely linked to economic development. A first step was to embrace the multilingualism in the community giving recognition to the local variety of Mam [mam] spoken there alongside Spanish. Signs were erected at the entrances to the town welcoming all to "Comitancillo, A Bilingual Community." Some stores and churches also began to use bilingual signage. In addition, a small community lending library was started that made both Spanish and Mam literature available. The municipal library is run and funded by local community leadership and it has now come to include a local "House of Culture."

In addition, several micro-enterprises were begun among the Mam-speaking population including a leather shop, a bookstore, a propane gas exchange and an apple cider business. There is also a local radio station that transmits programs, music, and discussion in both Spanish and Mam. These projects have linked Mam identity and language with success and economic wellbeing. All of these efforts increased the motivation of community members not only to use the local language with pride, but also to perceive the benefits of being able to access the growing body of literature being produced in it. As Multilingual Education was introduced in the community, parents were more willing to have their children participate (Wes Collins, personal communication).

Environment

Saami [sme]. In January 1992, following years of not very favorable language policies, the Norwegian government assigned official status to Saami alongside Norwegian. Instead of focusing on the "Norwegianization" of the Saami people, Norway's goal became the attainment of stable multilingualism among Saami speakers. Students were allowed to choose from three tracks in both primary and secondary school. The first track allowed students to have Saami as their first language and the language of instruction while taking Norwegian as a foreign language course. The second track identified Norwegian as the student's first language and the language of instruction while taking Saami as a foreign language course. The third track allowed students to classify Norwegian as their first language while requiring no exposure to Saami. The goal of the first two tracks was to help create stable multilingualism through appropriate exposure to each language for the individual student. The government and Saami people recognized that a monolingual Saami society was no longer viable. However, they hoped that through this school program Norwegian would not become overly dominant (Todal 1999:43).

Frisian [fry]: Negotiating a covenant. In the process of ensuring the status of Frisian in the context of the Netherlands, a formal agreement, called a covenant, was negotiated between the state and the local-language community. The agreement was time-bounded with the intention that it would be reassessed and renewed at the end of the stated term. The state agreed to provide funds for strengthening the infrastructure of the local language community (i.e., funding local language theater troupes, research institutions, broadcasting companies, and other entities associated with the speech community). The covenant also established how the minority language would be used in public administration and the judicial system (Gorter 2001:218).

Otomí/Ñahñú [ote]: Establishing a language academy. In 1986, the Academia de la Lengua Ñahñú was founded by graduates of a special ethnolinguistic program at the Centro de Investigaciones y Estudios Superiores en Antropología Social in Mexico. The purpose of the academy was to focus on activities that may reverse language shift in the Otomí language community. It was originally made up of voluntary bilingual teachers, but in 1989 they started receiving salaries. The government allows them to use a large room in a government building for their work. The group advocates and organizes the production of Otomí textbooks, sponsors forums in an attempt to regularize the orthography, organizes reading and writing courses for adults, and produces cassettes of Ñahñú songs and stories.

The academy has played a part in changing the government's implementation of their language policy and creating a more accepting environment for teaching Otomí (Lastra de Suarez 2001:142–165).

Differentiation

Machiguenga [mcb], Peru: Creating institutional support for literacy. "Subsequent to the introduction of literacy the Machiquenga have developed their own set of institutions (for example, community organizations, parents' associations, and mothers' clubs) and group customs (such as posting signs, letter writing, and labeling clothing) which require reading and writing. This cultural institutionalization of literacy has been an important factor in literacy retention" (Davis 2004:267).

Developing a discourse of sustainable use. Catalan [cat] is an example of a positive environment in need of a discourse of sustainable language use that is widespread among the population. In spite of a very positive set of language policies and strong implementation of the use of the language in schools, resulting in second-language acquisition by many who have immigrated to Catalonia, analysts of the situation are concerned that an adequate differentiation of the appropriate domains of use for Spanish and Catalan does not exist among the general population and especially among the younger generations. Some young people view Catalan as "artificially fostered by those in power." They note that many younger citizens will happily engage in conversations in either Spanish or Catalan even when interacting with other first-language speakers of Catalan. This lack of differentiation is seen as evidence that even with strong government support, a vibrant sense of local identity, and a considerable investment of resources in language acquisition and use in education, sustainable use of Catalan cannot be assured unless there are clearly differentiated associations of the language with specific functions (Strubell 2001).

A.3 Achieving Sustainable Orality

A.3.1 Cultivating the language (from EGIDS 6b, 7 to EGIDS 6a)

Functions

Working group strategy: identifying and documenting Functions. *Documentation group:* The responsibility of the documentation group is to provide materials and information for the greater use of the language for life-crucial functions. They are responsible to work out the logistics and the documentation needs and then to carry out the plan. Once this task is complete and funding is available, they work closely with the other working groups to decide what to spend time documenting (Hadjidemetriou 2008:39–43).

Acquisition

Working group strategy: Facilitating Acquisition. *Language Reintroduction group:* This group focuses on encouraging community members to use the local language in the home domain. They accomplish this by providing classes for both children and adults, creating a campaign that promotes the usefulness of the language, and developing materials for learning the language (Hadjidemetriou 2008:39–43).

Arapaho [arp]. Arapaho has a population of around 1,200, primarily located in Wyoming. The Arapaho people have endured genocide and forced migrations at the hand of the dominant culture and their language is suffering. The general attitude is a desire to shift to English for the economic benefits found thereby, but there is a sentimental attachment and desire to maintain their heritage culture and language. Arapaho is taught in schools as a subject language, starting in preschool. However, in order to fill in the developmental gap before the children came of age to go to preschool, the Arapaho Language Lodge developed a program aimed at parents of young children. The program connected parents with an older woman who provided instruction in the "language of nurturing and caring." This program is reinserting Arapaho into the home domain for the parents that take advantage of the opportunity (Greymorning 1999:6–16).

Motivation

Working group strategy: Facilitating awareness. *Awareness group:* The awareness group has two priorities. The most important is to educate those within the speech community to the importance of learning and transmitting the language to younger people. These activities contribute to motivation. The second priority is to raise awareness among the dominant society about the community's language development efforts. These activities contribute to motivation internally but also address the Environment condition. This can occur through media or outreach cultural events. The point is to create visibility and to increase the appreciation for the community's heritage language and culture outside of the community (Hadjidemetriou 2008:39–43).

Hainanese [nan], Jun, Mai, Danzhou, Danjia, Huihui, Li, Miao. In Sanya, a city on China's Hainan Island, there are eight indigenous languages spoken along with Putonghua (Mandarin [cmn]). Revitalization of the local languages was promoted through a bilingual speech competition. The goal was to create an environment where all the languages were on an equal footing and where awareness of the local languages could be promoted. In some cases this competition was the first time the participants had observed the use of the local languages in a formal environment alongside Mandarin. Some of the participants reported that prior to the competition they had not been aware of the existence of the local languages. The competition served to strengthen the identities of the local language communities (T'sou et. al. 2007).

Slovenian [slv]. The Slovene community in Carinthia (Austria) is geographically isolated from the larger Slovenian speech community found in Slovenia. The smaller group in Austria avoids being identified as Slovenes due to their treatment in Carinthia. Many have created "weekend" identities where they express their linguistic heritage in private on the weekend in their homes and more private community settings. As a result Slovenian was in decline in Carinthia. Mass media has played an important role in the maintenance of a Slovene identity. Members of the older generation still openly read Slovenian newspapers and watch Slovenian television programs. At the same time, this type of media allows members of the younger generations, who wish not to be associated as insiders, to absorb media in Slovenian anonymously. The media has been useful in uniting geographically separated members of the local group into a new type of social network. The newspapers and radio programs focus on relational topics that would, in the past, be heard in the village square or market. Now those who have left their home areas stay connected and in touch with the local news through Slovenian media (Busch 2001:35–39).

Irish Gaelic [gle]. Revitalization efforts have been attempted in Ireland even though the language has been in continuous, though declining, use for many years. In spite of the fact that overt success has not always been visible, the overall perception of these efforts is positive. It has been necessary to divide revitalization efforts between the Gaeltacht and the East of Ireland. The Gaeltacht consists of pockets of communities in western Ireland that were able to maintain Irish long after it was lost elsewhere. Efforts to reverse this language shift were originally focused on the Gaeltacht with the hope that if intergenerational transmission could be reached in these pockets of Gaelic-speaking communities, then they would become a help and inspiration in other parts of the country. Through government funding of numerous Irish language acquisition courses, the facilitation of Irish cultural and literary preservation, and other promotional efforts, motivation has been enhanced towards Irish once again becoming the language spoken throughout Ireland. That goal has not yet been achieved, but attitudes towards Irish are in a much better state than they would have been if these motivational activities had never been attempted (Fishman 1991:122–148).

Mayangna [yan]. The Mayangna people live along the Nicaraguan coast. They recently established two different radio programs that were initiated through a pilot program sponsored by the University of the Atlantic Region of the Caribbean Coast of Nicaragua. The first attempt was a daily fifteen minute time slot that focused on storytelling, the Bachelor's Degree program for bilingual and intercultural education, and local news. It lasted for one month and was so successful that a proposal was written to institute a daily hour-long program for three years. In 2001, two programs were designed for two different stations. There are two administrative centers for the Mayangna people: Rosita and Bonanza. By establishing a radio program in each town, all Mayangna people had access to the programs. The content includes support for bilingual education programs, Mayangna history and culture, nature conservation information, support for current education activities, music, and local announcements. Each program lasts for one hour daily in the afternoon. People are encouraged to participate by sending in announcements and interacting with the program designers about cultural and historical information. This activity has drawn the speech community together, sometimes over long distances. It has allowed for the preservation of cultural knowledge and motivation to use the language in this new sphere (Benedicto et. al. 2001:55–58).

Assyrian Neo-Aramaic [aii]. For Assyrians worldwide, the Internet has become a source of information supporting their ethnic identity. As well as a remnant in their homeland community in Iraq, a majority of the Assyrian population is located all around the world. Assyrian activists are therefore focusing language maintenance efforts on the Internet. Since many of the people are found in western countries, large segments of the speech community have access to the Internet and make use of language learning websites, internet radio programs, online dictionaries and grammars, and forums devoted to the promotion of Assyrian culture and the use of the language. They have created a virtual global community where they find others with a similar world view, cultural understandings, and where they can communicate in their own language (McClure 2001:68–75).

Environment

Tamazight online. Tamazight is an overarching label for the Berber languages found in Morocco, Algeria, Libya, and Tunisia. In spite of a fairly large overall population, the older generations are no longer transmitting these languages to younger generations and have endured years of political oppression. Both of these factors are causing attrition in language use that is leading to endangerment. There are many websites aimed at promoting the Tamazight language and encouraging Imazighen culture. Two of the most prominent websites are administered by the Amazigh Cultural Association of America and the Amazigh World Congress. Both are created by members of the community in the diaspora and thus have the potential to foster both a local and non local identity. The main goal of both websites is the documentation, preservation, and promotion of Tamazight. These websites are being used to raise awareness outside of the community about the suppression of basic human rights towards the Tamazight speech community while providing a public domain for documentation (Ouakrime 2001:61–67).

Tamazight language academy. In the past, the governments of Algeria and Morocco promoted an Arabization policy which disadvantaged other languages spoken within those countries. This policy resulted in active state-sanctioned suppression of the Tamazight language and culture in order to make way for Islam and the Arabic language. A Berber resistance movement responded to that suppression in an effort to defend their traditional Berber identity from eradication. In the mid-1900s, many Tamazight nationalists were exiled while others left to avoid the intolerant atmosphere. In 1967 in Paris, these exiles established the Berber Academy for the express purpose of bringing both in-group and out-group attention to the human rights violations being committed by Algeria. They disseminated information about Tamazight history, culture, language, politics, and anthropology through a nondescript newsletter that could be easily circulated within Algeria without drawing government attention. By establishing their academy outside of the language area, they were able to avoid the bans and legalities imposed by the governments. Their location also allowed them to reach out to community outsiders and bring international attention to their situation. The academy succeeded in increasing awareness among exiled Berbers towards their ethnic identity while reaching out to younger generations. Many youth returned to Algeria as new members of the Berber nationalist movement. The most important contribution the academy made to language and culture revitalization efforts was the discovery and implementation of an ancient Tamazight writing system called *Tifinagh*. The reintroduction of this ancient script deflated the Algerian military regime's propaganda that Tamazight was a substandard, unwritten dialect. A Latin script developed in the 19th century is still preferred over *Tifinagh* in daily use, but it has become an identity marker that is found at political rallies and demonstrations. Overall, the academy catalyzed the Berber nationalist movement both inside and outside of the language area by developing and promoting tangible identity markers (Mezhoud 2005:109–116).

Minority languages in Taiwan. In 1984, National Taiwan University students established a group called Yuanquanhui (Association to Promote Indigenous Rights) that appealed to the government for help with issues faced by the 14 minority communities in Taiwan. This organization developed into the Council of Indigenous People (CIP), which became an established government entity in 1996. The CIP focuses on development programs that involve the minority people in preservation of culture, political participation, education, social welfare, economics, and land affairs. In order to encourage language learning and use, the government allowed minority children easier access to higher level schools by accepting lower scores than non-minority students. They also made various scholarships available to minority students. In 2005, the government started requiring the students to present a certificate of mother tongue proficiency in order to receive those benefits. These types of policies affected parents as well as children, since the use of the local language became a means for financial gain. All of these policies were initiated and backed by the CIP (Tsukida and Tsuchida 2007:288–293).

Catalan [cat]. After forty years of repression under the Franco regime in Spain, Catalonia regained autonomy in 1979. Language development efforts were begun, aimed at eradicating the negative attitudes towards the use of Catalan. In 1982, the government of Catalonia implemented a "normalization campaign" that targeted both Castillian-speaking immigrants to the region and Catalan speakers. They adopted the slogan "Catalan belongs to everyone" and presented it to the public through a humorous, 10-year-old female cartoon character named Norma. Norma proclaimed the message on television, radio, and in newspaper advertisements. The campaign was considered a success. In 1983 the government adopted the Charter of the Catalan Language, which established equality between Catalan and Spanish in all government domains (Fishman 1991:287–336).

Differentiation

Diné [nav]. Until recently, the Navajo Nation has been able to maintain a high level of intergenerational transmission of their language, Diné. Just one generation ago nearly all Navajo people spoke the language, but there are fewer children growing up as native speakers now. There are several reasons for the shift from Navajo to English, but it is ultimately founded on the economic success associated with English. The Navajo Nation has the largest land base of any tribe in the United States (27,000 square miles), which gave them the ability to isolate themselves from U.S. culture to a certain degree. As subsistence farmers, they have largely relied on the land instead of moving off the reservation for wage-earning jobs. However, due to over-grazing and increases in population, people are increasingly forced to find work off the reservation resulting in increased use of English. One tool the Navajo have used to combat language shift is the signing of contracts between speakers and non-speakers. The contract is signed by a language teacher and a learner or by speakers and non-speakers in the same family. The contracts establish when and where the participants will speak Navajo with one another. The contracts provide an opportunity for the people to both learn the language and create a clear differentiation between the use of Navajo and English in daily life (Fishman 1991:187–229, Lee and McLaughlin 2001:23–43).

Cochiti Keres [kee]. In the mid-1980s, the Cochiti Tribal Council began a language and culture revitalization effort that was aided by the return of educated professional young adults that had a desire to address language loss in their community. Language coordinators were trained in order to raise awareness among community members about the status of the language and to cultivate members' felt needs in the form of long-term goals for the community. They decided to target language use in tribal offices. An early attempt, using language teachers, was unsuccessful but when they had fluent employees teach non-fluent employees for fifteen minutes at the beginning of each day, better results were achieved. The program was altered further to be more effective. Trained language coordinators taught the non-fluent employees three times a week for thirty minutes and optional evening classes were offered to continue language education. Overall, employees in tribal offices were encouraged to reserve business and interoffice communication for the local language, reclaiming that domain from English (Pecos and Blum-Martinez 2001:80).

Catalan [cat]. A program has been developed to address some of the social and psychological issues that arise when a local language has not been associated with very many functions or lacks prestige and acceptance. People who know the language may be reluctant to use it because of patterns of "learned helplessness" in which they automatically switch to the dominant language in contexts where they may feel insecure or unsure. These patterns of behavior are ingrained and automatic and changing them requires conscious effort as well as behavioral resources designed to re-enforce new language use patterns. The Catalan program takes the form of a workshop or retreat where participants examine their current language use and then make concrete plans aimed at reducing their level of discomfort and increasing their level of satisfaction in using their local language.

During the workshop, participants identify specific changes they wish to make in their language use and create for themselves resources that will help them achieve those changes. They are asked to begin with the easiest modifications and then can move to more difficult changes as they are successful. This behavior modification is facilitated in an atmosphere of respect and without coercion. The goal is to increase the level of comfort that each participant feels when using their heritage language (Suay 2015).

Pennsylvania German [pdc]. The Amish community in the United States historically has maintained strong boundaries separating themselves from the dominant culture for religious and traditional reasons. This desire for isolation has motivated them to make deliberate decisions about language use. The community recognizes the importance of being able to speak and interact within the dominant English culture, but only enough to maintain economic relationships with outsiders. With that mindset, Amish children are not exposed to the dominant language, English, until they enter school. Up until that point, children are monolingual speakers of Pennsylvania German. The community views school as part of the dominant culture and, because of this classification, it is an effective tool to teach their children as much about the dominant culture as they feel necessary for the community's economic survival. In the mid-1900s, the public schools attended by Amish children began to give parents less control over their child's education. At that point, the community began to develop private parochial schools that were community operated. The people made a deliberate decision to continue using English in their schools in order to establish the habit of using English for economic purposes but retained Pennsylvania German at home and when interacting within the community. Many scholars view education in the local language as a key component to language revitalization, but this case is the exact opposite. In order to minimize the impact of English on the use of Pennsylvania German, the speech community has been intentional in creating stable multilingualism in which the use of the dominant language in education clearly differentiates Pennsylvania German as the language of the community and English as the language of outsiders (Johnson-Weiner 1999:31–37).

A.3.2 Revitalizing the language (from EGIDS 8a, 8b to EGIDS 7)

Functions

Karajarri [gbd]. Karajarri is located in Western Australia. At EGIDS 8a, it is still spoken by the older generations while the younger generation only maintains a passive understanding. The language is not being transmitted to children even though the ability to speak the language is related to an individual's land affiliation. While children are growing up without knowledge of the language, they are associated with specific geographic territories by what language they *should* be able to speak. Various language revitalization efforts are underway and the people are aware of the need for these programs. One of the unexpected results of their fight for the Karajarri Native Title claim in 2001 was the discovery and subsequent use of historical language documentation in language revitalization. The researcher that helped with the Native Title claim visited the area in 2002 and spent time studying the old documents with two Aboriginal women. Other Karajarri people were involved in studying these texts which served to rejuvenate the people's desire for language maintenance through what they learned in the documents. The documents reminded the people of words and phrases that are currently out of use and old traditional stories that had been forgotten (Sharp 2003:20–25).

Lardil [lbz] Language Learner's Guide. The Lardil Projects Steering Committee of Mornington Island, Australia, recognized that there were few resources available to support language learners in the general community. They decided to develop a Lardil language learner's guide consisting of a booklet and an audio tape. The guide used a domain approach, organized around themes that were relevant to the daily life of the Lardil people. The themes reflected the land-sea dichotomy in Lardil life and culture (Ash, Fermino, and Hale 2001:22–23).

The Confederated Tribes of Warm Springs, USA: Kiksht [wac], Numu [pao], Ichishkiin [waa]. A cooperative relationship between Portland State University (Oregon, USA) and the Confederated Tribes of the Warm Springs Reservation was developed. The partnership connected members of the speech community, fieldworkers, and university representatives. Prior to this, the three languages included in the confederation were making attempts at revitalization, but finding that many outsider specialists would only come for short periods of time and were not part of a longer term program. The community needed ongoing training programs for national teachers, linguists to help develop materials for local language classrooms, and people experienced in collecting and archiving language data. The university had the resources and people to help the language group in those specific areas over a longer period of time. In turn, the university could diversify its programs while investing in the community (Kono and Finch 2004:225–226).

Acquisition

Indigenous languages of New South Wales, Australia. The Koori Centre was established at the University of Sydney in order to enrich the lives of indigenous Australians through easier access to university classes. The center is an autonomous entity based at the university for the purpose of facilitating and guiding indigenous Australians through their higher education experience. All management and a majority of the staff are indigenous Australians. The center offers a facility for students to interact with one another informally and meet with staff members that will advise them on how to best achieve their individual goals. They also provide teacher training courses that are only available to indigenous Australian students. The program includes several levels of accreditation. Students can take advantage of 6-week block classes which are formatted to meet the needs of the indigenous communities. The center's partnership with the University of Sydney allows them to produce students that are both educated in best teaching practices and who meet the requirements of the Australian government for educators (Hobson 2004:53–57).

Master-apprentice program. "The Master-Apprentice Language Learning Method is a mentored learning approach, created for people who may not have access to language classes but, instead, have access to a speaker. The program was originally designed in California for the endangered indigenous languages of the state.... This program is designed for communities in which there are elders who still know their language but rarely have an opportunity to speak it. It is for communities who want to preserve their native language and bring it back into use again. It is to help adults learn their languages of heritage so they can pass them on through programs at home, school, or in the community. It is also for individual members of the community who want to learn their language, just because they love it."

"The master-apprentice program is designed so that a highly motivated team consisting of a speaker and a learner can go about language teaching/learning on their own, without outside help from experts. The teaching and learning is done through **immersion**: the team members commit themselves to spending ten to twenty hours per week together, speaking primarily the language" (Hinton 2002:xiii–xiv, emphasis in the original).

The program has been implemented in the Karuk [kyh], Hupa [hup], Yurok [yur], Pomo [peb] [peq] [pej], Wukchumne [yok], Yowlumne [yok], Paiute [ute], Mojave [mov] and Chemehuevi [ute] languages of California and continues to gain widespread use (Hinton 2001b:223–225).

Anishinaabemowin [oji]: Acquisition in the home. Anishinaabemowin is the autonym for the Ojibwa languages spoken around the Great Lakes region of North America. In this context where English is the dominant language, parents face a challenge in passing the language to their children. One implementer has identified three basic stages to creating a bilingual home: crawling, walking, and running:

- Crawling consists of teaching learners how to think in the language based on its structure. This helps them to put the language into perspective and enables them to begin tapping into the worldview of their heritage culture.

- Walking is characterized by planned language lessons and artificial environments to practice what is being learned.

- Running happens when learners can use the language without thinking about it and are put into situations where they can use their language skills naturally (i.e., traditional events, talking with elders).

This approach combines naturalistic language use with more overt instruction and recognizes that language acquisition for emerging language users is a progression that takes a considerable amount of time. There are, as well, venues other than the home where language acquisition can take place and be encouraged (Noori 2009:11–22).

Acoma [kjq]. In 1997, after a language-use survey reaffirmed the general belief that the Acoma community in New Mexico was shifting to English, the tribal members organized a two-week immersion camp for Acoma children. The camp was a success and subsequently lengthened to six weeks in 1998. The camp was funded by a collaboration of tribal programs and staffed by 12 willing speakers.

Three hour-long language sessions were given to the elementary children in the morning and the secondary school children in the afternoon. Parents of the children were encouraged to attend the classes. Campers completed surveys at the end of camp where many commented on the presence of adults that were also learning the language, stating that it was encouraging to see them try to learn (and not always succeed).

Before the camp started, the staff spent significant time learning about the process of developmental language learning in children. Instead of immediately expecting the campers to respond and speak, they allowed the students to be comfortable in their passive understanding. The students were not encouraged to try speaking until the teachers had gained rapport and campers were at ease with their environment. During the six-week camp, the final project was a traditional storytelling through puppetry that would be presented to the community. This set the precedent for campers to start using what they learned in public. After the program, there was a lot of positive feedback from parents. Children continued to play the language games, songs, and stories they had learned at camp and passed them along to their siblings. The camp experience created positive attitudes in youth towards the local language and a desire to continue learning (Sims 2001:70–72).

Potawatomi [pot]. The Potawatomi have developed an extensive website to directly address language revitalization issues within their speech community. They have already established adult and school-based language classes, some of which are online. The website provides information about these classes while providing extra activities for language learning externally. One of the stated goals of the website is to bring language acquisition into the home through these activities. They are designed to encourage parents and their children to work together on vocabulary and grammar games. The website also incorporates review activities from the classroom and immersion programs that can be downloaded onto hand-held devices. Instead of resisting the encroachment of technology, which is usually associated with the dominant language, the creation of a website infuses the minority language with a contemporary image while simultaneously providing a means of language re-acquisition (Hannahville Potawatomi Indian Community, USA 2009).

Motivation

The American Indian Language Development Institute (AILDI): Increasing the value of indigenous languages. AILDI grew out of a project at San Diego State University called the Yuman Language Institute. Academic linguists and bilingual educators worked together to use linguistic knowledge to improve education for indigenous students. AILDI's primary aim is "to incorporate indigenous linguistic and cultural knowledge into school curricula in ways that affirm indigenous students' identities, support their academic achievement, and promote the retention of their languages and cultures" (McCarty et al. 2001:372).

"Over the years, AILDI has increased the value of the linguistic and cultural capital brought to school by indigenous students through its facilitation of curricula, programs, and personnel able to make use of that capital. Just as important, AILDI has helped transform indigenous linguistic and cultural resources into political capital. Recognition of the importance of indigenous languages and cultures does more than merely validate them; it increases their value and the power of those who speak and control those linguistic and cultural resources" (McCarty et al. 2001:376).

Environment

The Native American Languages Acts of 1990 and 1992. Language policy in the United States has often been cited as an example of the planned eradication of Indian languages with oppressive measures mandated in education and other public settings. Early statements regarding Native American languages in policy documents referred to them as "barbarous dialects" that should be "blotted out". Attempts to alter those policies have involved a process of successive attempts to reach a Congressional consensus that would result in a more favorable legislative and policy environment. A contemporary attempt to define such a policy was embodied in the Native American Languages Act of 1990 which repudiated past policies and declared that Native Americans had the right to use their own languages. This effort was itself influenced by the efforts in the state of Hawai'i to achieve the recognition of Hawaiian. Enactment of the bill was difficult to achieve, however, in light of strong sentiment against the use of any language but English in the United States. It was only through the use of some legislative strategies that the full text of the Native American Languages Act of 1990 was incorporated into another bill and passed into law.

In 1992 a separate bill was proposed that duplicated in large measure the contents of the 1990 legislation and included provisions for funding of development efforts in the Native American languages. It met with similar resistance but was given a great deal of support by members of Native American communities, linguists, and educators. After a lengthy and arduous process of negotiations and amendments, the bill was finally passed in both houses of Congress and signed into law by the President on October 26th, 1992 (Arnold 2001).

Differentiation

Welsh [cym] Civil disobedience. The Welsh Language Society was organized in the early part of the 20th century to promote the legal recognition of the Welsh language and used civil disobedience as a way to draw attention to their demands. They occupied public offices, refused to pay taxes using English-only forms, destroyed English-only road signs and were fined and sent to jail as a result. This very public and radical campaign of "differentiation" gradually gained popular support and laws were amended to recognize Welsh for legal transactions and many governmental and private institutions began to provide Welsh signage and printed forms and informative literature. Over the succeeding years, a place for Welsh in modern Wales has gradually expanded and gained resources. The Welsh movement was further advanced as traditional Welsh cultural activities gained in popularity and more contemporary cultural art forms have also become associated with the Welsh language. While Welsh continues to decline in rural and industrial communities, the ability to speak Welsh is seen as an advantage in local and national government, education, tourism, and in the communication industries (Morgan 2001:111–112).

A.3.3 Awakening the language (from EGIDS 9 to EGIDS 8b)

Functions

Resources for documenting language functions. Resources that offer useful checklists for planning corpus collection around the themes of functions and bodies of knowledge are: Orwig, 2008, Section 4.5.3 "Oral Tradition (pp. 56–64) and Questionnaire 18: Oral tradition (pp. 689–691) in Bouquiaux and Thomas 1992, and chapter 2, "Things to talk about in texts" (pp. 135–219) in Brewster and Brewster 1976.

The first offers extensive lists of functions of language that a language learner must master. These could be used in planning a language documentation corpus. It would be difficult for a documentation team to happen upon most of these functions using traditional methods of text collection. A group of willing volunteers might be found who could be recorded as they did role plays exemplifying these uses of the language.

The second resource offers many ideas about topics to probe in collecting texts over a wide range of bodies of knowledge. The discussion gives ideas concerning locations, landmarks, plants, animals, social organization, seasonal and nonseasonal activities, personal histories, and technology. It also offers an extensive list of text types.

The third resource contains prompting questions to stimulate exploration of over 130 functions of language and bodies of knowledge. See also the index of topics on pages 107–108.

Technologies for Language Documentation. "With the information technology revolution, the tools needed to document language in use are readily available. Digital sound recording, digital video, and digital photography can easily be combined with text in multimedia displays. Compiling a rich archive of numerous aspects of daily life, including language use, is now an achievable possibility, and language documentation is moving in this direction" (Amery 2009:143).

The Basic Oral Language Documentation (BOLD) methodology is an example of how digital technologies and participatory methods can be combined to document a wide range of language use even in contexts where there are no literate community members.

The BOLD methodology uses both audio and video recordings to document natural speech. Unlike traditional documentation, however, the transcription of the speech is produced through successive oral repetitions of the speech, first in a slower, fully elaborated rendition, followed by a translation of the utterance in a language of wider communication. Written transcriptions and linguistic analysis can be done later using both the audio and video materials.

There are several advantages to this approach: (1) It involves the community directly in the documentation work, often with older speakers providing the local language samples and younger speakers/hearers providing the oral transcriptions; (2) It allows for a fairly rapid collection of a variety of genres; (3) Both audio and video recordings aid in the written transcription and analysis. The BOLD methodology does rely on community members feeling comfortable and willing to be recorded and it requires some investment in creating an adequate recording site. Equipment needs are relatively modest and a simple, but adequate recording "studio" can be constructed using many local materials (Reiman 2010).

Acquisition

Lushootseed [lut] foreign language course. In 1972, the University of Washington began a Lushootseed foreign language course based on the stated interest of Lushootseed youth to learn the language. The course was specifically aimed at a Lushootseed demographic, but some linguistics students and Native American students from other tribes also took the course. After the pilot program established the popularity of the course, it was expanded to a two-year program that meets five times per week during the school year. Efforts are made to limit the artificiality of the classroom environment through field trips to ceremonies and gatherings, as well as introducing cultural games and food during class time (Hilbert and Hess 1982:71–89).

Home school language and culture textbook with CD-ROM. Textbooks are usually written and published for use in an institutionalized school environment. However, there are potential benefits to writing a textbook geared to children that are too young for school or simply for use in the home with older children.

By making the book user-friendly for non-teachers, some language acquisition can occur in the home and act as a motivator for the childbearing and elderly generations to teach the language to their children (and to themselves). These textbooks should be written with the goal of creating teachable moments for older generations to pass on language and culture information to children.

In communities that are technologically advanced, it is helpful to have digital media to accompany the textbook. The media supplement is meant to attract people that are 20–50 years old and to add prestige to the learning materials.

On the surface level, the at-home textbooks are a tool for language acquisition. However, in situations where the language is not being transmitted to the children and only the older generations are still using it, the textbooks can provide a deeper sentimental attachment (i.e., motivation) to the language among the childbearing generation.

Motivation

Culture groups for Saraguro Quichua [qvj] youth. Quechua [que] has 8–12 million speakers, concentrated in three countries. It is the most widely spoken indigenous language in the Americas, but it is considered threatened. For about 500 years, speakers of Quechua have endured adverse social and political conditions despite a brief period when Spanish and Quechua existed together in a diglossic relationship.

The current linguistic situation is quite complex. There are many different varieties of Quechua, and each has shifted in its own way. The Saraguro people that live in the Loja Province of Ecuador are, for the most part, monolingual in Spanish. Quichua is currently used by the older generations, to make jokes, and for traditional events. Youth culture groups that promote the revitalization of Saraguro culture are quite popular. They showcase traditional music, dancing, poetry, oration, and speak out against social injustice. These groups have been popular for about forty years, but are still limited to young people without children. The groups have not reached out to or developed any influence on the childbearing demographic. Despite this shortcoming, the emphasis on traditional music and culture brings with it a symbolic use of Quechua and attracts youth. Though the people do not learn the language through this activity, a sentimental attachment is developed that may reignite motivation to learn it (Hornberger and King 2001:73–175).

Itelmen [itl]. The Itelmen language is a highly endangered language found on the Kamchatka peninsula in eastern Russia. The only speakers left are members of the older generation and the only domain fulfilled by Itelmen is traditional ceremonies. Regardless of the lack of use, the people still find their identity in the language and culture. Based on this attitude, a revitalization project was begun that involved creating a new textbook (some school textbooks already existed) aimed towards children that had not yet entered school. The textbooks were written with a focus on combining important cultural and traditional information with language learning. The obvious goal was to begin teaching children about the language and culture at a young age within the home environment. The less obvious and probably more realistic goal was to create a sense of attachment to the language in the generations that no longer found speaking Itelmen beneficial. In order to attract the younger generations, the project managers created a CD-ROM to accompany the textbook. The CD piqued the interest of a technologically savvy generation and raised the prestige of the learning materials. Essentially, it was now more acceptable to buy and use the product (Kasten 2008:152–153).

Environment

Advocacy for language revitalization. Where language use has waned and revitalization is desired, a hostile or indifferent language policy can be addressed through proactive efforts to convince policy makers that the nation's linguistic heritage is valuable and worthy of preservation. This may be achieved through an appeal to international agreements, treaties, and accords which protect the rights of minority and indigenous peoples to maintain their languages and cultures. The international agreements that might be referenced include:

- African Charter on Human and People's Rights (1987)
- International Covenant on Civil and Political Rights (1966, 1976)
- Framework Convention for the Protection of National Minorities (1998)
- ILO Convention on Indigenous and Tribal People, no. 169 (1989)

- United Nations Declaration on the Rights of Indigenous Peoples (2007)
- European Charter for Regional or Minority Languages (1992)
- Convention for the Safeguarding of Intangible Cultural Heritage (2005)
- Convention against Discrimination in Education (1960)
- Some of these are regional in their focus and there may be others that apply specifically to a particular region. In addition, local laws which have not been adequately implemented or enforced may provide a basis for arguing for more equitable and favorable polices.

Differentiation

Welsh [cym]: Linguistic Rights Enforcement as differentiation. The effort to promote the ongoing use of Welsh can be supported through legal and judicial efforts to create and protect the rights of speakers to use the language. One incident involved judicial support for the right of a mother and daughter to speak to each other in Welsh, the daughter's first language, in a doctor's office. The doctor requested that they speak English. When the mother complained to the Welsh Language Commission, the commission ruled that the medical practice had ignored their right to speak the Welsh language (http://www.bbc.com/news/uk-wales-north-east-wales-29610299).

A.4 Achieving Sustainable Identity

A.4.1 Landing at Sustainable Identity (from EGIDS 8b to EGIDS 9)

Functions

Arctic languages in the Russian Federation. The focus of the Voices from the Tundra and Taiga research project, sponsored by the Netherlands Organisation for Scientific Research (NWO) from May 2002 to June 2005, was on languages close to extinction that the government was either unable or unwilling to spend resources on for preservation. Previous research was recovered through new technology, giving the project the ability to compare some of the target languages to recordings that had been made fifty years earlier. Both sets of sound recordings consist of folktales, fairy tales, songs, and normal conversations. The current project also oversaw and promoted the development of a training program for members of the speech communities so they can continue the work of preserving their languages (de Graaf 2004:158–159).

Tlingit [tli]. In 1994, the Southeast Alaska Native Subsistence Commission documented over 3,000 place names in Tlingit and other indigenous languages. These names provide crucial information vis à vis fishing, the people's history, and the people's culture. The elders identified the location of each place on a map for later use. The Tlingit people recognize that losing knowledge in this domain is also a loss of cultural knowledge. Children are no longer learning the true meaning of place names and are required to go to cultural interpreters in order to understand their significance. By carefully documenting the names and creating story maps, the knowledge will last beyond the elders and can be used to transmit the information to the children, strengthening their sense of identity (Thornton 2003:29–35).

Alamblak [amp]. In 2003, only one elderly Alamblak man in Papua New Guinea felt confident performing the indigenous signal drumming communication, played on the *nrwit* (Tok Pisin: *garamut*). Other local residents claimed to be able to "hear" the signals (understand them if they heard them) but were unwilling to perform the rhythmic patterns.

Neil R. Coulter, an ethnomusicologist, worked with this one elderly man from 2004 to 2006, learning the *nrwit* patterns from him and transcribing them—first in waveforms, then in percussion notation on a single-line staff. This activity did not lead to revitalization of the system, but the audio and written documentation is available for future generations who want to learn from it.

Coulter wondered if mobile phones (and particularly texting) might be the ultimate replacement for *nrwit* communication, but Alamblak people stated the significant distinction: signal drumming communicates to entire villages at once, but texting is only a one-to-one communication system. Community is an important factor, even in communication, and so the *nrwit* documentation may yet prove important for the Alamblak people (Coulter 2005:72–100).

Garrawa [wrk] and Yanyuwa [jao]. Garrawa and Yanyuwa are located in the Borroloola region of Northwest Territory, Australia. Many Aboriginal people have switched to English in order to avoid the mistreatment applied to them in the past and want to give their children better opportunities in the western context. In 1987, the Papulu Apparrkari Language Centre established the Borroloola Project with a goal of documenting and preserving the language before the last speakers passed away. They wanted to give children the opportunity to see and hear the language spoken, as well as learning about their history and culture. So they recorded on video and in writing the elderly speakers teaching about bush medicine, traditional uses for various plants, oral histories, basket weaving, traditional songs, and word lists. The project lacked funding and ended up being unable to turn the final recordings into teaching materials. However, the records now exist and can eventually be disseminated. They intentionally sent young children on the data-collecting trips enabling them to have intimate interactions with the speakers of the older generation (LoBianco and Rhydwen 2001:402–406).

Acquisition

Blackfoot [bla]. The younger generations of Blackfoot were no longer learning the language. They were identifying with the tribe ethnically, but not culturally. Inspired by an all-day immersion school in Hawai'i, speakers of Blackfoot established an immersion school in Montana in 1995.

Instead of working within the public school system, garnering federal funds, they raised the necessary money through friends, patrons, and private foundations. This was an intentional decision made in order to maintain independence from outside regulations.

The school teaches regular academic subjects while teaching the language and culture. Blackfoot children that had previously been unable to participate in traditional events were able to pray at tribal ceremonies after being educated at the all-day immersion school (Kipp 2009:1–9).

Motivation

Tlingit [tli], Haida [hai], Tsimshian [tsi]. Spoken in Alaska and Canada, these three languages have endured abuse at the hands of the church and government in the past. Some (not all) churches taught that the indigenous languages were unholy, leaving a deep impression on the people that God did not approve of their language. At government schools, students from these language groups were singled out and sent to speech therapy class to correct their English accents. Many elders and people of childbearing age have memories of harsh punishments associated with using the local language. One speaker states, "Whenever I speak Tlingit, I can still taste the soap" (Dauenhauer and Dauenhauer 1998:65).

The amount of damage done in the past affects the people's desire to revitalize their language. They support efforts in word, but in practice they refuse to send their children to language school or use it in the home out of fear that their children will experience the same negative reactions that they did. The three communities have established small groups that teach and perform traditional dances, songs, and wear traditional costumes. Despite the negative attitude towards the language, the people are proud of their heritage and culture. The dances and songs are relatively easy to learn and the traditional dress is bright and attractive. The cultural heritage groups do not address language and so will not directly increase language use, but they do bring people in closer contact with the language through positive interaction with cultural symbols (Dauenhauer and Dauenhauer 1998:67–68).

Environment

Irish [gle]: The effect of positive policy. The newly independent government of Ireland recognized the Irish language as official in 1922. Achieving that policy goal (moving from EGIDS 9 to EGIDS 1 in the predominantly non-Irish-speaking regions) has not been successful; it has, however created space for Irish maintenance and revitalization, as well as committing the government to the provision of resources in support of the language. In spite of this lack of broad success, the favorable policy environment has slowed down the process of language shift and has "clearly altered the spatial and social structure of bilingualism in Ireland." Only about 10% of those interviewed in surveys indicated that they have adequate levels of proficiency in Irish for day-to-day use and only about 5% of the national population identify Irish as their first or main language. Nevertheless, passive use of Irish has increased (Riagáin 2001:196–197, 201–202).

A.4.2 Reclaiming the language of identity (from EGIDS 10 to EGIDS 9)

Functions

Kaurna [zku]. Kaurna was spoken in the Adelaide Plains of Australia. The last time it was used was in the late 1800s. When language reclamation started in 1990, there were no speakers and no audio recordings that could be used in a language reclamation or revitalization program. The people had to rely on written records that were filled with gaps. In order to fill in lexical gaps, the people looked to related languages and developed their own vocabulary. In 2000, funding was provided for a workshop that would develop vocabulary for use in families and to study traditional funeral rites. This workshop brought together groups of people that were passionate about language reclamation. The first workshop turned into several more, and this core group of people ended up forming the Kaurna Warra Pintyandi, a committee that oversaw the promotion, development, and dissemination of Kaurna. The committee encouraged projects that include: welcome protocols, funeral protocols, radio programs, greeting cards, postcards, place names, strengthening community involvement in language reclamation, and creating a request database. The committee is the driving force behind the movement, keeping the community focused on their language goals (Amery and Rigney 2007:21–28; Grenoble and Whaley 2006:63–67).

Badjala, Australia: Rediscovering identity. The Badjala language of Gari (Fraser Island) in Queensland, Australia is part of the Gabi-Gabi language group [gbw]. There is no intergenerational transmission of the language and many who identify themselves as Badjala also identify with other Aboriginal languages. No one is a fluent speaker of the language, though there is documentation of the grammar and lexicon. Language revitalization activists have focused on teaching the language to children who have taken up using Badjala words and phrases when speaking Aboriginal English. Use of the language includes personal stories, traditional and modern music and dance, greetings, gestures, actions, names of body parts, seasons and elements, kinship terms for family members, numbers, and the names of land and sea animals. These uses of the language are viewed as being "critical to [their] identity and distinctiveness as Aboriginal people" and that "words seem to be enough for people to connect the language to their identity" (Bell 2007, 2013, and Bell and Bonner 2015, as cited by Dadd (2015:9).

Acquisition

Miamiya [mia]: Reawakening a language using documentary materials. The last fluent speaker of Miamiya died in the early 1960s. At that point the language was classified as extinct though there remained a sizeable community of people who retained their identity as members of the Miami tribe. By the 1980s, there were many Miami children who did not know a single word in the language. Using a large body of archival materials including documents from the 17th, 18th, 19th and early 20th centuries, the language is being awakened and brought back into use. Where the documentation is inadequate, the community is innovating, borrowing from related Algonquian languages, extending the semantic scope of known vocabulary, and bringing the language back into dynamic use in its contemporary context through the creation of neologisms. In the 1990s teacher training workshops were started supplemented by cultural immersion camps for young people, language learning materials, games, and some formal classroom-based learning opportunities. "There are now hundreds of Miami people with some knowledge of the language and perhaps about fifteen people with conversational proficiency" (Leonard 2008:25–26).

Motivation

Latin [lat] and other dead languages. Where no ethnic group that associates its identity with a particular language remains, efforts to motivate people to use the language may need to focus on factors other than identity, at least at the start. While few may be seriously considering the resurgence of the Roman empire, there are some who champion Latin, for example, not only as a language for liturgical uses, but for a broader, though still limited, set of functions. There are, for example, online user groups where Latin is used exclusively, Latin clubs, and groups which promote the production of contemporary Latin literature. There are podcasts of readings of Latin classical literature and numerous opportunities to learn Latin online or even in communal immersion settings. This activism serves to provide a sense of community among Latin activists that provides encouragement and motivation for those who participate. See http://www.latinteach.com as one repository of Latin resources.

Environment

Native American Programs Act of 1974. With many Native American communities in decline after decades of hostile policies, the Native American Programs Act of 1974 was an outcome of the "war on poverty" initiated by the administration of President Lyndon Johnson. The Act provided grants aimed at promoting economic development in Native American, Alaska Native, Native Hawaiian organizations and Native populations in U.S. dependencies throughout the Pacific basin. These grants are supervised by the Administration for Native Americans. Central among the programs promoted by the act are language revitalization and continuation projects. This reversal of Federal policy and the commitment of resources has assisted many local groups in their efforts to restore the vitality of their communities (http://www.acf.hhs.gov/programs/ana).

References

Ager, Dennis. 2005. Image and prestige planning. *Current Issues in Language Planning* 6(1):1–43.

Ah Suhn. 2015. Assessing the vitality of Akha in Myanmar with the Sustainable Use Model. M.A. thesis. Department of Linguistics, Payap University, Chiang Mai, Thailand.

Alisjahbana, S. Takdir. 1974. Language policy, language engineering and literacy in Indonesia and Malaysia, In Joshua A. Fishman. (ed.), *Advances in language planning*, 391–416. The Hague, Mouton.

Allard, R., and R. Landry. 1986. Subjective ethnolinguistic vitality viewed as a belief system. *Journal of Multilingual and Multicultural Development* 7(1):1–12.

Alloni-Fainberg, Yafa. 1974. Official Hebrew terms for parts of the car: A study of knowledge, usage and attitudes. In J. A. Fishman (ed.), *Advances in language planning*, 493–517. The Hague: Mouton.

Amery, Rob. 2009. Phoenix or relic? *Language Documentation and Conservation* 3(2):138–148. http://scholarspace.manoa.Hawaii.edu/bitstream/handle/10125/4436/amery.pdf. Accessed April 1, 2016.

Amery, Rob, and Alitya Wallara Rigney. 2007. Collaborative language revival: The work of Kaurna Warra Pintyandi. In N. Ostler (ed.), *Proceedings of the Eleventh Conference of the Foundation for Endangered Languages, University of Malaya, 26–28 October 2007*. Bath, UK: Foundation for Endangered Languages.

Araali, Bagamba B., and Douglas W. Boone. 2015. Challenges to applying the EGIDS in northeastern Democratic Republic of Congo. In Lewis and Simons, 70–104.

Arnold, Robert D. 2001. To help assure the survival and continuing vitality of Native American languages. In Hinton and Hale, 45–48.

Ash, A., J. L. D. Fermino, and K. Hale. 2001. Diversity in local language maintenance and restoration: A reason for optimism. In Hinton and Hale, 19–35.

Asian Development Bank. 2006. *Results based management explained.* Asian Development Bank. http://www.adb.org/sites/default/files/publication/29718/managing-development-results.pdf. Accessed April 2, 2016.

Baker, Colin. 1988. *Key issues in bilingualism and bilingual education.* Multilingual Matters 35. Clevedon, UK: Multilingual Matters.

Baldwin, Ruth, and Linda Orr Easthouse. 2005. Results-based management: The basics. Ms.

Batibo, Herman M. 2008. *Reversing attitudes as a key to language preservation and safeguarding in Africa.* Paper presented at UNU / UNESCO International Conference, United Nations University, 27–28 August. http://www.unu.edu/globalization/2008/files/UNU-UNESCO_Batibo.pdf. Accessed April 2, 2016.

Batibo, Herman M. 2009. Poverty as a crucial factor in language maintenance and language death: Case studies in Africa. In W. Herbert et al. (eds.), *Language and poverty,* 23–36. Clevedon, UK: Multilingual Matters.

Bell, J. 2007. Why we do what we do! Reflections of an Aboriginal linguist working on the maintenance and revival of ancestral languages. *Ngoonjook: A journal of Australian indigenous issues* 30:12–18.

Bell, J. 2013. Language attitudes and language revival/survival. *Journal of Multilingual and Multicultural Development* 34(4):399–410.

Bell, J., and J. Bonner. 2015. *Language ecology and Butchulla revitalisation.* Paper presented at 4th International Conference on Language Documentation and Conservation, February 26–March 1, 2015, Honolulu, HI. http://scholarspace.manoa.hawaii.edu/handle/10125/25341?show=full. Accessed April 2, 2016.

Benedicto, Elena et al. 2001. *Indigenous presence in the Nicaraguan media: The mayangna.* Paper presented at the Fifth Foundation for Endangered Languages Conference, 20–23 September 2001, Agadir, Morocco.

Bird, Steven, and Gary Simons. 2003. Seven dimensions of portability for language documentation and description. *Language* 79:557–582.

Bouquiaux, L., and J. M. C. Thomas. 1992. *Studying and describing unwritten languages.* Dallas, TX: SIL International.

Bourhis, Richard Y., and Howard Giles. 1976. The language of cooperation in Wales: A field study. *Language Sciences* 42:13–16.

Bourhis, Richard Y., Howard Giles, and Wallace E. Lambert. 1975. Social consequences of accommodation of one's style of speech: A cross-national investigation. *International Journal of the Sociology of Language* 6:55–72.

Bourhis, Richard Y., Howard Giles, and Doreen Rosenthal. 1981. Notes on the construction of a subjective vitality questionnaire for ethnolinguistic groups. *Journal of Multilingual and Multicultural Development* 2:144–155.

Bourhis, Richard Y., and Itesh Sachdev. 1984. Vitality perceptions and language attitudes: Some Canadian data. *Journal of Language and Social Psychology* 3:97–126.

Brenzinger, Matthias, Akira Yamamoto, Noriko Aikawa, Dimitri Koundiouba, Anahit Minasyan, Arienne Dwyer, Colette Grinevald, Michael Krauss, Osahito Miyaoka, Osamu Sakiyama, Rieks Smeets, and Ofelia Zepeda. 2003. *Language vitality and endangerment.* Paris: UNESCO Ad Hoc Expert Group Meeting on Endangered Languages. http://www.unesco.org/culture/en/endangeredlanguages Accessed March 10–12, 2003.

Brewster, E. Thomas, and Elizabeth S. Brewster. 1976. *Language acquisition made practical: Field methods for language learners.* Pasadena: Lingua House.

Brown, Roger, and Albert Gilman. 1960. The pronouns of power and solidarity. *American Anthropologist* 4(6):24–29.

Busch, Brigitta. 2001. *The virtual village square: Media in minority languages in the process of media diversification and globalisation—an example from southern Carinthia (Austria)*. Paper presented at the Fifth Foundation for Endangered Languages Conference, 20–23 September 2001, Agadir, Morocco.

Cahill, Michael. 2014. Non-linguistic factors in orthographies. In Cahill and Rice, 9–25.

Cahill, Michael, and Keren Rice eds. 2014. *Developing orthographies for unwritten languages*. Dallas: SIL International.

Campbell, Lyle, and Martha C. Muntzel. 1989. The structural consequences of language death. In Dorian, 181–196.

Chambers, Robert. 1983. *Rural development: Putting the last first*. Essex, UK: Longman Scientific & Technical.

Chambers, Robert. 1994. The origins and practice of participatory rural appraisal. *World Development* 22(7):953–969. http://ideas.repec.org/a/eee/wdevel/ v22y1994i7p953-969.html. Accessed April 2, 2016.

Chambers, Robert. 1995. Poverty and livelihoods: Whose reality counts? *Environment and Urbanization* 7(1):173–204. http://eau.sagepub.com/cgi/content/abstract/7/1/173. Accessed April 2, 2016.

Chang, Debbie. 2010. *Taps: Checklist for responsble archiving of digital language resources*. Dallas, TX: Graduate Institute of Applied Linguistics.

Chomsky, Noam. 1965. *␣Aspects of the theory of syntax*. Cambridge, MA: MIT Press.

Churchill, S. 1986. *The education of linguistic and cultural minorities in the OECD countries*. Clevedon: Multilingual Matters.

Chríost, Diarmait Mac Giolla. 2005. Prestige planning and the Welsh language: Marketing, the consumer-citizen and language behaviour. *Current Issues in Language Planning* 6(1):64–72.

Cooper, Robert L., ed. 1982. *Language spread: Studies in diffusion and social change*. Bloomington, IN: Indiana University Press.

Cooper, Robert L. 1989. *Language planning and social change*. Cambridge: Cambridge University Press.

Cooperrider, David. 2004. *Engaging the "whole system" in an appreciative inquiry summit*. http://www.ovationnet.com/worldvisioncasestudy.pdf. Accessed April 2, 2016.

Coulmas, Florian. 1984. *Linguistic minorities and literacy: Language policy issues in developing countries*. Berlin: Mouton.

Coulter, Neil R. 2005. Signifying names and places on the Alamblak garamut: Some initial observations of a traditional sign system. *Ethnodoxology* 3(2):15–19.

Cox, Philip, Sherry Kozak, Louise Griep, and Lisa Moffat. 2004. *Splash and ripple: Planning and managing for results*. PLAN:NET Limited. http://www.hc-sc.gc.ca/ahc-asc/pubs/_contribution/ripple-ricochet/index-eng.php. Accessed April 1, 2016.

Cox, Philip. 2005. *Managing for change: Introducing the art of Results-Based Management*. PLAN:NET Limited. http://www.focusintl.com/RBM010-Management%20For%20Change.pdf. Accessed April 1, 2016.

Cummins, James. 1980. The construct of language proficiency in bilingual education. In James E Alatis (ed.), *Georgetown University Round Table on Languages and Linguistics*, 81–103. Washington D.C.: Georgetown University Press.

Crystal, David. 2000. *Language death*. Cambridge: Cambridge University Press.

Dauenhauer, Nora Marks, and Richard Dauenhauer. 1998. Technical, emotional, and ideological issues in reversing language shift: Examples from southeast Alaska. In L. A. Grenoble and L. J. Whaley (eds.), *Endangered languages: Language loss and community response*, 57–98.

Dadd, Kathy. 2015. Analysing Badjala language revival activities with EGIDS and the Sustainable Use Model. Kangaroo Ground, Australia. Ms.

Davis, Kathryn Anne. 1994. *Language planning in multilingual contexts. Policies, communities and schools in Luxembourg*. Philadelphia: John Benjamins.

Davis, Patricia M. 2004. *Reading is for knowing: Literacy acquisition, retention, and usage among the Machiguenga*. Publications in Language Use and Education. Dallas, TX: SIL International.

de Graaf, Tjeerd. 2004. *The status of endangered languages in the border areas of Japan and Russia*. Paper presented at the Eighth Foundation for Endangered Languages Conference, 1–3 October 2004, Barcelona, Spain.

Dimmendal, Gerrit J. 1989. On language death in eastern Africa. In Dorian, 13–31.

Dorian, Nancy C. 1973. Grammatical change in a dying dialect. *Language* 49:413–438.

Dorian, Nancy C. 1977. The problem of the semi-speaker in language death. *International Journal of the Sociology of Language* 12:23–32.

Dorian, Nancy C. 1978. *East Sutherland Gaelic: The dialect of the fisherfolk of Brora, Golspie, and Embo*. Dublin: The Dublin Institute for Advanced Studies.

Dorian, Nancy C. 1980a. Language shift in community and individual: The phenomenon of the laggard semi-speaker. *International Journal of the Sociology of Language* 25:85–94.

Dorian, Nancy C. 1980b. Linguistic lag as an ethnic marker. *Language in Society* 9(1):33–41.

Dorian, Nancy C. 1981. *Language death: The life cycle of a Scottish Gaelic dialect*. Philadelphia: University of Pennsylvania Press.

Dorian, Nancy C. 1986. *Abrupt transmission failure in obsolescing languages: How sudden the "tip" to the dominant language in communities and families?* Paper presented at Proceedings of the Annual Meeting of the Berkeley Linguistic Society.

Dorian, Nancy C. 1987. The value of language-maintenance efforts which are unlikely to succeed. *International Journal of the Sociology of Language* 68:57–67.

Dorian, Nancy C., ed. 1989. *Investigating obsolescence: Studies in language contraction and death*. Cambridge: Cambridge University Press.

Dorian, Nancy C. 1994. Varieties of variation in a very small place: Social homogeneity, prestige norms, and linguistic variation. *Language* 70(4):631–696.

Eastman, Carole M. 1983. *Language Planning: An introduction.* San Francisco: Chandler & Sharp Publishers Inc.

Edwards, John. 1977. Ethnic identity and bilingual education. In H. Giles (ed.), *Language, ethnicity and intergroup relations.* London: Academic Press.

Edwards, John. 1985. *Language, society and identity.* Oxford: Basil Blackwell.

Edwards, John. 1988. Bilingualism, education and identity. *Journal of Multilingual and Multicultural Development* 9(1 & 2):203–210.

Edwards, John. 1994. *Multilingualism.* London: Routledge.

Edwards, John and Joan Chisholm. 1987. Language, multiculturalism and identity: A Canadian study. *Journal of Multilingual and Multicultural Development* 8(5):391–408.

Elwell, Vanessa M. R. 1982. Some social factors affecting multilingualism among Aboriginal Australians: A case study of Maningrida. *International Journal of the Sociology of Language* 36:83–103.

Fasold, Ralph W. 1984. *The sociolinguistics of society,* vol. 5. Language in society. Oxford: Blackwell.

Ferguson, Charles A. 1959. Diglossia. *Word* 15:325–340.

Ferguson, Charles A. 1968. Language development. In J. A. Fishman, J. Das Gupta, and C. A. Ferguson (eds.), *Language problems of developing nations 3-16.* NY: Wiley & Sons.

Fierman, William. 2005. *Kazakh language from semi-endangerment to partial recovery.* Paper presented at the Ninth Foundation for Endangered Languages Conference, 18–20 November 2005, Stellensbosch, South Africa.

Fishman, Joshua A. 1964. Language maintenance and language shift as a field of inquiry. *Linguistics* 9:32–70.

Fishman, Joshua A. 1964/1978. Language maintenance and language shift as a field of inquiry. In J. A. Fishman, L. Davidowicz, E. Ehrlich and S. Ehrlich (eds.), *Language loyalty in the United States,* 424–458. New York: Arno Press.

Fishman, Joshua A. 1965. Language maintenance and language shift: The American immigrant case within a general theoretical perspective. *Sociological Journal for Empirical Social Psychology and Ethnic Research* 10(1):19–39.

Fishman, Joshua A. 1965. Who speaks what to whom and when? *Linguistique* 2:67–88.

Fishman, Joshua A. 1967. Bilingualism with and without diglossia; diglossia with and without bilingualism. *Journal of Social Issues* 13(2):29–38.

Fishman, Joshua A. 1968. Societal bilingualism: Stable and transitional. In J. A. Fishman (ed.), *Language in sociocultural change,* 135–152. Stanford, CA: Stanford University Press.

Fishman, Joshua A. 1972a. Domains and the relationship between micro- and macro-sociolinguistics. In J. J. Gumperz and D. Hymes (eds.), *Directions in sociolinguistics,* 435–453. Oxford: Blackwell.

Fishman, Joshua A. 1972b. The relationship between micro- and macro-sociolinguistics in the study of who speaks what language to whom and when. In J. A. Fishman (ed.), *Language in sociocultural change: Essays by Joshua A. Fishman*, 244–267. Stanford, CA: Stanford University Press.

Fishman, Joshua A. 1973. Language modernization and planning in comparison with other types of national modernization and planning, *Language in Society* 2(1):23–43.

Fishman, Joshua A. 1986. Language maintenance and ethnicity. In J. A. Fishman et al. (eds.), *The rise and fall of the ethnic revival: Perspectives on language and ethnicity*, 57–76. The Hague: Mouton.

Fishman, Joshua A. 1990. Empirical explorations of two popular assumptions: Inter-polity perspective on the relationships between linguistic heterogeneity, civil strife, and per capita gross national product. In G. Imhoff (ed.), *Learning in two languages: From conflict to consensus in the reorganization of schools*, 209–225. New Brunswick, NJ: Transaction Publishers.

Fishman, Joshua A. 1991. *Reversing language shift.* Clevedon, UK: Multilingual Matters.

Fishman, Joshua A. 2000. Reversing language shift: RLS theory and practice revisited. In Kindell and Lewis, 1–26.

Fishman, Joshua A, ed. 2001. *Can threatened languages be saved? Reversing language shift, revisited: A 21st century perspective.* Multilingual Matters 116. Clevedon, UK: Multilingual Matters.

Foerster, Liz, and Mary Beth Saurman. 2013. *Producing culturally relevant language development materials for a mother tongue-based education program. Workshop Manual and Handouts.* Edition 3–November 2013. Chiang Mai, Thailand: Payap University and SIL International. http://tinyurl.com/pyxszna

Fox News Latino. 2013. *Baktun: The first telenovela made by Mayans, for Mayans.* Fox News Network LLC. http://latino.foxnews.com/latino/lifestyle/2013/08/02/baktun-first-telenovela-made-by-mayans-for-mayans/. Accessed January 24, 2015.

Friedman, Thomas. 2005. *The world is flat: A brief history of the twenty-first century.* New York: Farrar, Strauss and Giroux.

Gal, Susan. 1996. Language shift. In H. Goebl et al. (eds.), *Kontaktlinguistik, contact linguistics, linguistique de contact*, 586–593. Berlin: Walter de Gruyter.

Giles, Howard, Richard Y. Bourhis, and D. M. Taylor. 1977. Towards a theory of language in ethnic group relations. In H. Giles (ed.), *Language, ethnicity and intergroup relations*, 307–348. European Monographs in Social Psychology, 13. London: Academic Press.

Giles, Howard, and Patricia Johnson. 1987. Ethnolinguistic identity theory: A social psychological approach to language maintenance. *International Journal of the Sociology of Language* 68:69–100.

Gippert, Jost, Nikolaus P. Himmelmann, and Ulrike Mosel, eds. 2006. *Essentials of language documentation.* Berlin: Mouton De Gruyter.

Golla, Victor. 2007. North America. In C. Moseley (ed.), *Encyclopedia of the world's endangered languages*, 1–96. London: Routledge.

Gómez de García, Julie, Melissa Axelrod, and Jordan Lachler. 2002. *"If you play with fire: Literary production in Jicarilla Apache*. Paper presented at the Sixth Foundation for Endangered Languages Conference, 8–10 August 2002, Antigua, Guatemala.

Goody, Jack R. 1968. *Literacy in traditional societies*. Cambridge: Cambridge University Press.

Goody, Jack R. 1982. Alternative paths to knowledge in oral and literate cultures. In D. Tannen and W. Chafe (eds.), *Spoken and written language: Exploring orality and literacy,* 201–216. Norwood, NJ: Ablex Publishing Corporation.

Gorter, Durk. 2001. A Frisian update of reversing language shift. In Fishman, 215–233.

Grenoble, Lenore A., and Lindsay J. Whaley. 1998. *Endangered languages. Language loss and community response.* Cambridge: Cambridge University Press.

Grenoble, Lenore A., and Lindsay J. Whaley. 2006. *Saving languages: An introduction to language revitalization.* New York: Cambridge University Press.

Greymorning, Stephen. 1999. Running the gauntlet of an indigenous language program. In J. Reyhner et al. (eds.), *Revitalizing indigenous languages,* 6–16. Flagstaff, AZ: Northern Arizona University. http://jan.ucc.nau.edu/jar/RIL_2.html. Accessed April 2, 2016.

Grimes, Barbara F., ed. 1974. *Ethnologue: Languages of the World.* 8th edition. Huntington Beach, CA: Wycliffe Bible Translators, Inc.

Grimes, Barbara F. 1992. Notes on Oral Proficiency Testing (SLOPE). In E. Casad (ed.), *Windows on bilingualism.* Dallas, TX: Summer Institute of Linguistics and University of Texas at Arlington.

Grin, François. 1990. The economic approach to minority languages. *Journal of Multilingual and Multicultural Development* 11(1):153–173.

Grin, François and, François Vaillancourt. 1997. The economics of multilingualism: Overview and analytical framework. *Annual Review of Applied Linguistics* 17:43–65. http://dx.doi.org/10.1017/S0267190500003275. Accessed April 2, 2016.

Grinevald, Colette. 1998. Language endangerment in South America: A programmatic approach. In Grenoble and Whaley, 124–159.

Gumperz, John J. 1968. The speech community. *International Encyclopedia of Social Sciences* 9:381–386.

Haarman, Harald. 1990. Language planning in the light of a general theory of language: A methodological framework. *International Journal of the Sociology of Language* 86:103–126.

Hadjidemetriou, Chryso. 2008. *Attempting to document and revitalize Kormakiti Maronite Arabic.* Paper presented at the Twelfth Foundation for Endangered Languages Conference, 24–27 September 2008, The Netherlands.

Hale, Ken, Michael Krauss, Lucille J. Watahomigie, Akira Y. Yamamoto, Colette Craig, Jeanne LaVerne Masayesva, and Nora C. England. 1992. Endangered languages. *Language* 68:1–42.

Hannahville Potawatomi Indian Community. 2009. *Language revitalization: Providing for future generations.* http://www.potawatomilanguage.org/revitalization.php. Accessed April 2, 2016.

Hanawalt, Charles, Bryan Varenkamp, Carletta Lahn, and Dave Eberhard. 2015. *A guide for planning the future of our language.* Preliminary edition–July 2015. Dallas, TX: SIL International. http://www.leadimpact.org/language. Accessed April 2, 2016.

Harris, R. 1990. On redefining linguistics. In H. Davis and T. Taylor (eds.), *Redefining linguistics,* 18–52. London: Routledge.

Harrison, K. David. 2007. *When languages die. The extinction of the world's languages and the erosion of human knowledge.* Oxford: Oxford University Press.

Haugen, Einar. 1966a. Dialect, language, nation. *American Anthropologist* 68:922–35.

Haugen, Einar. 1966b. Linguistics and language planning. In W. Bright (ed.), 50–71.

Headland, Thomas N. 2010. Why the Philippine Negrito languages are endangered. In M. Florey (ed.), *Endangered languages of Austronesia,* 110–118. Oxford: Oxford University Press.

Heath, Shirley Brice. 1978. Bilingual education and a national language policy, In *Monograph Series on Language and Linguistics,* 53–66. Washington D.C.: Georgetown University Press.

Henderson, Brent, Peter Rohloff, and Robert Henderson. 2014. More than words: Towards a development-based approach to language revitalization. *Language Documentation and Conservation* 8:75–91. Manoa, HI: University of Hawaii Manoa. http://hdl.handle.net/10125/4611. Accessed April 2, 2016.

Hilbert, Vi, and Thom Hess. 1982. The Lushootsesed language project. In R. St. Clair and W. L. Leap (eds.), *Language renewal among American Indian tribes,* 71–89. Washington D.C.: National Clearinghouse for Bilingual Education.

Hill, Jane H., and Kenneth C. Hill. 1980. Mixed grammar, purist grammar and language attitudes in modern nahuatl. *Language in Society* 9:321–348.

Hill, Jane H. 2002. "Expert rhetorics" in advocacy for endangered languages: Who is listening and what do they hear? *Journal of Linguistic Anthropology* 12(2):119–133.

Himmelmann, Nikolaus P. 1998. Documentary and descriptive linguistics. *Linguistics* 36:161–195.

Hinton, Leanne. 2001a. Language revitalization: An overview. In Hinton and Hale, 3–18.

Hinton, Leanne. 2001b. The master-apprentice language learning program. In Hinton and Hale, 217–226.

Hinton, Leanne. 2002. *How to keep your language alive. A commonsense approach to one-on-one language learning.* Berkeley: Heyday Books.

Hinton, Leanne, and Ken Hale, eds. 2001. *The green book of language revitalization.* San Diego, CA: Academic Press.

Hirsch-Dubin, F. 2010. *Ethnomathematics in a Mayan context: Mathematics as integral to cultural ways of knowing in the highlands of Chiapas, Mexico.* NASGEm News 2, 7–8. Estes Park, Colorado: North American Study Group on Ethnomathematics.

Hobson, John. 2004. *Learning to speak again: Towards the provision of appropriate training for the revitalization of indigenous Australian languages in New South Wales.* Paper presented at the Eighth Foundation for Endangered Languages Conference 1–3 October 2004, Barcelona, Spain.

Holmes, J. 1992. *An introduction to sociolinguistics.* London: Longman.

Hopper, P. 1998. Emergent grammar. In M. Tomasello (ed.), *The new psychology of language,* 155–175. Mahwah, NJ: Erlbaum.

Hornberger, Nancy H. 1988. Language ideology in Quechua communities of Puno, Peru. *Anthropological Linguistics* 30(2):214–235.

Hornberger, Nancy H. 1993/1994. Language policy and planning in South America. *Annual Review of Applied Linguistics* 14:220–239.

Hornberger, Nancy H. 2002. Multilingual language policies and the continua of biliteracy: An ecological approach. *Language Policy* 1:27–51.

Hornberger, Nancy H. 2006. Frameworks and models in language policy and planning. In Ricento, 24–41.

Hornberger, Nancy H., ed. 2003. *Continua of biliteracy: An ecological framework for educational policy, research and practice in multilingual settings.* Clevedon, UK: Multilingual Matters.

Hornberger, Nancy H., and Kendall King. 2001. Reversing Quechua lnaguage shift in South America. In Fishman, 166–194.

Hornberger, Nancy H., and Ellen Skilton-Sylvester. 2000. Revisiting the continua of biliteracy: International and critical perspectives. *Language and Education* 14(2):96–122.

Hult, Francis M. 2005. A case of prestige and status planning: Swedish and English in Sweden. *Current Issues in Language Planning* 6(1):73–79.

Husband, Charles, and Verity Saifullah Khan. 1982. The viability of ethnolinguistic vitality: Some creative doubts. *Journal of Multilingual and Multicultural Development* 3(3):193–205.

Hymes, Dell. 1972. Models of the interaction of language and social life. In J. J. Gumperz and D. Hymes (eds.), *Directions in sociolinguistics: The ethnography of communication,* 35–71. New York: Holt, Rinehart and Winston.

ISO. 2007. ISO 639 3:2007: Codes for the representation of names of languages—Part 3: Alpha-3 code for comprehensive coverage of languages. Geneva: International Organization for Standardization. http://www.iso.org/iso/home/store/catalogue_tc/catalogue_detail.htm?csnumber=39534. Accessed April 2, 2016.

Jancewicz, Bill, and Marguerite MacKenzie. 2002. Applied computer technology in Cree and Naskapi language programs. *Language Learning and Technology* 6(2):83–91. http://llt.msu.edu/vol6num2/jancewicz/default.html Accessed June 30, 2010.

Johnson, Patricia, Howard Giles, and Richard Y. Bourhis. 1983. The viability of ethnolinguistic vitality: A reply. *Journal of Multilingual and Multicultural Development* 4(4):255–269.

Johnson-Weiner, Karen M. 1999. *Educating in English to maintain Pennsylvania German: The old order parochial school in the service of cultural survival.* Paper presented at the Third Foundation for Endangered Languages Conference, 17–19 September 1999, Maynooth, Ireland.

Jones, Randall L., and Bernard Spolsky. 1975. *Testing language proficiency.* Arlington, VA: The Center for Applied Linguistics.

Joseph, John Earl. 2004. *Language and identity: National, ethnic, religious.* Houndsmills, Basingstoke, Hampshire: Palgrave Macmillan.

Kahane, Henry. 1986. A typology of the prestige language, *Language* 62:3:495–508.

Karan, Mark E. 2000. Motivations: Language vitality assessments using the perceived benefit model of language shift. In Kindell and Lewis, 65–78.

Karan, Mark E. 2011. Understanding and forecasting ethnolinguistic vitality. *Journal of Multilingual and Multicultural Development* 32(2):137–149.

Karan, Mark E. 2015. Motivation as a condition for sustainable language use. In Lewis and Simons, 26–34.

Kasten, Erich. 2008. *Preserving endangered languages or local speech variants in Kamchatka.* Paper presented at the Twelfth Foundation for Endangered Languages Conference, 24–27 September 2008, The Netherlands.

Kelman, Herbert C. 1971. Language as an aid and barrier to involvement in the national system: The motivation and rationalization for language policy. In J. Rubin and B. Jernudd (eds.), *Can language be planned? Sociolinguistic theory and practice for developing nations,* 21–51. Honolulu: University of Hawaii Press.

Kim, Amy. 2015. Towards a language vitality profile of Bangladesh. In Lewis and Simons, 57–69.

Kindell, Gloria E., ed. 1991. *Proceedings of the Summer Institute of Linguistics International Language Assessment Conference.* Dallas, TX: Summer Institute of Linguistics.

Kindell, Gloria E. and M. Paul Lewis (eds.). 2000. *Assessing ethnolinguistic vitality: Theory and practice,* Vol. 3. SIL Publications in Sociolinguistics. Dallas, TX: SIL International.

King, Kendall A. 2001. *Language revitalization processes and prospects: Quichua in the Ecuadorian Andes.* Clevedon, UK: Multilingual Matters.

King, Kendall, Natalie Schilling-Estes, Lyn Fogle, Jia Lou, and Barbara Soukup. 2008. *Sustaining linguistic diversity: Endangered and minority languages and language varieties.* Washington, D.C: Georgetown University Press.

Kipp, Darrell. 2009. Encouragement, guidance and lessons learned: 21 years in an immersion school. In J. Reyhner and L. Lockard (eds.), *Indigenous language revitalization: Encouragement, guidance and lessons learned,* 1–9. Flagstaff, AZ: Northern Arizona University. http://jan.ucc.nau.edu/~jar/ILR/ILR-1.pdf. Accessed April 2, 2016.

Kono, Nariyo, and Tim D. Finch. 2004. *Developing partnerships between universities and language communities: Top-down and bottom-up integration.* Paper presented at the Eighth Foundation for Endangered Languages Conference, 1–3 October 2004, Barcelona, Spain.

Kosonen, Kimmo, Catherine Young, and Susan Malone eds. 2006. *Promoting literacy in multilingual settings.* Bangkok: UNESCO.

Krauss, Michael. 1992. The world's languages in crisis. *Language* 68(1):4–10.

Krauss, Michael. 2007. Classification and terminology for degrees of language endangerment. In M. Brenzinger (ed.), *Language diversity endangered,* 1–8. Berlin: Mouton de Gruyer.

Laakso, Johanna, Anneli Sarhimaa, Sia Spilpoulou Åkermark, and Reeta Toivanen. 2013. *ELDIA Comparative Report.* ELDIA Project.
Labov, William. 1972a. The social motivation of a sound change. *Word* 19:273–309.
Labov, William. 1972b. *Sociolinguistic patterns.* Philadelphia: University of Pennsylvania Press.
Lamy, Paul. 1979. Language and ethnolinguistic identity: The bilingualism question. *International Journal of the Sociology of Language* 20:23–36.
Landry, Rodrigue, and Réal Allard. 1991. *Ethnolinguistic vitality and subtractive identity.* Paper presented at "Recent Advances in the study of ethnolinguistic vitality and cultural identity" Annual Conference of the International Communication Association, May 23–29, 1991, Chicago, IL.
Landweer, M. Lynn. 1991. Schlie-Landweer priority allocation assessment device: Rationale paper. In Kindell, 49–67.
Landweer, M. Lynn. 1998. Indicators of ethnolinguistic vitality: Case study of two languages: Labu and Vanimo. In N. Ostler (ed.), *Endangered languages: What role for the specialist? Proceedings of the Second Foundation for Endangered Languages (FEL) Conference,* 64–72. Bath, UK: Foundation for Endangered Languages.
Landweer, M. Lynn. 2012. Methods of language endangerment research: A perspective from Melanesia. *International Journal of the Sociology of Language* 2012(214):153–178.
Lastra de Suarez, Yolanda. 2001. Otomí language shift and some recent efforts to reverse it. In Fishman, 142–165.
Lee, Tiffany S., and Daniel McLaughlin. 2001. Reversing Navajo language shift, revisited. In Fishman, 23–43.
Leonard, Wesley Y. 2008. When is an "extinct language" not extinct? Miami, a formerly sleeping language. In King et al., 23–34.
LePage, Robert B., and Andrée Tabouret-Keller. 1985. *Acts of identity.* Cambridge: Cambridge University Press.
Lewis, M. Paul. 1993. Real men don't speak Quiché: Quiché ethnicity, Ki-che ethnic movement, K'iche' ethnic nationalism. *Language Problems and Language Planning* 17(1):37–54.
Lewis, M. Paul. 2000. Power and solidarity as metrics in language survey data analysis. In Kindell and Lewis, 79–102.
Lewis, M. Paul. 2006. *Towards a categorization of endangerment of the world's languages.* Dallas, TX: SIL International. http://www-01.sil.org/silewp/2006/silewp2009-^902.pdf?_ga=GA1.2.380451782.1457483895. Accessed April 4, 2016.
Lewis, M. Paul. 2008. Evaluating endangerment: Proposed metadata and implementation. In K. King et al., 35–49.
Lewis, M. Paul, ed. 2009. *Ethnologue: Languages of the world.* 16th edition. Dallas, TX: SIL International.
Lewis, M. Paul, and Gary F. Simons. 2010. Assessing endangerment: Expanding Fishman's GIDS. *Revue Roumaine de Linguistique* 55(2):103–120. http://www.lingv.ro/RRL%202%202010%20art01Lewis.pdf. Accessed April 4, 2016.

Lewis, M. Paul, and Gary F. Simons, eds. 2015. *Ecological perspectives on language endangerment: Applying the Sustainable Use Model for language development.* Dallas, TX: SIL International. http://leanpub.com/ecologicalperspectives.

Lewis, M. Paul, Gary F. Simons, and Charles D. Fennig. (eds.) 2016. *Ethnologue: Languages of the World.* 19th edition. Dallas, TX: SIL International.

Lewis, M. Paul, and Barbara K. Trudell. 2008. Language cultivation in contexts of multiple community languages. In B. Spolsky and F. M. Hult (eds.), *The handbook of educational linguistics,* 266–279. Oxford: Blackwell.

Litteral, Robert. 1999. *Four decades of language policy in Papua New Guinea: The move towards the vernacular.* Dallas, TX: SIL International. http://www.sil.org/resources/publications/entry/7823. Accessed April 4, 2016.

LoBianco, Joseph, and Mari Rhydwen. 2001. Is the extinction of Australia's indigenous languages inevitable? In Fishman, 391–422.

Lyon, Jean. 1996. *Becoming bilingual: Language acquisition in a bilingual community (bilingual education and bilingualism).* Clevedon, UK: Multilingual Matters.

Mackey, William F. 1968. The description of bilingualism. In J. A. Fishman (ed.), *Readings in the sociology of language,* 554–584. The Hague: Mouton.

Malone, Susan, ed. 2004. *Manual for developing literacy and adult education programmes in minority language communities.* Bangkok: UNESCO.

Malone, Susan. 2007. *Advocacy kit for promoting multilingual education: including the excluded.* Bangkok: UNESCO. http://unesdoc.unesco.org/images/0013/001351/135164e.pdf. Accessed April 4, 2016.

Marmor, T. W., and E. Bartels. Forthcoming. *Managing language programs: Perspectives, processes, and practices.* Dallas, TX: SIL International.

May, Stephen. 2001. *Language and minority rights: Ethnicity, nationalism and the politics of language.* Essex, UK: Pearson Education.

May, Stephen. 2006. Language policy and minority rights. In Ricento, 255–272.

McAllister, I., and A. Mughan. 1984. The fate of language: Determinants of bilingualism in Wales. *Ethnic and Racial Studies* 7:321–341.

McCarty, Teresa L., Lucille Watahomigie, Akira Yamamoto, and Ofelia Zepeda. 2001. Indigenous educators as change agents. Case studies of two language institutes. In Hinton and Hale, 371–383.

McClure, Erica. 2001. *The role of language in the construction of ethnic identity on the internet: The case of Assyrian activists in diaspora.* Paper presented at the Fifth Foundation for Endangered Languages Conference, 20–23 September 2001, Agadir, Morocco.

Melander, Björn. 2007. *Language planning in developed contexts: The case of Sweden.* Paper presented at the American Association for Applied Linguistics Annual Meeting, April 22, 2007, Costa Mesa, CA.

Mesthrie, Rajend, Joan Swann, Ana Deumert, and William L. Leap. 2000. *Introducing sociolinguistics.* Edinburgh: Edinburgh University Press.

Mezhoud, Salem. 2005. *Salvation through migration: Immigrant communities as engine rooms for the survival and revival of the Tamazight (Berber) language.* Paper presented at the Ninth Foundation for Endangered Languages Conference, 18–20 November 2005, Stellenbosch, South Africa.

Moore, Robert E., Sari Pietikainen, and Jan Blommaert. 2010. Counting the losses: Numbers as the language of language endangerment. *Sociolinguistic Studies* 4(1):1–26.

Morgan, G. 2001. Welsh. In Hinton and Hale, 107–113.

Muehlmann, S. 2012. Von humboldt's parrot and the countdown of last speakers in the Colorado Delta. *Language and Communication* 32(2):160–168.

Muldrow, William. 1976. Languages of the Maji area. In M. L. Bender (ed.), *The non-Semitic languages of Ethiopia*, 603–607. East Lansing, MI: African Studies Center, Michigan State University.

Nettle, Daniel, and Suzanne Romaine. 2000. *Vanishing voices: The extinction of the world's languages.* Oxford: Oxford University Press.

Neustupny, Jirí V. 1974. Basic types of treatment of language problems. In J. A. Fishman (ed.), *Advances in language planning*, 37–48. The Hague: Mouton.

Newman, Paul. 2000. *The Hausa language: An encyclopedic reference grammar.* New Haven: Yale University Press.

Noori, Margaret. 2009. *Wanesh waa osjkii-bmaadizijig noondamowaad?* What will the young children hear? In J. Reyhner and L. Lockard (eds.), *Indigenous language revitalization: Encouragement, guidance and lessons learned*, 11–22. Flagstaff, AZ: Northern Arizona University.

Obiero, Ogone John. 2010. From assessing language endangerment or vitality to creating and evaluating language revitalization programmes. *Nordic Journal of African Studies* 19(4):201–226.

Ong, Walter J. 2002. *Orality and literacy: The technologizing of the word.* 2nd edition. New York: Routledge.

Orwig, C. J. 2008. Common purposes or functions of language. In C. J. Orwig (ed.), *Preparing for language learning*, Dallas, TX: SIL International.

Ostler, Nicholas, and Blair Rudes (eds.). 2000. *Endangered languages and literacy. Proceedings of the Fourth FEL Conference, Charlotte, North Carolina, September 21–24, 2000.* Bath, UK: Foundation for Endangered Languages.

Ouakrime, Mohamed. 2001. *Promoting the maintenance of endangered languages through the internet: The case of Tamazight.* Paper presented at the Fifth Foundation for Endangered Languages Conference, 20–23 September 2001, Agadir, Morocco.

Patrick, Peter L. 2002. The speech community. In J. K. Chambers et al. (eds.), *Handbook of language variation and change. 1st edition*, 573–597. Oxford: Blackwell.

Paulston, Christina Bratt. 2000. Ethnicity, ethnic movements, and language maintenance. In Kindell and Lewis, 27–38.

Paulston, Christina Bratt, and G. Richard Tucker (eds.). 2003. *Sociolinguistics: The essential readings.* Oxford: Blackwell.

Paulston, Christina Bratt, and Kai Heidemann. 2006. Language policies and the education of linguistic minorities. In Ricento, 292–310.

Pecos, Regis, and Rebecca Blum-Martinez. 2001. The key to cultural survival: Language planning and revitalization in the Pueblo de Cochiti. In Hinton and Hale, 75–82.

Pool, Jonathan. 1972. National development and language diversity. In J. A. Fishman (ed.), *Advances in the sociology of language,* vol. 2, 213–230. The Hague: Mouton.

Quakenbush, J. Stephen. 2015. Some lessons learned in applying EGIDS and the Sustainable Use Model. In Lewis and Simons, 119–126.

Reiman, D. 2010. Basic oral language documentation. *Language Documentation and Conservation* 4:254–268.

Riagáin, P. Ó. 2001. Irish language production and reproduction 1981–1996. In Fishman, 195–214.

Ricento, Thomas, ed. 2000. *Ideology, politics and language policies: Focus on English*. Amsterdam: John Benjamins.

Ricento, Thomas. 2006a. Language policy: Theory and practice—an introduction. In Ricento, 10–23.

Ricento, Thomas. 2006b. Theoretical perspectives in language policy: An overview. In Ricento, 1–9.

Ricento, Thomas, ed. 2006. *An introduction to language policy: Theory and method* (Language and social change 1). Oxford: Blackwell.

Romaine, Suzanne. 1995. *Bilingualism*. 2nd edition. Oxford: Basil Blackwell.

Romaine, Suzanne. 2008. Linguistic diversity, sustainability, and the future of the past. In K. King et al. (eds.), *Sustaining linguistic diversity: Endangered and minority languages and language varieties,* 7–22. Washington, D.C.: Georgetown University Press.

Rubdy, Rani, and Lubna Alsagoff. 2014. The cultural dynamics of globalization: Problematizing hybridity. In R. Rubdy and L. Alsagoff (eds.), *The global-local interface and hybridity: Exploring language and identity,* 1–14. Clevedon, UK: Multilingual Matters.

Ruiz, R. 1984. Orientations in language planning. *NABE Journal* 8(2):15–24.

Ryan, Ellen Bouchard. 1979. Why do low-prestige language varieties persist? In H. Giles and R. N. St. Clair (eds.), *Language and social psychology,* 145–157. Baltimore, MD: University Park Press.

Sallabank, Julia. 2005. Prestige from the bottom up: A review of language planning in Guernsey. *Current Issues in Language Planning* 6(1):44–63.

Saussure, Ferdinand de. 1966. *Course in general linguistics 1916*. C. Bally and A. Sechehaye (eds.). New York: McGraw Hill.

Schroeder, Leila. 2004. Mother-tongue education in schools in Kenya: Some hidden beneficiaries. *Language Matters Studies in the Languages of Africa* 35(2):376–389.

Sharp, Janet. 2003. *Karrajarri, historical and contemporary connections with country and kin.* Paper presented at the Seventh Foundation for Endangered Languages Conference, 22–24 September 2003, Broome, Western Australia.

Sijens, Hendrik. 2008. *How information and commumicaiton technology (ICT) can help language preservation and education.* Paper presented at the Twelfth Foundation for Endangered Languages Conference, 24–27 September 2008, the Netherlands.

SIL International. 2014. *Rapid word collection*. Dallas, TX: SIL International. http://www.sil.org/dictionaries-lexicography/rapid-word-collection-methodology. Accessed April 5, 2016.

Simons, Gary F. 2006. *Ensuring that digital data last: The priority of archival form over working form and presentation form.* Dallas: SIL International. http://www-01.sil.org/silewp/2006/003/SILEWP2006-003.htm. Accessed Aprl 5, 2016.

Simons, Gary F. 2011. *On defining language development.* Paper presented at the 2nd International Conference on Language Documentation and Conservation, 11–13 February 2011, University of Hawaii.

Simons, Gary F., and M. Paul Lewis. 2012. *The SUM Assessment Grid.* Dallas, TX: SIL International. http://www.sil.org/resources/archives/57632. Accessed April 5, 2016.

Simons, Gary F., and M. Paul Lewis. 2013. The world's languages in crisis: A 20 year update. In E. Mihas et al. (eds.), *Responses to language endangerment. In honor of Mickey Noonan: New directions in language documentation and language revitalization,* 3–19. Studies in Language Companion Series 142. Philadelphia: John Benjamins.

Sims, Christine P. 2001. Native lnaguage planning: A pilot process in the Acoma Pueblo community. In Hinton and Hale, 63–73.

Skutnabb-Kangas, Tove. 1984. *Bilingualism or not: The education of minorities.* Clevedon, UK: Multilingual Matters.

Skutnabb-Kangas, Tove. 2000. *Linguistic genocide in education—or worldwide diversity and human rights?* Mahwah, NJ: Lawrence Erlbaum Associates.

Skutnabb-Kangas, Tove. 2006. Language policy and linguistic human rights. In Ricento, 273–291.

Skutnabb-Kangas, Tove. 2008. Bilingual education and sign language as the mother tongue of Deaf children. In C. J. Kellett Bidoli and E. Ochse (eds.), *English in international Deaf communication,* 75–94. Bern: Peter Lang.

Smith, Karla J. 2012. *Heritage language playschools for indigenous minorities.* 2nd edition. Kuching, Sarawak, Malaysia: Dayak Bidayuh National Association in association with SIL Malaysia.

Spolsky, Bernard. 2004. *Language policy.* Cambridge: Cambridge University Press.

Street, Brian V. 2008. New literacies, new times: Developments in literacy studies. In B. V. Street and N. H. Hornberger (eds.), *Encyclopedia of language and education, vol. 2,* 3–14. New York: Springer.

Strubell, M. 2001. Catalan a decade later. In Fishman, 260–283.

Suay, Ferran. 2015. *Psychological aspects of multilingualism with a special focus on the challenges in facilitating a change towards more assertive linguistic speakers of lesser-used languages.* Paper presented at Multilingualism in Baltic-Sea Europe, 13–16 April 2015. Universität Johannes Gutenberg, Mainz, Germany.

T'sou, Benjamin et al. 2007. *Critical multilingual shift in Sanya, China: Accelerated urbanization and possible sociolinguistic repair.* Paper presented at the Eleventh Foundation for Endangered Languages Conference, 26–28 October 2007, Kuala Lumpur, Malaysia.

Tabouret-Keller, A. 1968. Sociological factors of language maintenance and language shift. In J. A. Fishman et al. (eds.), *Language problems of developing nations.* NY: Wiley & Sons.

Thornton, Thomas F. 2003. *Place names and the language of subsistence in Southeast Alaska.* Paper presented at the Seventh Foundation for Endangered Languages Conference, 22–24 September 2003, Broome, Western Australia.

Todal, Jon. 1999. *The use of the Saami language in Norwegian schools.* Paper presented at the Third Foundation for Endangered Languages Conference, 17–19 September 1999, Maynooth, Ireland.

Tollefson, James W. 1991. *Planning language, planning inequality.* London: Longman.

Tollefson, James W. 2006. Critical theory in language policy. In Ricento, 42–59.

Trainum, Michael W. 2012. *Life access technology trust: About shellbooks.* http://www.lifeaccesstech.org/shellbook.html. Accessed April 5, 2016.

Trudell, Barbara K. 2006. Local agency in the development of minority languages: Three language committees in northwest Cameroon. *Journal of Multilingual and Multicultural Development* 27(3):196–210.

Trudgill, Peter. 1972. Sex, covert prestige and linguistic change in the urban British English of Norwich. *Language in Society* 1:179–195.

Tsukida, Naomi, and Shigeru Tsuchida. 2007. Indigenous languages of Formosa. In O. Miyaoka et al. (eds.), *The vanishing languages of the Pacific rim,* 285–300. New York: Oxford University Press.

UNESCO. 1996. *Manual on establishing effective and sustainable mechanisms for literacy programmes.* Paris: UNESCO/UNDP. http://unesdoc.unesco.org/images/0010/001036/103689E.pdf. Accessed April 5, 2016.

UNESCO. 2005a. *First Language First: Community-based literacy programmes for minority language contexts in Asia.* Bangkok: UNESCO Bangkok.

UNESCO. 2005b. *Towards knowledge societies. UNESCO world report.* Paris: United Nations Educational, Scientific, and Cultural Organization. 226 http://unesdoc.unesco.org/images/0014/001418/141843e.pdf. Accessed April 5, 2016.

Wardhaugh, Ronald. 2002. *An introduction to sociolinguistics,* 4th edition. Oxford: Basil Blackwell.

Warren, Kay B. 1998. *Indigenous movements and their critics. Pan-Maya activism in Guatemala.* Princeton: Princeton University Press.

Warner, Sam L. No'Eau. 2001. The movement to revitalize Hawaiian language and culture. In Hinton and Hale, 133–144.

Woodbury, Anthony C. 2003. Defining documentary linguistics. In P. Austin (ed.), *Language Documentation and Description* 1:35-51. London: School of Oriental and African Studies.

Wright, Sue. 2004. *Language policy and language planning: From nationalism to globalisation.* Houndsmills, Basingstoke, Hampshire: Palgrave Macmillan.

Index

Acquisition condition, 6, 10, 125, 126, 134–137, 147, 152, 161, 166, 174, 175, 178, 180–182, 186–188, 194, 196, 198, 200
acquisition infrastructure, 135
acquisition planning, 49, 51–54, 58, 59, 66, 163, 167, 197
Acquisition scale, 134–137, 197
acts of identity, 32
advocacy, 53, 54, 175, 176, 180, 189, 192
advocacy, internal, 179
agency, 48, 57, 61
Ager, Dennis, 167
Ah Suhn, 221
Alisjahbana, S. Takdir, 168
Allard, Réal, 96
Alloni-Feinberg, Yafa, 51
Alsagoff, Lubna, 13
Amery, Rob, 121, 236, 242
Arnold, Robert D., 235
Ash, Anna, 232
Asian Development Bank, 58, 212
attitudes, 175, 194
awareness and perspective, 204
Axelrod, Melissa, 218
Bagamba, B. Araali, 152
Baker, Colin, 13
Baldwin, Ruth, 58
Bartels, Eric, 8, 213
Batibo, Herman M., 150, 219
Befus, Mariann, 58
Bell, Jeanie, 242
Benedicto, Elena, 228
best guess, 92, 94, 95

bilingual proficiency, 13
Bird, Steven, 121
Blommaert, Jan, 30
Blum-Martinez, Rebecca, 230
bodies of knowledge, 3, 7, 10, 36, 44, 51, 63, 66–68, 72, 132, 143, 145, 152, 153, 155–160, 162–164, 166, 167, 170, 173, 175, 180, 182, 183, 185, 186, 190, 193, 196, 197, 199, 206, 215
Bonner, Joy, 242
Boone, Douglas W., 152
Bouquiaux, Luc, 236
Bourhis, Richard Y., 96, 106
Brenzinger, Matthias, 96, 108, 109
Brewster, E. Thomas, 236
Brewster, Elizabeth S., 236
Brewster, Steve, 58
Brown, Roger, 32
Buckley, Molly, 58
Busch, Brigitta, 227
Cahill, Michael, 161, 167
Campbell, Lyle, 96
capacity, 152
capacity building, 54, 150, 205, 206, 208
capacity, community, 206, 207, 210
capacity of the language, 206
capacity, organizational, 206–208, 210
capacity, resourcing, 208
Chambers, Robert, 57, 60
Chang, Debbie, 121
Chisholm, Joan, 121
Chomsky, Noam, 29
Chríost, Diarmait Mac Giolla, 167

Churchill, Stacey, 151
COD (Capacity, Opportunity, Desire), 152
code-switching, 13
codification, 50, 51, 61, 168, 202
Collins, Wes, 224
communication genres, 2, 63, 68
communicative motivations, 150
community, 16, 40
community-based language development, 9, 35, 36, 42, 45, 46, 50, 52–54, 56, 58, 64
community capacity, 177
community development, 36, 59, 207
community, local, 2
community organizing, 207
compartmentalization, 71, 73, 147, 151, 152, 168
competence, 29
complementary distribution, 129, 143, 145, 165
contact, 1, 2
Cooper, Robert L., 14, 58, 151, 167, 168
Cooperrider, David, 58
corpus development, 190
corpus planning, 49–52, 54, 58, 59, 66, 150, 157, 159, 167, 168, 185, 186, 206
Coulmas, Florian, 168
Coulter, Neil R., 240
covert prestige, 167
Cox, Philip, 58, 212
Coyne, Kathy, 58
critical theory, 168
Crystal, David, 31, 33, 96
cultivation planning, 151
Cummins, James, 13
Dadd, Kathy, 242
Dauenhauer, Nora Marks, 241
Dauenhauer, Richard, 241
Davis, Kathryn Anne, 168
Davis, Patricia M., 225
de Graaf, Tjeerd, 239
Deaf associations, 174
Deaf schools, 174
decision tree, 92
desire, 152

diachronic variation, 32
diagnostic questions, 92, 95
dialects, 29
diastratic variation, 32
diatopic, 32
Differentiation condition, 6, 10, 125, 129, 145, 147, 151, 152, 161, 165, 166, 168, 175, 177, 180, 184, 190, 192, 195, 199
Differentiation scale, 143–145
diglossia, 10, 70–73, 97, 120, 130, 151, 152, 167
diglossia, broad, 74
Dimmendal, Gerrit J., 87, 96
diversity policy, 151, 167
domains of use, 9, 10, 65–67, 70–72, 130, 149, 152, 166
Dorian, Nancy C., 96, 98, 167
dormant, 118
Easthouse, Linda Orr, 58
Eastman, Carole M., 167
Eberhard, Dave, 95
economic development, lack of, 12
economic empowerment, 150
economic motivations, 150
educational use, 103
Edwards, John, 13, 121
EGIDS, *see* Expanded Graded Intergenerational Disruption Scale
EGIDS 0 (International), 81
EGIDS 1 (National), 82
EGIDS 2 (Provincial), 83
EGIDS 3 (Wider Communication), 83
EGIDS 4 (Educational), 84, 132, 134, 139, 141, 145, 171, 172, 178–180, 203
EGIDS 5 (Developing), 85, 132, 136, 139, 142, 172, 174–177, 179, 180
EGIDS 6a (Vigorous), 86, 132, 133, 136, 139, 142, 145, 172, 182, 184, 186, 203
EGIDS 6b (Threatened), 86, 133, 137, 139, 142, 181, 182, 184, 186, 188, 190
EGIDS 7 (Shifting), 87, 133, 137, 140, 143, 146, 186
EGIDS 8a (Moribund), 88, 133
EGIDS 8b (Nearly Extinct), 88

EGIDS 9 (Dormant), 89, 133, 137, 140, 143, 146, 171, 186, 190, 192, 193, 196–198
EGIDS 10 (Extinct), 90, 133, 134, 137, 140, 143, 146, 197
elaboration, 50, 61, 162–164, 167, 178
Elwell, Vanessa M. R., 74
emergent language, 100
empowerment, 150
Endalew, Tefera, 222
Environment condition, 6, 10, 125, 127, 128, 140, 142, 147, 150–152, 175, 176, 180, 183, 187, 192, 199, 204, 206, 226
Environment scale, 140–143
Ethiopia, 22
ethnolinguistic vitality, 146
Expanded Graded Intergenerational Disruption Scale (EGIDS), 4, 6, 56, 79, 80, 90, 91, 96, 102, 111, 117, 123, 130, 148, 156, 169–171, 180, 186, 199–202, 205, 215
external knowledge, 22, 68, 157–159, 162, 164, 166, 185, 198, 205
FAMED conditions, 6, 10, 11, 130, 143, 146, 149, 150, 156, 167, 169–171, 175, 180, 186, 200, 202, 203, 205, 210, 215, 217
Fasold, Ralph W., 12, 13, 71, 72, 74
Fennig, Charles D., 13, 29, 81, 84–86, 88, 90, 151
Ferguson, Charles A., 61, 70, 72, 73, 76, 167
Fermino, Jessie Little Doe, 232
Fierman, William, 220
Finch, Tim D., 232
Fishman, Joshua A., 12, 33, 71, 73–76, 79, 96, 103, 105, 120, 149, 167, 227, 229, 230
Foerster, Liz, 219
forgotten languages, 116
Fox News Latino, 52
Friedman, Thomas, 13
functional assignments, 9, 56, 66, 67, 129, 143
functional distribution, 63, 64, 70, 166
functional language identification, 29
functions, 9, 45, 48–51, 63–72
Functions condition, 6, 10, 11, 125–133, 139, 143, 145–147, 149, 151–153, 155–157, 159, 161–168, 172, 173, 175–178, 180–182, 184–186, 190–199, 202, 203, 206, 207, 215, 220
functions, dominant-language, 199
functions, High, 77
functions, instrumental, 69, 76
functions, intimate, 68
functions, local-language, 199
functions, Low, 77
functions, non-intimate, 68
functions, private, 68
functions, public, 68
Functions scale, 131–133
functions, sentimental, 69, 76
Gal, Susan, 72
GIDS, see Graded Intergenerational Disruption Scale
Giles, Howard, 96, 106, 107
Gilman, Albert, 32
Gippert, Jost, 121
globalization, 12
Golla, Victor, 89
Goody, Jack R., 121, 122
Gorter, Durk, 224
Graded Intergenerational Disruption Scale (GIDS), 90, 96, 102, 103, 107, 108
Grenoble, Lenore A., 28, 33, 96, 109, 121, 242
Greymorning, Stephen, 226
Griep, Louise, 58
Grimes, Barbara F., 13, 107
Grin, François, 152
Grinevald, Colette, 100
Gumperz, John J., 33, 57
Gómez de Garcia, Julie, 218
Haarman, Harald, 58, 59, 167
Hadjidemetriou, Chryso, 226
Hale, Ken, 14, 178, 179, 232
Hanawalt, Charlie, 95
Harris, Roy, 30
Harrison, K. David, 31, 33, 96
Haugen, Einar, 29, 30, 61, 167
Headland, Thomas N., 20
Heath, Shirley Brice, 168

Heidemann, Kai, 168
Henderson, Brent, 31
Henderson, Robert, 31
Henson, Bonnie, 38
Hess, Thom, 237
High language, 68
Hilbert, Vi, 237
Hill, Jane H., 30, 168
Hill, Kenneth C., 168
Himmelmann, Nikolaus P., 101, 120, 121
Hinton, Leanne, 149, 178, 179, 189, 200, 233
Hirsch-Dubin, Faviana, 221
Hobson, John, 101, 232
Holmes, Janet, 13
Hopper, Paul, 30
Hornberger, Nancy H., 28, 33, 57, 60, 122, 151, 167, 238
hostile environment, 127
Hult, Francis M., 167
human rights, 189
Husband, Charles, 96
hybridization, 13
hybridized identities, 22
Hymes, Dell, 33
identity, 32, 103
identity construction, 13
impact, 209, 210
informal functions, 69
inside knowledge, 67, 119
institutional support, 84
instrumental functions, 69, 76
intangible heritage, 24
intergenerational transmission, 103, 137, 182, 186, 190, 194, 196, 200, 230
internal advocacy, 179
internal knowledge, 22, 37, 68, 157–159, 162, 166, 185, 186, 198, 205
ISO 639-3 standard, 29
Jancewicz, Bill, 219
Johnson, Patricia, 96, 106, 107
Johnson-Weiner, Karen M., 231
Jones, Randall L., 13
Joseph, John Earl, 121
Kahane, Henry, 167
Karan, Mark E., 96, 150

Kasten, Erich, 238
Kelman, Herbert C., 76
Khan, Verity Saifullah, 96
Kim, Amy, 104
Kindell, Gloria E., 96
King, Kendall A., 57, 96, 97, 238
Kipp, Darrell, 240
knowledge, *see* bodies of knowledge *or* life-crucial knowledge
knowledge, external, 21, 185
knowledge, internal, 185
knowledge management, 2, 4
knowledge transmission, 176, 201, 202, 205
Kono, Nariyo, 232
Kosonen, Kimmo, 57, 149, 168
Krauss, Michael, 14, 96, 108
Laakso, Johanna, 153
Labov, William, 30
Lachler, Jordan, 218
Lahn, Carletta, 95
Lamy, Paul, 96
Landry, Rodrigue, 96
Landweer, M. Lynn, 96, 110
language capacity, 208
language change, 48
language choice, 13
language community, 30, 43, 45, 46
language contact, 13
language cultivation, 59
language death, 3, 4, 14
language development, xiii, 2, 4–7, 9, 10, 36, 47, 59, 150, 152, 167, 208
language development, definition of, 66
language development effort, 208
language development programs, 210
language documentation, 193
language ecology, 63, 65
language empowerment, 175
language endangerment, 4, 14
language engineering, 59
language, heritage, 193
language, local, 2
language loss, 4, 193
language maintenance, 2, 163
language mixing, 13

language planning, 47, 52–54, 58, 59, 151, 157, 167, 168
language policy, 53, 127, 151, 180
language projects, 210
language revitalization, 193
language shift, 3, 4, 13, 72, 181
language spread, 14
language transmission, 137
language vitality, 5, 123
Language Vitality and Endangerment (LVE) framework, 108, 109
language vs. dialect, 29
langue, 28–30
Lastra de Suarez, Yolanda, 225
Lee, Tiffany S., 100, 230
Leonard, Wesley Y., 103, 242
LePage, Robert B., 32
levels of sustainable use, *see* sustainable levels of language use
Lewis, M. Paul, xv, 6, 12–14, 29, 32, 57, 60, 77, 81, 84–86, 88, 90, 95, 96, 98, 99, 102, 107, 151, 167
life-crucial knowledge, 2, 3, 6, 8, 9, 16, 20, 22, 24, 31, 35, 37, 53, 55, 64, 67, 68, 111, 131–133, 139, 144, 145, 147, 155, 156, 159, 164, 166, 169, 172, 175, 176, 178, 179, 181, 182, 186, 190, 191, 196–198, 202, 205, 209, 215
linguistic diversity, 1, 12
linguistic ecology, 1, 9, 13, 67, 205
linguistic empowerment, 150
linguistic hygiene, 168
linguistic repertoire, 3, 6, 9, 17, 22, 36, 43, 45, 64, 67, 201, 202
linguistic rights, 189
literacies, 166, 167
literacy acquisition infrastructure, 136
literacy skills, 149, 166
Litteral, Robert, 168
LoBianco, Joseph, 240
local communities, 2
local languages, 2, 201, 202
local speech communities, 1, 16
Low language, 68
Luft, Murray, 58
LVE, *see* Language Vitality and Endangerment

Lyon, Jean, 13
MacKenzie, Marguerite, 219
Mackey, William F., 72
Majangir, 22, 45
Malone, Susan, 57, 149, 167, 168, 172, 177
Marmor, Thomas W., 8, 213
May, Stephen, 151, 168
McAllister, Ian, 74
McCarty, Teresa L., 235
McClure, Erica, 228
McLaughlin, Daniel, 100, 230
Mesthrie, Rajend, 33, 57
Mezhoud, Salem, 229
micro-environments, 128, 140, 177
MLE, *see* multilingual education
mobility, 1
modalities, 23, 45, 68, 156
modernization, 168, 202
Moore, Robert, 30
Morgan, Gerald, 236
Mosel, Ulrike, 121
Motivation condition, 6, 10, 59, 125, 126, 147, 150, 152, 164, 166, 175, 177, 179, 182, 183, 185–188, 192, 194, 195, 198, 206, 226, 237
Motivation scale, 138–140, 150
motivations, 52, 59, 150
Muehlmann, S., 30
Mughan, Anthony, 74
Muldrow, William, 87
multilingual education, 12, 168, 178
multilingualism, 13
Muntzel, Martha C., 96
Nettle, Daniel, 25, 31, 33, 96
Neustupny, Jiri V., 151
Newman, Paul, 84
Noori, Margaret, 233
norms of use, 143, 144, 152, 155, 199
Obiero, Ogone John, 96
official recognition, 104, 151
Ong, Walter J., 122
opportunity, 152
oral literacies, 166
oral literature, 122
oral modality, 145
orality, 118
Orwig, Carol J., 236

Ostler, Nicolas, 101
Ouakrime, Mohamed, 228
outcomes, 209–211
outputs, 210, 211
outside knowledge, 67, 69
overt prestige, 167
parole, 28–30
Patrick, Peter L., 57
Paulston, Christina Bratt, 29, 61, 96, 168
Pecos, Regis, 230
Perceived Benefit Model, 150
perceived benefits, 126, 150, 194
performance, 29
persistence, 71
Pietikainen, Sari, 30
policy environment, 10, 143
policy planning, 151
Pool, Jonathan, 12
Potawatomi, Hannahville Indian Community, 234
power, 32, 69
prestige planning, 52–54, 59, 66, 164, 167
products, 153
Quakenbush, J. Stephen, 105
Rapid Word Collection, 158
RBM, *see* Results-Based Management
reawakening, 91
reestablishing, 91
reflective practitioners, xiii, 2, 5
Reiman, Duane, 237
religious motivations, 150
Results-Based Management (RBM), 57, 208, 209, 212
results plan, 209
revitalizing, 91
Rhydwen, Mari, 240
Riagáin, Padraig Ó., 200, 241
Rice, Keren, 167
Ricento, Thomas, 30, 33, 58, 60, 167, 168
Rigney, Alitya Wallara, 242
Robinson, Sheila, 58
Rohloff, Peter, 31
Romaine, Suzanne, 13, 25, 31, 33, 72, 96
Rosenthal, Doreen, 96

Rubdy, Rani, 13
Rudes, Blair, 101
Ruiz, Richard, 12, 60
Ryan, Ellen Bouchard, 167
Sachdev, Itesh, 96
Sallabank, Julia, 167
Saurman, Mary Beth, 219
Saussure, Ferdinand de, 28
Schlie, Perry, 110
Schroeder, Leila, 223
semi-speaker, 100
sentimental functions, 69, 76
shalom, 27
Sharp, Janet, 232
Sijens, Hendrik, 223
Simons, Gary F., xv, 6, 13, 14, 29, 47, 81, 84–86, 88, 90, 95, 96, 99, 102, 121, 151
Sims, Christine P., 234
Skilton-Sylvester, Ellen, 33, 167
Skutnabb-Kangas, Tove, 28, 168, 189
Smith, Karla J., 218
social motivations, 150
social networks, 65
sociopolitical empowerment, 150
solidarity, 32, 69
specialization, 74
speech community, 3, 6, 9, 30, 33, 42, 43, 45, 63, 64, 68, 169, 202
Spolsky, Bernard, 13, 60
stability, 71
stable multilingualism, 10, 63, 64, 67, 70, 71, 117, 129, 130, 143, 147, 152, 157, 168, 224, 231
standardization, 11, 29, 50, 51, 159, 160, 163, 164, 167
status planning, 49–52, 54, 58, 59, 66, 129, 157, 167
Street, Brian V., 167
Strubell, Miquel, 225
structural language identification, 29
Suay, Ferran, 231
SUM, *see* Sustainable Use Model
SUM Assessment Grid, 95, 148, 149
Sustainable History, 10, 108, 116–118, 126, 133, 134, 195, 196

Sustainable Identity, 10, 117, 118, 126, 133, 137, 140, 146, 160, 163, 193, 194, 196–198
sustainable institutions, 135
sustainable language use, 63, 72, 115, 149, 152, 163, 171, 185, 190, 208, 215, 216
sustainable levels of language use, 6, 10, 50, 111, 115, 123, 126, 130, 143, 156, 157, 160, 169–171, 198, 202, 204, 205, 207, 210, 212, 215
Sustainable Literacy, 10, 119, 120, 126, 132, 134, 141, 145, 160, 164, 171, 175, 177, 180, 203, 209, 210
Sustainable Orality, 10, 103, 118, 119, 126, 132, 133, 136, 145, 160, 164, 186
Sustainable Use Model (SUM), xiv, xv, xvii, xviii, 1, 2, 4–9, 12, 35, 50, 56, 65–67, 70, 80, 108, 111, 113, 123, 150, 152, 155, 156, 165, 169–172, 185, 197, 201–203, 205–208, 210, 215, 216
T'sou, Benjamin, 226
Tabouret-Keller, Andrée, 32, 96
Taylor, Donald M., 106
Thomas, Jacqueline M. C., 236
Thornton, Thomas F., 239
Todal, Jon, 224
Tollefson, James, 59, 168
topics, 67, 157
Trainum, Michael W., 31
transmission of knowledge, xiii, 2, 18, 22, 35–37, 55, 67
Trudell, Barbara K., 12, 57, 60, 151, 167
Trudgill, Peter, 167
Tsuchida, Shigeru, 229
Tsukida, Naomi, 229
Tucker, G. Richard, 29, 61
UNESCO, 31, 57, 104, 149
urbanization, 1
Vaillancourt, François, 152
Varenkamp, Bryan, 95
vehicular languages, 83, 84, 93
vehicularity, 94, 104
Wadhwa, Bava, 58
Wardhaugh, Ronald, 13

Warner, Sam L. No'Eau, 101, 220
Warren, Kay B., 33
Whaley, Lindsay J., 28, 33, 96, 109, 121, 242
Woodbury, Anthony C., 121
Wright, Sue, 167
written modality, 145
Young, Catherine, 57, 149, 168, 221

About the Authors

Paul Lewis and Gary Simons have been leaders in a decade-long process of reflection and discussion that has involved a large number of experienced colleagues regarding what SIL International has learned after 80 years of working in local language communities. The result was the Sustainable Use Model (SUM) of language maintenance and advancement which is explained and applied in this book. This book is deliberately aimed at those who are "on the ground," working with a community to address the issues that arise from language and culture contact. The hope is that many in this reading audience will themselves be members of those communities. The book is designed to be both a textbook for learning about and applying the SUM approach, and to be a handbook for reference purposes.

©Wong Kong Seng

M. Paul Lewis served as General Editor of *Ethnologue®: Languages of the World*, from 2005 to 2016. He is now a Senior Consultant in Sociolinguistics with SIL International, having previously served as International Sociolinguistics Coordinator for SIL. His first fieldwork was in Guatemala, where he focused on the K'iche people. His primary research and publication interests are in language maintenance, shift and death; language policy and planning; and language documentation. He holds a Ph.D. in sociolinguistics from Georgetown University, and has engaged in consulting and training in Africa, Australia, Asia, Europe, Central America, North America, and South America.

©SIL International

Gary F. Simons is the Chief Research Officer for SIL International and Executive Editor of the *Ethnologue®*. He is also Adjunct Professor of Applied Linguistics at the Graduate Institute of Applied Linguistics (Dallas, TX). Early in his career he was involved in language development in Papua New Guinea and Solomon Islands, and was an early pioneer in the use of portable computers in fieldwork. He developed the PTP computer programming language, as well as resources for doing language survey. More recently, Simons has contributed to the development of cyberinfrastructure for linguistics as co-founder of the Open Language Archives Community and co-developer of the ISO 639-3 standard of three-letter identifiers for all known languages of the world. He was also a developer of GOLD, the General Ontology for Linguistic Description, and co-authored with Steven Bird the influential *Language* article, "Seven dimensions of portability for language documentation and description." He holds a Ph.D. in linguistics (with minor emphases in computer science and classics) from Cornell University.

Selected Bibliography:

Simons, Gary F., and M. Paul Lewis. 2013. The world's languages in crisis: A 20 year update. In Elena Mihas, Bernard Perley, Gabriel Rei-Doval and Kathleen Wheatley (eds.), *Responses to language endangerment. In honor of Mickey Noonan*. Studies in Language Companion Series 142. Amsterdam: John Benjamins. Pp. 3–19.

Lewis, M. Paul, and Gary F. Simons. 2010. Assessing endangerment: Expanding Fishman's GIDS. *Revue Roumaine de Linguistique* 55(2):103–120. http://www.lingv.ro/RRL%202%202010%20art01Lewis.pdf.

Bird, Steven, and Gary Simons. 2003. Seven dimensions of portability for language documentation and description. *Language* 79(3):557–582.

Lewis, M. Paul. 2001. K'iche': A study in the sociology of language. *SIL Publications in Sociolinguistics 6*. Dallas: SIL International.

Lewis, M. Paul, and Gloria Kindell, eds. 2000. Assessing ethnolinguistic vitality: Theory and practice. *SIL Publications in Sociolinguistics 3*. Dallas: SIL International.

www.ingramcontent.com/pod-product-compliance
Lightning Source LLC
Chambersburg PA
CBHW080408300426
44113CB00015B/2445